MW01195018

MONTANA
WASHINGTON
OREGON
IDAHO
CALIFORNIA
NEVADA
UTAH
Fort Colville
Seattle
Ellensburgh
Olympia
Spokane Falls
Sprague
Missoula
Dayton
Lewiston
Lapwai
Mt. Idaho
Ainsworth
Walla Walla
Portland
Goldendale
Umatilla
Centerville
Pendleton
The Dalles
Pilot Rock
Wallowa
Union
Salem
Baker City
Brownsville
Prineville
Canyon City
Idaho City
Boise City
Hailey
Burns
Silver City
Goose Creek
Lakeview
Fort Bidwell
Winnemucca
Elko
Kelton
Toano
Chico
Eureka
Reno
Virginia City
Sacramento
San Francisco
Pioche
NORTHERN PACIFIC R.R.
N. PACIFIC R.R.
OREGON R.R.
OREGON & CALIFORNIA R.R.
OR. R. & N. NAVIGATION CO.
UNION PACIFIC R.R.
CENTRAL PACIFIC R.R.
DANCING CRANE'S
MAP OF
IDAHO, OREGON,
NEVADA, WASHINGTON,
W. UTAH, W. MONTANA
AND
NORTHERN CALIFORNIA
1884

(Courtesy Sophia Riede)

Although he had a reputation as a horse thief, Hank Vaughan posed as a gentleman for this studio portrait when he was about forty years old, ca. 1890.

HANK VAUGHAN
(1849-1893):

A Hell-Raising Horse Trader of the Bunchgrass Territory

A Biography by

Jon M. Skovlin
and
Donna McDaniel Skovlin

Reflections Publishing Co.
P.O. Box 121
Cove, Oregon 97824

Copyright © 1996 by
Jon M. Skovlin and Donna McDaniel Skovlin

All rights reserved. No part of the material protected by this copyright notice may be reproduced or utilized in any form or by any means, electronic or mechanical, including photocopying, recording or by any informational storage system without written permission from the copyright owner. Printed in the United States of America.

ISBN (paperback) 0-9649449-1-X

ISBN (hardcover) 0-9649449-0-1

Library of Congress Catalog Card Number: 96-70169

Cover photo,
Charles M. Russell painting "Best Wishes for your Christmas" (detail),
courtesy of the Montana Historical Society, MacKay Collection.

Printed by
Maverick Publications
P.O. Box 5007
Bend, Oregon 97708

CONTENTS

ACKNOWLEDGEMENTS

We are indebted to many people in preparing this biography. Information has been graciously supplied by a number of Hank Vaughan's relatives, especially Mrs. Laura Belle Rogers. Other relatives who have been most helpful were Mrs. Courtney Del Curto, Mrs. Thelma Martin, Mrs. Cordelia Vaughan Winters, Mrs. Sophia Reide, Mrs. Sylvia Brandt, and Mrs. Grace Bower. Mrs. Virginia Atchison and Mr. and Mrs. Royal Robie also deserve thanks. Tribute is due the late Jack Brandt for valuable genealogical material.

Others who have been generous in providing records and reference material are Mrs. Margaret Keillor, Reference Archivist, Oregon State Library, Terry Abraham, formerly Manuscript Archivist, Washington State University, Howard Hickson, Director, Northeastern Nevada Historical Society, Laurence Dodd, Archivist, Whitman College, and M. Gary Bettis, Archivist, Idaho State Library. Grateful thanks goes to John Evans and John Reister, formerly Librarians, Eastern Oregon State College, for making available microfilm and other references in a seemingly endless search. Others who generously contributed information are Judge James H. Sturgis, Mrs. Areta Barrett, Bill Knight, Gerald Tucker, Ron Donoho, and Kerry Ross Boren. We also thank H.W. Hawley, Historian, Oregon State Sheriffs' Association, for helpful assistance and encouragement.

Institutions deserving acknowledgement are the National Archives and Records Service, court clerks for innumerable counties in Oregon, Washington, Idaho, Utah, Nevada, and Arizona; libraries of Umatilla and Union counties, the Bancroft Library, historical society libraries of Washington, Oregon, Idaho, Utah and Nevada and the central libraries of all these states.

PREFACE

Legend and western folklore say Hank Vaughan was an outlaw and a horse thief, that he was a gunman, a desperado, a gambler and a drunk. Those who knew him remember him as a jokester, a story teller, a man of his word and a gentleman. All recognized his ingenuity, ambition and skillful leadership.

Little has come to light of this man's true character, but after more than a hundred years, tales of his exploits are still retold around cow camps and branding fires, behind rodeo chutes and across mahogany bars in smoke-filled cowtown saloons. Occasionally *True West* or *Frontier Times* print stories of Hank and his daring deeds, but the skeptical reader satiated with TV and movie bad guys discounts the story as the product of another writer's vivid imagination.

Jon first heard Hank Vaughan stories in 1955 while working cattle on the Starkey range in northeastern Oregon. Ten years later he started searching through reels of newspaper microfilms and other records from the National Archives and found that many of the stories about Vaughan stemmed from actual events. More often than not the original happening was more hair-raising and audacious than the legend that survived.

The main object of this work is to provide a portrait of the life of an aggressive character who took advantage of a lawless period in the development of the West. Eventually, law and order prevailed bringing an end to the activities of the likes of Hank Vaughan and the Pacific Northwest became a relatively safe place for common folk to live.

Vaughan lived during harsh and exciting times in Oregon. He began his reputation in the early 1860s when gold discoveries in the interior brought about a period of rapid growth and development to the new state. He ranged around the frontier settlements of The Dalles, Pendleton, Spokane Falls, Boise City, and Elko wherever there was money to be made. He died in 1893 after contributing greatly to the folklore of the west when it was wild.

There are gaps in this report of Hank's life when no records are available. For example, during his early twenties, there is a period of three years when nothing was uncovered about him. These were prime years in this man's life, years when people and events would have greatly influenced the directions of his later actions. But since the evidence of these experiences remains hidden, so must much of the reasons why he turned out as he did.

Liberal quotes from old newspapers and documents are included as well as reminiscences of old-timers and our own interpretations. Hopefully, all these sources have been identified so the reader can separate them in his mind and recognize the bias inherent in each. The wording of much of the original material has not been changed in an effort to preserve the flavor of a journalistic period when editors said what they thought with no fear of libel.

We have attempted to show the change in people's attitudes during the period from 1850 through the 1890s when a single generation witnessed the evolution from absolute wilderness to a settled society. Today, not many people remember that the Inland Empire of the Pacific Northwest was the last stronghold of the wilderness. Fewer realize that this tranquil territory between the Cascades and the Rockies spawned desperados of such notoriety as Hank Vaughan.

In presenting this biography, we hope to have successfully portrayed Vaughan's complex character without having done injustice to those brave elements of law and order that he so often mocked.

I.

SETTING THE STAGE
(1849-1864)

It was a cold Sunday morning on December 21, 1881. Inside the saloons that bordered the frozen rutted street running through the middle of Prineville, cowboys lounged around potbellied wood stoves keeping warm preparing to wait out another idle winter day. Today, however, there was a feeling that something unusual might be developing that would break the monotony of their normal routine. Little did they anticipate that this seemingly ordinary day would produce a bloody shootout, the worst this Oregon frontier town ever experienced.

Only two men would take part in the bloodletting; one was a local cowboy, the other was the stranger who had ridden into town yesterday. His arrival had been the topic of considerable speculation amongst those hanging around the bars once it was realized that the newcomer was Hank Vaughan, the man thought to be the brains behind the biggest rustling operation in eastern Oregon. He also had a reputation as a man who was quick to use his guns and even here in Prineville everyone had heard at least one version of how he had shot a sheriff and killed a deputy before he was even sixteen years old.

The watchful residents wondered at his reason for coming to Prineville. Surely, if this man were as clever as he was claimed to be, he knew that the big cow operators around this Crooked River area were losing patience with the losses they suffered from rustlers. They were organizing and preparing to rid the region of all cattle and horse thieves. If Vaughan knew about the Prineville vigilante movement, he apparently wasn't afraid of it. Perhaps he came to test the ranchers' strength.

When Vaughan made his appearance, he wasted no time moving into enemy territory. He entered Graham's Saloon which was considered to be the headquarters of the vigilante group and here he singled out Charlie Long, a mild-mannered little cowboy, tough as a rawhide rope, who had worked as cow boss on several big cattle ranches. Presently he was employed by Colonel Thompson, one of the ranchers most outspoken on the issue of rustling.

Hank and Charlie drank whiskey together and began to play cards. The more they drank, the more unorthodox their game became. With no explanation, they moved their cards from the round card table to the rough plank floor. Now the game took on a more deadly tone. Long drew his bowie knife and pinned Hank's buckskins to the floor. Hank followed suit sticking his knife through Charlie's leather chaps holding him to the wood. At this point, Graham stepped in to separate the duelists and the two drifted apart.

Later that afternoon, Long was with his cronies in Till Glaze's Singer Saloon when Vaughan entered and threw his gold piece on the bar offering to set up drinks for all. This time Charlie refused and Hank took offense. The two men like fighting cocks in a pit started a ritual of abuse which continued until the final challenge was offered and accepted. "Charlie," Vaughan ordered, "drink with me like a gentleman or pull your gun and we'll commence shooting."

Much as they wanted to observe the action, the bystanders quickly cleared the room as Vaughan and Long grabbed left hands and began firing their revolvers at each other. Long, who had the least experience in this type of gunplay, was allowed the first shot. He fired off a ball which grazed Vaughan's head, opening a wound in the scalp that started blood pouring down his face. Then, leaping and whooping like an Indian in combat, Vaughan pumped four bullets into Long's body. Before his shooting arm was rendered useless, Long improved his aim and fired a slug which thudded into Vaughan's chest where it ranged through his left lung and came to rest near his spine.

With that, the bloody battle and the Sunday ended. The contenders, punctured and bleeding, were carried off to a quiet place to rest and heal their wounds. Both survived to continue on separate trails—Charlie riding in support of the vigilantes and Hank just keeping out of the reach of their ropes.

This was one episode in the life of Henry C. Vaughan who was reported to have killed thirteen men during his relatively short existence. His life spanned a remarkable period in western history. Hank lived during that time of the West when ranchers policed the rangelands for lack of better law enforcement. He travelled by horseback before trains and railroads replaced the trails. Automobiles were not even imagined. Electric power was not available. The telephone and telegraph were yet to be invented, but word of Vaughan's activities somehow preceded him wherever he went. He gained notoriety not so much for his lawlessness as for his bizarre behavior which kept reporters busy relating his activities in every town that could support a newspaper. These reports covered barroom brawls, violent shooting scrapes, and wild buggy rides. Occasionally papers considered it newsworthy to simply tell their readers that Hank Vaughan had been in town.

Few writers knew much about Vaughan and little effort was spent in getting background for stories about him. In 1890, when a man named McDonald came to Pendleton planning to shoot Hank to avenge his brother's death, the *East Oregonian* neither verified nor disproved the claim that Hank had killed his brother. When Hank shot Pitt Smith in front of the Overland Hotel in Boise City, the *Tri-weekly Statesman* gave no clue as to the motive.

Most of those who later reminisced about Vaughan did not know where he came from. William Parsons, the Umatilla County lawyer, said, "It is claimed he was born in the Willamette Valley, but he was probably a native of Missouri."[1] Parsons was proud of other Oregon products and perhaps he didn't wish to claim Vaughan as a native son, but Hank Vaughan was indeed an Oregon product, born there before that frontier became a state. He never attached much importance, however, to being one of the first Oregonians. His later activities showed he cared

*(Courtesy Lane County Museum)**

FIGURE 1—Hank's grandparents, William Tyler Vaughan and Phoebe Hazlett Vaughan, were among the earliest people to settle in Oregon's Willamette Valley. William arrived first in 1845. He returned in 1847 with his wife and their nine children.

little about belonging to any one part of the land. He ranged back and forth across the western territories of Oregon, Washington, Idaho, Nevada and occasionally into Arizona and Montana.

Hank grew up among restless men. His grandfather was one of them and Hank never tired of hearing how he as a young man moved his wife and their multiplying brood of children from Virginia to Kentucky, from Illinois to Missouri (fig. 1). They were in Platte County, Missouri, in 1845 when William Tyler Vaughan first learned of the opportunities offered in the Oregon frontier. He quickly signed on as a cattle drover with Sol. Tetherow on one of the earliest wagon trains of emigrants heading for Oregon.

In later years, the route of the Oregon Trail would be easily identifiable by the deep ruts forced on the land by thousands of wagon wheels, but, in 1845, when Grandpa Vaughan first traveled it, the trail was dim and every wagon master was looking for a better, quicker route. At Fort Boise, Col. W.G. T'Vault, captain of Vaughan's group, followed Stephen Meek south around the Blue Mountains into the Malheur region. They spent three desperate weeks wandering through the empty

* Figures not credited were provided by the authors.

desert of central Oregon.[2] Unshaken by this grim ordeal which cost the lives of twenty pioneers, Hank's grandfather was so taken by the Willamette Valley he returned to Missouri to bring back his family.

Hank greatly respected his grandfather who spent that winter splitting rails and other jobs earning money to make the return trip East. He travelled alone with little more than a couple of horses, a gun, a frying pan and some flour and made it back across the mountains and plains to Missouri.[3] Grandma Phoebe Hazlett Vaughan also came in for her share of respect from Hank. He had often heard the story of how she loaded their provisions into two big Conestoga wagons and with her nine children around her courageously crossed the plains with her husband.

When the grandparents reached the Oregon frontier, they chose a site along the slopes of the Cascade Range in the Waldo Hills near present day Coburg where they began turning a timbered wilderness into a farm. Alexander "Aleck," their oldest son, helped Captain Billy and Phoebe work their donation claim homestead that first winter, but he soon was making plans of his own with young Elizabeth Fields whose family arrived in the Willamette Valley the same year as the Vaughans.

In the spring of 1848, Aleck and Elizabeth were married (fig. 2). Choosing to stay in the same area as their parents, the young couple dutifully set about providing themselves with a farm, a home, and children. It was into this rural frontier setting and from this union Hank Vaughan was born on April 27, 1849.[4]

Henry Clay Vaughan was one of the first babies born in Oregon Territory. It took Joseph Lane and Joe Meek six months to bring word to the Willamette Valley that the U.S. Congress had officially recognized the boundaries of the Oregon Territory and located its capitol in Oregon City. By that time, the settlers were less interested in their own political development than they were in another development taking place several hundred miles south. Gold had been discovered in California and nearly every able bodied man had rushed there to seek his fortune.

Among those who headed for California were Hank's father, grandfather and several uncles.[5] These men had reached the West with no cash reserves and the chance of discovering gold in any quantity was enticing. With gold they could invest in seeds, and trees and livestock. Gold could buy an easier life. Some were lucky and did find the elusive mineral, but what small amount Hank's father brought back was soon gone. Wresting a living out of this new land continued as hard as before.

From the beginning, young Hank showed little enthusiasm for farming. While some people seem born with a love for the soil which keeps them contentedly in the field from daylight to dark, through spring, summer and fall, from plowing through harvest, Hank found such activity boring and tedious. If there was anything about the farm he liked, it was the horses his father kept. While these were a motley assortment of broken down and lame nags acquired from travellers headed past the farm, Hank would one day ride some of the best and fastest horses bred in the west.

Aleck, too, found farm life not at all appealing. In about 1862, he got tired of pulling stumps to convert forests into farmland and left his family to find more profitable and exciting work. As the oldest son, Hank stayed with his mother who was expecting another child, and his younger sisters, ten-year-old Amanda, five-year-old Almina Sarah, and two-year-old Nancy.

Aleck may first have tried mining with his uncle, John Q. Vaughan, who was prospecting in the Idaho City or west Bannock area as early as 1861.[6] When he

(Courtesy Sophia Riede)

FIGURE 2—Hank Vaughan's parents, Elizabeth Fields Vaughan and Alexander H. Vaughan, as they appeared in 1866. Hank's father is holding Francis Marion "Little Aleck," one of their seven children.

tired of mining, Aleck came back as far as The Dalles, a river front town which was beginning to grow and prosper as a supply point for the men headed for the gold mines in the remote inland regions of Oregon and Idaho Territory.

When Aleck sent word for his family to join him, there was a fair amount of tears shed as Elizabeth prepared to leave the comfort of her family and the home she had helped put together over the past twelve years. Now that baby Fannie had arrived, Aleck said they should come as soon as possible. He also instructed them to bring butter and cheese and any other food stuff they could for these items were selling at unbelievably high prices in The Dalles. Hank was only twelve when he was entrusted with the job of trading off their milk cows and extra horses. They kept the wagon and a team, however, to carry the produce and family to Portland.

The family joined the stream of wagons hauling Willamette Valley produce to Portland. Their route took them to the docks where ocean-going ships moored alongside the small stern- and side-wheeled steamers which served the upper Columbia. There they found hundreds of Idaho-bound miners thronging the docks clamoring for passage.

Through the help of Uncle George Washington Vaughan[7], a captain on one of the river boats, Hank and his mother found space on a vessel scheduled to leave soon for The Dalles. They then made the necessary arrangements to sell the horses and wagon. As Aleck predicted this provided enough cash to pay for the shipping costs on their farm produce plus the family's passage up river.

The steamer *Carrie Ladd* which would take Hank and his family for part of their journey was loaded at night. Food and equipment for the mines and miners up river were put aboard into her hull from the drays strung out along Front Street. By 4:30 a.m. the passengers began to arrive. By 5 a.m. with all the freight stowed aboard, the pilot climbed into the wheel house and upon his signal black smoke began to roll from the tall stacks.

After the first few lazy turnings, the great wheel began threshing the water, easing the prow of the boat from the dock. The pillar of steam from the escape pipe signalled the long white vessel's turn into the current of the Willamette River and a flurry of foam followed as the steamer slipped downstream. Hank's mother and her excited brood shared with the other passengers the thrill of the unfamiliar in their water born adventure.

The noise of the engine took on new dimensions when the *Carrie Ladd* left the Willamette and turned upstream forcing its way against the power of the mighty Columbia River. The smell of spring freshness filled the morning air as the heavily burdened paddle-wheeler cut a slow rolling wake through the Columbia, running bank full with the snow melt of mountain ranges as far inland as the Rockies.

By mid morning passengers gathered on deck to view the spectacular scenery of the gorge. Slowly the fir-covered hills moved higher and closer to the river, pierced by tall grey basalt outcrops rising in sheer columns from the river's edge hundreds of feet to their tops. While young Amanda gazed in awe at the spectacle of the myriad of falls cascading down the face of the cliffs, each mile upstream bringing another more spectacular view, Hank shifted his interests to his fellow passengers.

Among them was a group of California miners. These were hardened veterans of gold fevers caught and lost in mountain streams from the Caribou to California.

They were in high spirits believing the ship carried them nearer the golden lodes which were awaiting them in the Boise Basin of Idaho Territory. Miners were expected to be a rough lot, but these Californians were much more crude and coarse than normal and were mostly shunned by the more conservative Oregonians. Hank saw in their behavior a self confidence and boldness that he seldom noticed in the work-worn valley farmers. Hanging around listening to their stories and watching their antics made the time pass quickly for the boy.

Shortly before noon, the boat reached the lower cascade, a thundering rapid which created the first barrier to upstream traffic. From here, a train of the Cascades Portage Railway awaited the passengers. All freight had to be trundled by handcart out onto the wharf and into the stubby freight cars. The Vaughans with other passengers proceeded in tramcars which to their amusement were pulled by mules over a wooden roadbed on wooden rails. The six-mile ride took them alongside the rapids on a ledge below the steep cliff to the upper cascades where the small steamer *Idaho* waited to carry the passengers and freight on the next leg of their journey up the Columbia.

By early afternoon the *Idaho* still under full power paddled into full view of The Dalles. Hank's mother looked for the buildings of the Methodist mission which she remembered from her trip through here in 1846. That small mission station had been a welcome sight to the weary pioneers nearing the end of their journey on the Oregon Trail. This was the first white settlement they had seen since Boise Valley. The mission appeared to have grown in the fifteen years since but the number of Indian tipis and long houses spread along the rocky ledge upstream seemed about the same.

Anticipating the ship's arrival at the dock, the scow hands, stevedores and Mexican packers increased their activity as they prepared to receive passengers and freight. Empty wagons behind teams of pawing mules waited for supplies to fill the uptown stores while other wagons arrived loaded with cordwood to fuel the ship's engines for the downstream trip.

From where the *Idaho* would dock, four rows of drab rough cut wooden buildings appeared to fill a quarter mile of land up and down the river. Hank's eyes were drawn above those to the fort on the hill where three platoons of blue mounted cavalry drilled in tight formation, kicking up dust which spread across the low barracks to the officers' quarters under the yellow barked ponderosa pines. This force of regulars had come from the eastern states just a dozen years before, built their fort, and learned to fight against the Yakima, Palouse and Cayuse Indians. They would soon be called back to strengthen the Union forces fighting to hold on to the breakaway southern states in America's Civil War.

Hank felt the loss of momentum as the *Idaho* cut power and glided toward the wharf, her wheel lying dead in the water. At the proper instant on command from the captain, life surged back through the engines to the great wheel which now reversed, slowing the ship to rest with a grinding nudge against the rough planking of the wooden pier.

Hank was a boy of twelve when he first stepped foot in The Dalles. Up until then his experiences had been as a farm youth living in a quiet rural setting surrounded by family and friends. Here in The Dalles he would quickly absorb the excitement of this town involved as it was in the passage of men and goods to the

(Courtesy Oregon Historical Society)

FIGURE 3—The Dalles in the mid 1860s was the main supply point for all mining development in the interior northwest. The fort and military post is visible on the bench land behind town in line with Mt. Hood. The Vaughan house was on the same level but far to the left near the timber's edge.

inland mines up river. Located on the south bank of the Columbia River between two nearly impassible cascades, The Dalles was the main supply point for the interior mines (fig. 3).

According to Henry Dosch, an early-day merchant selling mining supplies for Black, Miller and Co., The Dalles was a wide open town:

> The Dalles [1864] had a population of not less than 2,700, and it was always thronging with transients on their way to or from the mines. There was more life in The Dalles in a day than there was in Portland in a month.[8]

As the most important outfitting point east of the Cascades, The Dalles was also the hangout of gamblers and their prey (fig. 4). According to frontiersman, Andrew J. Splawn:

> . . . Gambling hells with music and songs were on every side; clinking of coins around the tables told the old story that the fools were not all dead yet . . . it was the rendezvous of border ruffians . . . Matt Bledso [sic], red-headed cutthroat who had become notorious for killing a few innocent men, was here. The noted Hank Vaughn [sic]**, then a boy, was also attending this school of science; his later career showing him to have been an apt pupil.[9]

** Future misspellings of Vaughan will not be recognized.

(Courtesy Oregon Historical Society)

FIGURE 4—In 1864, mining outfitters at The Dalles did a brisk business during spring and summer months. When mining activity closed down for the winter, it was the bars, casinos and hostels that received the miners' earnings.

Hank did learn from the people who thronged through the town. He stored in his mind the atmosphere surrounding the swaggering ruffians who spent the slack winter months gambling and carousing as they waited for the warm weather that signalled their chance to head back to the hills in their search of the Eldorado.

It is known the Vaughans spent about five years in The Dalles. Pioneer historian, Lulu Crandall, said:

> Hank Vaughn lived in The Dalles in the very early "sixties," and went to school here. The family lived in a house, long ago gone, on the edge of the bluff east of The Dalles hospital. I remember him as one of the "big boys" and recall his name rather than his personality. . . . [10]

During that time, according to lawman, Oliver C. White, "Henry Vaughan was a terror." It is not known what Hank did to gain that reputation so young. He did go to school, said White, but not long enough to learn to write.[11] As for schooling, Hank probably had little chance to attend classes. He was the oldest child and although only in his early teens, in those frontier times, he was considered old enough to share in the work of supporting the family. Besides schools for older children were not often available and for someone like Hank who never had any great liking for what he considered the confinement of a classroom, there was little to be gained in forcing him to attend school.

If Aleck and Elizabeth could not find work for Hank, it was certain a job would be found somewhere for him through the extended Vaughan family. And there was plenty of family around. Hank had eleven aunts and uncles in the Oregon Territory, all descendants of Capt. Billy and Grandma Phoebe. Besides Billy and Phoebe, other Vaughan families had come from the East with those early wagon trains and now their children were spreading out over the territories making their living in a variety of ways.

Many continued agricultural pursuits in the Willamette Valley area. The problem faced by these early farmers was not lack of fertile and plentiful soil. There was that in vast abundance. Once the trees were grubbed out and the wild land tamed, there was more than enough produce for immediate consumption. No, the problem was not lack of land or laborers—it was lack of markets.

In the early 1860s two separate events occurred to change the fortunes of these farmers. First, the harsh winter of 1860-61 killed thousands of cattle in the interior Pacific northwest. The remaining herds were thinned dramatically by the equally killing winter of 1861-62. In the Willamette Valley where winter conditions were less severe, cattle were in surplus. There was a big demand for these animals to restock the ranges so recently decimated in the Columbia basin and in nearby Washington Territory. Second, gold was discovered along the inland mountain rivers bringing an influx of fortune seekers like Aleck and his kin. Both events opened up the markets the valley farmers were seeking.

Some of the Vaughan's chose to go prospecting as they had earlier to the rich gold fields of California. But after weighing the uncertainties of fortunes to be made in discovery against the certainty of making a living supplying the miners, the older Vaughan men like Capt. Billy encouraged the younger Vaughans to deliver the abundant produce from their farms to the needy mining communities.

There was a great sense of urgency about all this as no one could predict how long the bonanza would last. While nuggets were still being discovered, the miners were hungry consumers and would pay whatever price was demanded to get the foodstuffs they needed. Once the mineral veins played out, miners departed as quickly as they had come and markets departed with them. So for the Willamette Valley Vaughans with extra beef, dairy products, produce from their gardens and orchards, flour ground at the family mills, salted pork and dried fish, the challenge was to take advantage of the first strikes and get their goods to the miners quickly.

This was no easy undertaking. In good weather, a herd of cattle-or horse-drawn wagons full of farm produce could make the trip from Coburg to The Dalles in about ten days. The only overland route in the early 1860s was the Barlow Toll Road which wound over the Cascade Range, that steep forested barrier to the inland valleys. This route had not improved much since it was opened to wagon use in 1846.

At first everything the Vaughans brought over the mountains could be sold in The Dalles. But as local producers got into the market, it became necessary for the Vaughans to take their foodstuff to Canyon City two hundred miles south and east of The Dalles. Hank's dad was involved in freighting goods to and from Canyon City, gaining valuable experience which later put him into a position to become a part of the profitable freighting business in Idaho Territory.

The community of Canyon City had come into existence after gold was discovered along Canyon Creek late in 1861. At first it was just a tent city strung along the three-mile length of the canyon. The miners were too busy sifting out the precious ore trapped above bedrock to erect any permanent facilities, but, as the strikes continued and cash flowed in, a town grew up to supply the needs of the miners. The usual assortment of stores, livery, saloons, eating houses, and hotels began to appear until by 1864 there were churches, law offices and even an official post office. The contract for the post office was issued to Henry H. Wheeler whose contributions to the area was recognized when Wheeler County was named after him.

The Vaughans refined their marketing somewhat after 1863 when they began keeping a small herd of cattle in the Canyon City area. Young Hank, who had always liked working with horses and cattle, was a natural to help his uncles take care of their profitable beef herd here. He proved able to deal with this part of the operation and was gradually given more responsibility in maintaining this small herd, selling animals when possible.

In the process he began pasturing horses for miners and townspeople, herding their animals on the grassy foothills north of town. In this way, he made friends with the owners of the animals he kept and with the local butchers he supplied with beef. It was here he met Dick Donica who would remain a lifelong friend. He also made friends with Indians of the Warm Springs and northern Paiute tribes and through them learned the fine points of bartering their ponies to sell to miners. These years were times of learning for Hank. Although he neglected his formal education, he was gaining valuable experience buying, selling and handling livestock.

Hank was in Canyon City and only fifteen years old when he got into his first serious trouble with the law.[12] It is assumed the problem had something to do with his business dealings. Hank and his buddies had been supplying meat to the local butchers and taking care of horses for the past two years. They had also started buying and selling horses and Hank was learning how to deal in this tricky venture and come out ahead. On the occasion when he got into trouble in Canyon City, it is most probable that a miner had bought some horses from the young trader and was now unwilling to come up with the cash for the final payment.

Perhaps the man, William Headspot, had lost his money while drinking and gambling. At any rate when Hank accosted him and demanded payment, Headspot tried to bluff the boy. He figured he was dealing with a youngster, albeit one who was armed and acting pretty tough, but still a boy who could be outwitted. However, Hank was no ordinary farm youth. He had been more or less on his own for the past two years, living on the trail or in temporary camps while he and his friends herded small bands of horses and cattle. Dealing with butchers and beef was fairly straight forward, but in branching out into horse trading the rules of transactions took on new character. Horse traders had to be shrewder and tougher than cattle traders especially when they were dealing with transient groups like miners. If a deal wasn't cash on delivery the seller could expect problems in collecting later.

This was the situation young Hank faced. The horse had been delivered to Headspot with only partial payment. Hank knew he would have trouble collecting the balance. To give himself courage and get into the proper mood to approach the older man, Hank visited the bar for a drink of whiskey. He wasn't unknown in town and he probably found friends willing to buy him a drink and listen to his problem. The first time he sought out Headspot and demanded payment, he was told there was no money, that he'd lost everything in a poker game. Hank argued with Headspot and insisted if he couldn't pay then he'd take back the horse. He said he'd give Headspot a couple hours to come up with the full payment or the horse, and then went back to the bar with his friends and waited.

Two hours later, fortified with more drink and encouragement from his buddies, Hank again went after Headspot. This time Headspot jeered at the young, tipsy cowboy, repeated that he had no money to pay and no horse to return and added a further insult that the deal was no good anyway as the horse Hank sold him was stolen. That was an answer Hank wouldn't accept and being accused of stealing horses in front of his friends was an insult he couldn't let go by. In a fury, according to eye witness G.W. Anderson, Hank drew his Colt revolver and fired. His aim was high and the bullet knocked Headspot down as it glanced across the top of his forehead, drilling a furrow through his scalp.[13]

Hank left town immediately. It wasn't until seven days later that the deputy located and arrested him on charges of assault with a deadly weapon.

That drinking and belligerence were the causes of the shooting is indicated by the lack of vigilante action. If the charge had been more serious like horse theft or claim jumping, it is likely the miners would have punished Hank on the spot themselves. Before these mining towns had any strong formal government services, the vigilantes served a necessary community function—operating quite openly to bring frontier justice to the mining districts. Justice was usually swift and final; guilty verdicts were not subject to appeal. Hank didn't experience the wrath of a vigilante mob this time, but it was only a matter of time before he would.

Hank didn't stay in custody long. Two days later, he went free on bail after $400 was posted by bondsmen, A.W. Marchand and C.H. Rolfe. Perhaps Hank's friends brought in enough horses to cover his bail. It is hard to believe that the bondsmen knew him well enough to be assured that he would hang around to stand trial.

He was free for six weeks and did stay around Canyon City tending the cattle and horses as before. But by August 14, the bondsmen became worried over threats they had heard him make against G.W. Anderson who had filed the original complaint for his arrest. They brought Hank back to the lawmen and asked for their bond money back. Again Hank only spent two days in custody before two new bondspersons appeared. This time John Thomas and Grace Darling set Vaughan free. This would not be the last time Grace Darling would cross trails with Hank.

That day Hank stayed in town. While drinking with his friends in the bar to celebrate his new found freedom, Hank repeated his grievances against Anderson and Headspot and boasted he'd shoot either one on sight. When Anderson did appear, the drunken Hank drew his pistol and before he could be restrained fired off a shot that hit the man.

Bondsmen Darling and Thomas promptly handed him over to Deputy Sheriff M.P. Berry in the presence of Justice of the Peace B. Whitten. He was then taken from Canyon City to The Dalles, the only proper jail east of the Cascade range, and locked up in custody of Sheriff Charles M. White pending the next session of

Circuit Court. The charges against him now also included assaulting one "John Doe" with a pistol with intent to murder him. For some unknown reason, Anderson declined to sign the complaint after Hank's rearrest.

Hank spent four months in jail before his case came to trial. He was a problem prisoner, according to Sheriff White who chained him to a ring bolt in the center of the cell floor, because he shouted and sang ribald songs which disturbed the neighborhood for blocks around the courthouse.[14]

That Hank had an unsavory reputation in The Dalles became evident when many citizens who were called for jury duty were dismissed because they were found to be biased against the defendant, ". . . possessed of a state of mind which would preclude a fair trial." A jury was eventually picked from a slate of ranchers and businessmen, many of whom became well known and successful, such as Henry Heppner, Sam Ladd, Geo. R. Snipes, James Fulton, A.C. Phelps, and N.W. Wallace.

The first case involving Headspot was dropped, but the trial proceeded for the alleged assault on John Doe. Four witnesses were subpoenaed for the state, Deputy Dugall Walker, David Koontz, Isaac Jewell and Dr. Desch, who had probably attended the victimized Anderson. One witness, Anna Smith, appeared in behalf of Vaughan.[15]

When the jury could not agree on a verdict they were discharged. Vaughan's legal counsel then bargained with the judge to allow Hank to change his plea to guilty. Hank's family also appeared before the judge and because of a suggestion they made regarding Hank's future, Judge J.G. Wilson fined Hank $1.00 and cost and released him to Sheriff White until the sum was paid.

The family's suggestion was that Hank be inducted into the First Oregon Volunteer Infantry. This group was now recruiting members to fill the gap left when the regular army troops were ordered east to fight in the Civil War. The family hoped this disciplined life would keep Hank under control until he could mature into a law abiding citizen. On the same day he received his sentencing, January 2, 1865, not only Hank but also his father, Aleck, and two of his cousins enlisted in this Oregon volunteer guard.

The family remembers that Hank did not go along with this idea willingly. He convinced his father to go first in the induction line to "learn the procedure" as he said. In the confusion of enlistment, Aleck was not too attentive. After he filled out the papers, signed his name and handed the documents back to the recruiting officer, he turned to explain the process to Hank. But Hank was no where to be found.[16]

He did return later that same day under escort of his family and/or the law as he is shown on the January 2, 1865, muster roll as Entry No. 90. His father was No. 78; cousins Charles D. and Abner M. Vaughan of Hillsboro were Nos. 81 and 82. Both Aleck and Hank were assigned to Company G.

It was quickly apparent that Hank was not suited for this kind of regimentation. Six weeks later, on February 17, 1865, Lt. Wm. Kapus, U.S. Army, signed a Muster and Descriptive Roll which showed Henry C. Vaughan being "rejected and discharged . . . by reason of general unfitness for the service."[17]

REFERENCES

Chapter 1

1. Parsons, William, and W.S. Shiach. *History of Umatilla and Morrow County*. Spokane: W.H. Lever, 1902.
2. Clark, Keith, and Lowell Tiller. *Terrible Trail: The Meek Cutoff, 1845*. Caldwell: Idaho, Caxton Printers, Ltd., 1966.
3. Moore, Lucia. *The Wheel and The Hearth*. New York: Ballantine, 1953, 248.
4. Census, United States, Report of the Census Bureau, Washington, D.C., 1850. Henry C. Vaughan was first officially recorded as a resident in House No. 68 of Linn County (later Lane County); born in Oregon Territory to Alexander Vaughan, age 22, and Elizabeth Vaughan, age 19.
5. Anon. *Portrait and Biographical Record of the Willamette Valley Oregon*. Chicago: Chapman Publishing Co., 1903, 1356.
6. Bancroft, Hubert Howe. *History of Washington, Idaho, and Montana 1845-1889*. Vol. 31, San Francisco: The History Company, 1890, 634-5.
7. North Pacific History Company. *History of the Pacific Northwest: Oregon and Washington*. Vol. 2, Portland: 1889, 15.
8. Lockley, Fred. *Reminiscences of Colonel Henry Ernst Dosch*. Eugene: Koke-Tiffany, 1924, 9.
9. Splawn, Andrew J. *Kamiakin-Last Hero of the Yakimas*. Portland: Metropolitan Press, 1944, 199.
10. The Dalles *Chronicle*, July 22, 1926.
11. The Dalles *Chronicle*, September 23, 1926
12. Wasco County Circuit Court, Criminal Case File No. 55-51, Oregon State Archives, Salem. The plaintiff may have been William Hudspeth whose name was variously spelled. "Headspot" did not appear to press charges and clarify the spelling. Hudspeth was later a prominent rancher in southeastern Oregon (see Western Historical Publishing Company, *History of Baker, Grant, Malheur and Harney Counties*. Spokane: W.H. Lever Company, 1902, 401.)
13. Taylor, Daniel M. "Recollections of Hank Vaughn," Works Project Administration, General History No. 11, Umatilla County, Biographies-Hank Vaughn, 2 p., Oregon State Archives, Salem.
14. The Dalles *Chronicle*, September 23, 1926.
15. Wasco County Circuit Court, Criminal Case File No. 55-51. *op. cit.*
16. Personal interview, Mrs. Sophia Riede, Boise, Idaho, February 7, 1973. The late Mrs. Riede was a grandniece of Hank Vaughan.
17. Military Department Records, File No. 59-36 and 60-28, Oregon State Archives, Salem.

II.

GAINING A REPUTATION
(1865)

Hank Vaughan's dishonorable discharge from the Army was not well received by his mother and family. They had sincerely believed, if he were given a few years to mature while he gained experience in some useful vocation, he would stay out of the kind of trouble he had been into in Canyon City. The family supported him through the ordeal of his recent trial, accepting that he had been provoked into the Canyon City shooting, but they also felt it would be wise to get him out of the area long enough for people to forget about his youthful clash with society.

Although Judge Wilson and Hank's family may have felt a period in the military would be good for him, Hank bitterly resented his forced induction. His belligerent behavior may have been without purpose at first, but he so disliked the army he cultivated a style of behavior that within six weeks got him a discharge from the service. Once he was out of the army, he wasted little time making his own plans for getting away from The Dalles.

Winter time in the Pacific Northwest was a slack season for mining and The Dalles was the gathering point for miners as they awaited the spring thaw when they could again take up prospecting. The town was crowded with men who spent their time gambling, drinking, telling tall tales about their adventures, and speculating on how soon they would be able to head back to the hills to seek their fortune. Hank had always been attracted to this type of rowdy men and he spent a great deal of his time on the fringe of this crowd as he laid his future plans.

He became acquainted during this period with a young man by the name of Dick Bunton. Bunton who grew up on one of the early farms in the vicinity of Umatilla Landing had gravitated to making a living buying and selling horses. Since some of these horses were reportedly not always legally his, he often came to the attention of the law. Sheriff White in The Dalles was watching him, but as there was not enough evidence against him at this time he was free and a part of the winter crowd in The Dalles.

Finding they shared both an interest in horses and a strong desire to relocate as soon as the weather permitted, Hank and Bunton formed a loose partnership with the object of financing their entry into Idaho Territory through their horse trading abilities.

There was risk involved but Hank even at this age was not one to let that stop him. He was developing an ability to analyze a situation and figure out how he could exploit it. If the conditions seemed risky, he didn't seem to mind. He understood horses and knew they were a valuable commodity. Good saddle horses were selling for $200 in Boise City. Hank calculated the sale of one horse would equal more than what he might make in a month as a packer with a mule train or in a year herding stock for his uncles. What he needed was a companion with like interests who was familiar with the country that lay between The Dalles and Idaho Territory. He seemed to have found that person in Dick Bunton.

The two left The Dalles on a warm spring day in early April of 1865. They headed up the Columbia River on horseback following the wagon route along the boulder strewn terraces which marked the ancient levels of the relentless river as it carved its way down to its present channel. The hills were carpeted with clumps of bunch grass pushing new leaves through the silvery remains of last year's growth. The trail dropped in and out of the draws to the streams that fed into the main river, their courses lined with the shimmering yellow-green of the willows and cottonwood trees.

The pair travelled lightly. They had been successful in trading some of their possessions to get a few Indian ponies and the barest essentials necessary for camping. If any loose horses presented themselves along the way, they intended to add them to their band. They would repeat this trading process wherever they met a concentration of Indians. The Indians coveted good racing horses and they prized the white man's faster horses. If Hank and Dick could acquire a good blooded horse from a rancher, they might trade it for two or three Indian ponies which in turn could be sold at inflated prices to footsore miners.

It would take the two young men three to four days to reach the foothills of the Blue Mountains. Their plan was to keep to the less used Indian trails that Bunton knew. They avoided the little community which was growing up around the bridge Moses Goodwin built across the Umatilla River. They went four or five miles on beyond where they joined a group of Cayuse Indians and set up camp nearby. They spent about a month here. It was a good spot and one Hank would return to many times.

When Hank and Bunton felt they were ready to move on, they made a raid on a local rancher, relieving him of a couple good horses. They crossed the Blue Mountains not on the Meacham Road but on the old military road or Daley Road which skirted the Umatilla Indian Reservation, crossing the mountains by way of Starkey prairie.[1] Legitimate travellers, though trespassing on the reservation, would be taking the much improved Meacham Road which went more directly over the Blues.

At this time in the spring, the only people they would expect to encounter along the Daley route would be family groups of Cayuse Indians who were there digging camas roots and snagging steelhead trout from the swollen tributaries of the Grande Ronde River. These Indians paid little attention to Vaughan and Bunton but other riders would soon follow who were very interested in where the pair had gone.

While the Meacham Road entered the Grande Ronde Valley and passed through the tiny community of Brownsville, the Daley route kept to the mountains where there was no habitation. Hank and Dick could almost be certain they would not see other travellers until they came out of the forks in the lower Powder River Valley near the present site of North Powder. Here they could have picked up the Oregon Trail, but not wanting to be seen by anyone using this main route to Fort Boise they crossed the Powder River and kept to the sagebrush hills, south of the Wallowa Mountains. It was late in the afternoon when they set up their camp.

Vaughan and Bunton chose their overnight camp with care. The young men had good reasons to be cautious. They knew from their Cayuse friends that a group of Snake Indians suspected of stealing Cayuse ponies was in the area and were being followed by warriors from the Umatilla Reservation.[2] The Vaughan-Bunton duo didn't want to get mixed up in these Indian affairs so they chose their overnight camp fairly close to the Express Ranch knowing the Indians would stay further away.

On the other hand, they camped off the main route because of the uncertain ownership of some of the horses in their care. They didn't want their presence known by too many white travellers. Their plans were to get a very early start the next morning, keeping as many miles as they could between themselves and any lawmen who might be tracking them.

The camp site they chose was several miles east of the Express Ranch and a mile before the Burnt River cuts through the narrow canyon above Weatherby Station (fig. 5). At this point, a small stringer meadow along Swayze Creek entered

FIGURE 5—This site east of Durkee is thought to be where Hank Vaughan and his partner, Dick Bunton, had the midnight gun fight with the Umatilla County lawmen. The area is along Swayze Creek just north of where Burnt River enters the canyon gorge. Bunton's unmarked grave is somewhere nearby.

the valley from the north. Scattered willow and alder followed the creek to the cottonwood lined river below. Here, one-half mile from the river in a clump of willow about fifty feet from Swayze Creek, the two horse drovers dropped camp and turned all but two saddle horses loose.

The saddle horses were staked on picket ropes close to their willow bush camp where they could be quickly mounted if their owners needed to leave in a hurry. The riders expected to be followed, but, up until now, they had no reason to believe that they were.

However, they were wrong. When Umatilla County Sheriff Frank Maddock received the reports of stolen horses from around the boundaries of the Indian reservation, he immediately deputized several men and with them started tracking the thieves. He had been watching Hank and Dick the past month as Sheriff White had alerted him upon their departure from The Dalles and entry into Maddock's territory.

When a quick check revealed the boys had recently slipped out of the country, Maddock was sure the missing horses were with them. He left Pendleton with his deputy, Jackson "John" Hart, planning to stop them before they could reach Boise City or Placerville and dispose of their excess stock.

It was late in the afternoon of May 14 when Sheriff Maddock and Deputy Hart reached the Express Ranch (fig. 6). After hearing the report that two cowboys with a small band of horses had been noticed camping off the main trail, Maddock, suspecting the outfit to belong to Bunton and Vaughan, laid plans to approach the camp at night. Before leaving the ranch, Maddock secured fresh horses from Ira Knight. When asked if he might need some help in making the arrest, Maddock scorned any assistance as he considered Hank and his comrade only boys.[3]

After surveying the camp's location and knowing that the boys would undoubtedly be planning an early departure, probably before daybreak, they decided their best bet was a surprise attack. A late-rising half moon would give the officers enough light to see the necessary features of the camp and the positions of their sleeping quarry. Without the moon, they would have been forced to wait until daybreak.

Maddock and Hart tied their horses near the main trail along Burnt River. On foot with loaded revolvers in hand, they approached the quiet camp, separating about five hundred feet from the sleeping boys. Hart was to cover Hank while Maddock got into a position to control Bunton. As Maddock reached for Bunton's bedroll, he cried out. "Throw up your hands!"

The side canyon of Swayze Creek erupted in gunfire as Hank and Bunton woke up shooting. The officers returned the fire and the soft light of the moon was charged with the flash of exploding gun powder. The tethered horses snorted, jerked free of the picket ropes, and clattered up the canyon toward the loose band.

For a moment, all was quiet. Hart and Bunton were dead, killed instantly during the brief exchange. Sheriff Maddock had been hit by a bullet which crashed into his left cheek, passing through his head and emerging at the base of his skull. He lay on the ground, bleeding profusely, unable to move. Hank, too, was bleeding from a wound in his thigh and one in his scalp where a bullet had creased his skull, but he found he could move. He heard the horses of the lawmen nickering and threshing around but still tied near the trail. Making his way as best he could to

(Courtesy McCord Collection)

FIGURE 6—The Express Ranch run by C.W. Durkee was an important relay station on the Burnt River. Three stage and freight lines, Thomas and Ruckel, Hailey and Ish, and Greathouse and Company which competed in transporting goods and passengers between Boise City and Umatilla Landing, intersected here.

these animals, he cut one free, caught and mounted the other one, and rode far up into Swayze Canyon.

The gunfight was heard back at the Express Ranch and C.W. Durkee and others saddled up and came to investigate. Upon finding the dead and wounded, they brought Maddock back to the ranch, recruited a posse and proceeded to track down Vaughan. In his wounded condition, he was not able to elude the posse for long and they brought him into custody the following day.

The body of Dick Bunton was buried without ceremony not far off the trail from where he died. Oliver White, son of the Wasco County sheriff, said he saw the fresh grave while riding down Burnt River the following year.[4]

Maddock survived but he was in no condition to return Hank to Umatilla County. Word was sent to Auburn where on May 17, 1865, Sheriff J.H. Ingraham and Judge Neill Johnson issued a Baker County warrant for Vaughan's arrest, charging him with murder.

As soon as Vaughan could travel, he was taken to Auburn to stand trial. Auburn, the Baker County seat, was a thriving mining camp not unlike Canyon City (fig. 7). It had sprung into being three years earlier when gold was discovered in Griffin's Gulch late in the fall of 1861. Within a year it was estimated the district contained a floating population of between four and five thousand people. Isaac Hiatt, Baker County historian, said the influx was terrific. General stores, saloons, blacksmith shops and livery stables were put up and nearly every space down Blue Canyon for a mile was occupied.[5]

What happened after Hank was delivered to Auburn would indicate that feelings were running high against him over the killing of a lawman. It was late in the afternoon when an hostile mob began converging on the jail threatening to take the

(Courtesy Oregon Historical Society)

FIGURE 7—The upper end of Auburn's main street in 1864 shows log and shake roof buildings perched on the hillside. The two-story building to the right of the forked pine tree was the site of Vaughan's trial.

law in their hands. As speakers urged short circuiting the law and lynching the youthful killer and horse thief, the crowd outside the building where he was held became more and more agitated. Hank had to have been worried as he knew the fate of suspected criminals at the hands of such an aroused mob. He and his late companion had thoroughly discussed the fate of Bill Bunton at the hands of the Montana vigilantes who rid that territory of the notorious Plummer gang only the year before.

Fortunately for Hank, John Hailey, Sr., was in Auburn at that time. Striding to the jail and standing at its door, he drew his two revolvers. Calmly facing the mob, he announced that the prisoner would be tried by a regular court and anyone attempting to rush the jail would be shot. Hailey, a very imposing and respected man, was courageous enough to stand in front of this vigilante group bent on dealing out quick justice.[6] The crowd, knowing his reputation as a dead shot, milled about muttering threats and then dispersed into the night.

Hank's alleged crimes were to be considered in two separate trials. On May 25, Vaughan was properly arraigned. He was charged with the theft of a black mare belonging to Ira Knight and while in the commission of this felony having shot and killed John Hart.[7] He was prosecuted by State District Attorney W.A. George in the circuit court of J.G. Wilson, the same judge who had tried Hank in The Dalles only a few months before.

Vaughan was represented by R.F. Boham and James H. Slater, who later became a United States senator from Oregon. Vaughan entered a plea of not guilty. His attorneys asked for a postponement in view of the fact that the principal witness for the defense was dead and the only material witness, Dick Donica, of Marion County, was not available. Hank hoped his father would appear in his behalf as Aleck was serving with the First Oregon Volunteer Infantry somewhere in the vicinity of Fort Harney, but somehow the older Vaughan never got to Auburn in time to assist his son.

Acting without hesitation, the court considered and then overruled the motion to postpone. Trial proceeded on the larceny count. Witnesses for the state were Ira W. Knight, John Hailey, Sr., C.W. Durkee, J.J. Jarvis, S. Lowry, and Anthony Augustus, all men involved in the Burnt River posse. Although Vaughan claimed he had a contract to purchase the horse referred to in the indictment from the deceased Dick Bunton, the jury after a short deliberation returned a verdict of guilty. On Monday morning May 29 at 9 a.m. Vaughan was sentenced for larceny of a horse and given ten years in the state penitentiary.

That gloomy day in court continued for Hank with the selection of a new jury to hear the murder charge against him. Many of the impaneled jurors were found unfit to serve and the sheriff was ordered to fill the panel from the group of bystanders. The trial began with the defense giving a good accounting despite heavy odds against them. The state again called the former witnesses and, in addition, one William Henry was called as a witness for the defendant.

The jury took somewhat longer in this case, but, in due time, the foreman, David Collins, announced a verdict of guilty of second degree murder as charged. The counsel for Vaughan immediately submitted a motion for a new trial but the motion was denied. Sentencing was deferred until 5 p.m. the following day. At that appointed time, Henry C. Vaughan was sentenced to life imprisonment.

He remained in the Auburn jail for nearly two weeks before arrangements could be made to transport him to prison. Public sentiment was strong against him as evidenced by an item in The Dalles *Weekly Mountaineer* of June 16, 1865:

> Henry Vaughan, the boy thief and murderer, arrived at The Dalles yesterday in custody of an officer on his way to the penitentiary, where he is to pass the remainder of his life. This fellow is a youth—probably seventeen years of age—yet he is steeped in crime, and regarded as one of the worst villains that ever cursed the country. It is to be hoped that he is not permitted to escape, as in the event of his return to this county he is sure to be hung.

One of the reasons for the vehemence expressed in the press was the resentment over the killing of Jackson Hart. As pioneer freighter, George Waggoner, eulogized:

> Jack was a typical frontiersman, as genial a comrade and as brave a man as ever rode upon the Idaho trails. Straight as an Indian and almost as dark, he stood six feet two in his stockings and sat his horse as though born for the saddle. Like all truly brave men, Jack was tender-hearted and averse to shedding blood, and here I may remark that this trait of character cost him his life while arresting Hank Vaughn, a desperado, near Express Ranch, ...[8]

Public sentiment was not all against Vaughan, however. Oliver White gave an explanation for this:

> The plea of the boys that they thought they were being attacked by Indians was made in Hank's trial and lessened the sentence, [for] . . . it was pretty well known that Indians shot first, and talked afterwards. Hank supposed that he would be followed by father [Sheriff Charles M. White], and I think, told father that he thought he was shooting at him.[9]

On commitment to the penitentiary, Vaughan was listed as Case No. 172 in the Great Register. He was described as being sixteen years old, 5 feet 5 inches tall, of a straight build and weighing 119 pounds. He had light auburn hair, blue eyes and a light complexion. The Great Register added that he had a long scar in the hairline on the left side of his head which was the result of a gunshot wound.[10]

Although it wouldn't be long before the penitentiary was moved to Salem, Vaughan's term in prison started in Portland, the location of the Oregon Territorial Prison. Since territorial prisons were meant to be tougher than the meanest outlaw ever sentenced there, conditions in most of them were grim. The Oregon institution did not acquire the notoriety of hellhole as did some in the West, but that was not to infer this prison was much better. Suffice it to say, Vaughan found prison life bad enough that once he was out he avoided ever returning.

REFERENCES

Chapter 2

1. Tucker, Gerald J. "The Pilot Rock Emigrant Road." Manuscript, Umatilla County Library, Pendleton, Oregon. 10.
2. Ruby, Robert H., and John A. Brown. *The Cayuse Indians: Imperial Tribesmen of Old Oregon.* Norman: University of Oklahoma Press, 1972. 284.
3. Drake, Lee D. Original Manuscript. No Date, 10. Typescript in possession of James H. Sturgis, Curator, Blue Mountain College Museum, Pendleton.
4. The Dalles *Chronicle*, September 26, 1926.
5. Hiatt, Isaac. *Thirty-one Years in Baker County.* Baker City, Oregon: Abbott and Foster, 1893, 38.
6. Drake, *op. cit.*
7. Baker County Circuit Court, May Term 1865, Criminal Case File No. 19, Baker City, Oregon.
8. Waggoner, George A. *Stories of Old Oregon.* Salem: Statesman Publishing Co., 1904. 224.
9. The Dalles *Chronicle*, September 26, 1926.
10. The Great Register, Vol. 1., Oregon State Archives, Salem, 18-19. Commitment Papers, Oregon State Penitentiary, Vol. 1857-1878, 120-122.

III.

LIFE IMPRISONMENT
(1865-1870)

"Life imprisonment." Those words pronounced by Judge J.G. Wilson weighed heavily on Hank Vaughan. The four months he spent in The Dalles jail waiting trial had been unbearable. How was he to survive life in prison? When he shared those thoughts with his lawyers in Auburn, their positive advice was: Don't cause any trouble. Cooperate with the authorities. The state's case against you is too weak. We are sure we can get you a pardon.

On the journey from Auburn to Portland, there were several times when he felt he could have escaped but the cold metal of the handcuffs, reminding he was quite securely in custody of Marshal Standefer, and the hope that a pardon might be forthcoming kept him an obedient prisoner.

He had been a keen observer of the developments in the courtroom in Auburn as his trial unfolded. He understood the defense plan his lawyers devised and appreciated how they had exploited the weakest arguments of the prosecution while drawing out the smallest detail that favored Hank's innocence. The logic of their arguments and how valuable they had been in pleading his case was imbedded in his mind. Now in analyzing his new situation, he decided the best course was to trust the advice of the lawyers, be a cooperative prisoner and wait for a pardon or at least an early release on parole.

Hank's life sentence began in the penitentiary in Portland. His only other experiences in a restrained environment was a very brief period of service in the Oregon militia, his time in The Dalles jail and a few weeks in custody in Canyon City. His dislike of the disciplined life in the army was so apparent he was quickly discharged and, according to Sheriff White, his behavior while in jail was totally belligerent.

Apparently he adapted quite well to prison life. Several reasons contributed to this good adjustment. One, the Oregon prison was not the hell hole most early prisons were described as being. Two, during the time he served his sentence, a new penitentiary was being constructed, a situation which provided a less confining atmosphere than the normal prison scenario, and, three, his "life sentence" was almost assured to be cut short.

Until now Hank would have had little reason to know much about the Oregon penal system. Its short history was greatly influenced by funding—usually the lack of it. The first jail, a two-story blockhouse in Oregon City, was built only two decades before when the territory fell heir to $875 from the estate of early day stockman, Ewing Young.[1] The building was only in service briefly, as in 1846, a spiteful ex-prisoner burned it to the ground.

The first territorial prison was located in Portland due to the efforts of Hugh D. O'Bryant who was that city's first mayor. He was appointed to oversee the erection of this facility which was intended to house the worst of Oregon's criminals. Until the territorial assembly appropriated money for the penitentiary, the convicts had been lodged in a variety of shelters and leased out during the day to work for their board and room.

Before the new brick and stone building where Hank would first be lodged could be completed, the monies appropriated for its construction were expended. When George Sloan took over as prison superintendent early in 1857, he found the exterior walls were up, but the iron doors not yet installed.[2] Sloan continued to farm out the prisoners to the city, not only because it reduced the cost of their upkeep, but also because it was the social belief of the period that hard labor and a disciplined life could change dissipated men into first class laborers. It was common to see small groups of convicts working on the streets of Portland, restrained by a ball and chain.

When Oregon became a state in 1859, the new governor continued the effort to make the penitentiary self-sufficient and contracted with Robert Newell and Levi English to lease the facility along with custody of the prisoners for a five-year period. The contract was sublet to Luzerne Besser who put the convicts out to labor in brickyards and lumber mills, as well as to construct and maintain Portland streets.

This leasing system was abolished by the state in 1862 because of the high rate of escape. At one time, Besser was chagrined to report to the state that all the prisoners had escaped, some from inside the enclosures and the rest from work gangs in the city.[3] When the reporter on The Dalles *Mountaineer* expressed the hope that Vaughan would not be permitted to escape, he had good reason to question the security system at the Portland penitentiary.

Under Superintendent A.C. Shaw security was tightened and the usually critical *Oregonian* praised his efficiently run organization. When Hank Vaughan began serving his sentence, Shaw was still superintendent and J.C. Gardner was warden. An innovation of Shaw's that Hank would have benefitted from was the establishment of a saddle and harness shop where the prisoners worked and learned a skill. Warden Gardner was also an innovator. He perfected the design of a shackle, the "Oregon Boot," which would later be used to insure Hank's secure confinement.

Conditions did not sound good at the Portland prison when Hank started his sentence in 1865. According to the report given the legislative session, the convicts there were:

> [a]. . . small disorganized mob of reckless men—dangerous to come in contact with—wretched and degraded from continual punishment being inflicted without having it tempered with justice—insolent from hunger; and driven to despair by

disease, which held them more surely as prisoners than the guards placed over them.[4]

Fortunately for Hank, within a year of his internment, this situation would change dramatically. As part of the relocation of all state institutions to the new state capitol, prisoners would be moved to Salem where they would build their own prison.

On May 16, 1866, Vaughan and his fellow inmates began their trek to Salem—on foot. It had been raining hard and the Willamette River was running high when the convicts were ferried across it at Portland. The muddy conditions only made it more miserable for this odd company of men and their mounted guards as they trudged south on the market road. For added security, the prisoners were chained in small groups. This entourage which included hospital, chuck and supply wagons, could proceed at a rate of only eight to ten miles a day. During the week-long trek, the procession was watched with much interest by citizens all along its route.

On arriving at the new prison grounds, the convicts went to work clearing the area for their new quarters. The federal government had advanced $40,000 toward construction of a prison facility on a twenty-five acre plot of land along Mill Creek east of Salem.[5] The first concern of Warden Gardner was the erection of a temporary pole shelter with a fourteen-foot high log stockade surrounding it. Next, preparations were begun for a brickyard along with the tilling and planting of a garden plot.

In their first report to Governor A.C. Gibbs, the prison commissioners noted it had been impossible in the unfinished state of the stockade fence and buildings to hold the prisoners with maximum security, and, at the same time allow them to work under humane conditions. In other words it was necessary to shackle the prisoners to their work. One of the holding devices in use was the one patented by Warden Gardner.[6]

Known as the "Oregon Boot," these shackles weighed from five to twenty-eight pounds each, depending on the size of the prisoner and his particular need for restraint. The boot consisted of a heavy iron ring which was locked around one ankle and rested upon another iron band which was supported by braces attached to the heel of the wearer's boot (fig. 8).

Although hampered in their movements, Hank and the other convicts continued to work and the temporary wooden prison began to take shape. It was a rectangular building 90 feet long by 36 feet wide, set on a solid foundation, with walls 4 inches thick. These walls were made of plank laid horizontally and nailed so as to be strong and hopefully impenetrable to saw or ax.[7]

The windows were large and afforded abundant light and ventilation, a great improvement over most early prisons. The iron gratings protecting the windows were salvaged from the old penitentiary building in Portland. The cells were made of double wood planking and arranged down the center of the prison, stacked two tiers high in double rows. Although designed to hold only one prisoner, many of the forty cells were soon holding two as the number of inmates increased. About two new prisoners per month were added to the roster while Hank was there.

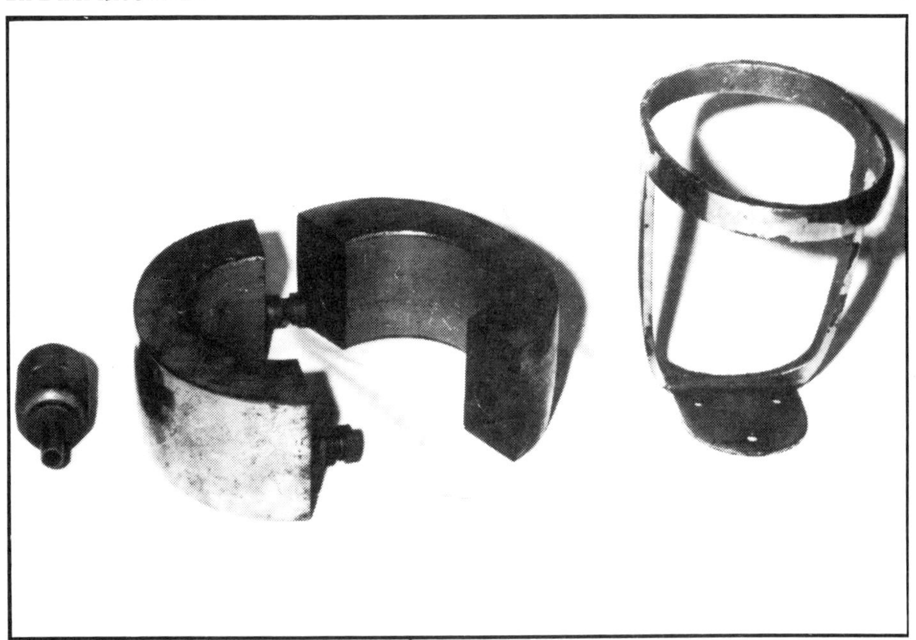

(Courtesy Oregon State Sheriffs' Association)

FIGURE 8—The Gardner shackle or "Oregon Boot" was worn by prison inmates after mid 1860. This efficient restraining device was used on Vaughan and other prisoners as they built the stockade around the new facilities in Salem. The heavy iron ring (above) fit loosely atop the rigid frame (below) which was attached to the heel of the prisoner's boot.

While some prisoners worked on the buildings and stockade, others were engaged in producing brick for construction of the permanent prison as well as other public buildings being erected in the capitol city. Superintendent Shaw ordered the shackles removed from the prisoners who were making brick as it was noted the devices slowed their work, galled their ankles and lamed their hips and backs.

Shaw was to regret that thoughtfulness as on 26 August, 1866, a group of prisoners seized him, Warden Allard and the brickyard foreman. They were taken as hostages to the still open section of the stockade fence where they were left unharmed as the escaping prisoners ran for the woods. Once the prison officials were freed, the guards opened fire. One convict was killed in the escape attempt while nine escaped.

The majority of the convicts, including Hank Vaughan, remained quiet during the outbreak, making no attempt to join in the escape.[8] This bloody breakout led the authorities to change administration and press for speedy completion of the brick structures. Another primary concern with the wooden buildings was fire danger. It was suspected that the prisoners only refrained from setting fire to the shelter because they realized they would surely lose their own lives in the resulting holocaust.

Three weeks after the breakout, Governor Biggs replaced Superintendent Shaw and Warden Allard with regular Army officers and initiated a new get-tough policy. Major Montgomery P. Berry became superintendent and a Lieutenant Gale was named warden.[9] These men served two terms and were Vaughan's keepers for the remainder of his prison stay.

By September 1868, when Major Berry made his first report to the state legislature conditions seemed greatly improved. He saw no comparison with the convicts now and the "small disorganized mob of reckless men" who had been brought down from Portland two years earlier. He noted there had been no escapes for the past two years, attributing this to the instructions given guards to "hold the prisoners at all hazards." Hank and his fellow inmates, interpreting this to mean that guards would shoot first and ask questions later, were most reluctant to try an escape.

Discipline for Vaughan and others was enforced by a graded punishment system. The first offense brought a lecture from the officer immediately in charge of the prisoner. The second offense was reported to the warden who admonished the culprit more strongly. The third offense brought shackling—two shackles if one was already worn—and loss of merit marks. The superintendent himself was notified of a fourth offense and he usually ordered the offending prisoner put "in the hole" on a diet of bread and water which meant from one to ten days in solitary confinement. Flogging was the last resort and supposedly used only when the prisoner had broken every rule of discipline. It is doubtful if Hank ever experienced the more severe disciplinary measures.

Fighting among prisoners had been a problem until guards were ordered to fire on the combatants. It was felt, according to Major Berry's report, that some prisoners entered the prison with the idea:

> . . . they could 'run the institution,' *bluff the officers, or leave when they were inclined.* With such men, an immediate war for supremacy commenced, and

> without being specially severe toward them, they generally succumbed as they became 'prisonwise,' but in some instances rough methods had to be applied.[10]

Hiring and keeping competent guards was also a problem. Warden Berry observed that only about one in fifteen men was fit for this occupation. He found that the constant vigilance required by their job so drained their energy that they either retired voluntarily or became so careless they had to be removed.

Communication between guards and prisoners was discouraged. Such exchange was viewed as destructive to the guard's usefulness as this personal contact brought out sympathy toward individual inmates. This sympathy was described as a disease—sometimes curable by granting the guard leave of absence for a short time to permit recuperation. If that didn't correct his attitude, the guard was discharged. While the public, from their more distant perspective, considered prisoners contemptible, many of the men who guarded them developed sympathy and friendships with them.

One of the regular guards was Oliver C. White, whose father as sheriff of Wasco County had numerous contacts with Hank Vaughan. Young White seemed to have formed a friendly relationship with Hank and came to support Hank's version of the shooting of Sheriff Maddock and his deputy.

In this rigid, no-nonsense military-style discipline, a school of sorts was offered. Every evening after supper, the mess hall tables were cleared for classes. School was optional for the older prisoners, but all the young men, including Vaughan, were required to attend.

Those attending classes lined up, marched to the hall and for one hour were taught "the various branches of the common schools." The more well-educated prisoners were utilized as teachers. Some of these proved to be fully competent instructors. This was where Hank improved upon his reading and writing skills and received the formal education he had neglected earlier in life.

Hank Vaughan was a quick student, observant both in and out of the prison school. Unfortunately, he was learning from everyone he came in contact with and some of them were not of the best moral character. For example, Matthew "Matt" Bledsoe, considered a cutthroat of the worst kind, was in prison with Hank. Bledsoe who had lived in The Dalles was the leader of the prison break which took place during Hank's term.

It was here that Hank was introduced to William Mason Roe, alias William "Bill" Moore or "Desperate Dick".[11] Roe also came to the penitentiary from The Dalles after being convicted of stealing a stocking footed bay mare in Walla Walla. After Roe served his three years for grand larceny and was released, he continued a life of crime that allegedly involved Vaughan in later years.

Another inmate at the time was J.C. McCarty, age 30, who was incarcerated from Coos County after "rioting" with John Short and using knives and pistols in C.G. Shandley's Saloon at Coos Bay. J.C. was such a bad character that his first indictment on a rather common charge landed him in prison. This association may have been Hank's first contact with one of the notorious McCarty family who became involved in bank and train robberies along with Butch Cassidy and Matt Warner.

The stories of brutality, crowded conditions, and filth attributed to many early prisons were not often used in describing the Oregon penitentiary. From reports to the legislative bodies after the prison was moved to Salem, it would appear that prisoners were reasonably well-treated at least during the period Hank was there.

Young Vaughan was fortunate to have served his sentence during the time when the new facilities were being built. This allowed him to be out in the open in a less confined situation which more suited his nature. This minimum security situation gave him a certain feeling of freedom. Because of the construction activity, he did learn some skills of brick making, blacksmithing and carpentering but as his later actions showed, he never put them to use.

While Vaughan was tolerating his confinement, Sheriff Maddock of Pendleton continued his law enforcement duties but was greatly hampered by the injury received to his jaw in the same Burnt River shootout which landed Hank in prison. An article in The Dalles *Daily Statesman* of July 14, 1865, related:

> Frank Maddock, Sheriff of Umatilla County who it will be recalled was seriously wounded in an encounter with a band of horse thieves, a few weeks since, arrived at Dalles by yesterday's boat. His wound continues to give him great inconvenience. It is understood that he comes here for medical treatment.

Maddock who was Umatilla County's first sheriff was only twenty-seven years old when he took office in June of 1864. He had served less than a year when he had the run in with Hank Vaughan. His youth and inexperience as a lawman were probably responsible for his ill-fated decision to approach the Bunton and Vaughan camp in the middle of the night. For his role in the Vaughan episode, the county court at Umatilla City paid Maddock $1,000 ". . . to compensate him in part for his injury and reward him for his bravery. . . ." Maddock was to become known as an outstanding lawman.

In another matter connected with the act that brought Hank to prison, a petition was filed with the Legislature for the relief of Mrs. Hart and her two small children. The petition, which was signed by over fifty people, stated that Vaughan, a horse thief, notorious desperado, and all around bad man, killed Hart and desperately wounded Sheriff Maddock. The petition was recorded September 1, 1867, but the extent to which it was acted upon is unknown.[12]

Whether Bunton or Vaughan shot the fatal bullet that killed Deputy Hart was never really known. It was obvious, however, that there was no question in the mind of the jury, possibly because the dead Bunton was beyond punishment.

One more note must be added here before Bunton is forgotten as it gives credence to some of the stories that circulated that Vaughan was riding with known horse thieves. Among those associates of the notorious sheriff, Henry Plummer, who was brought to justice by a dedicated vigilante group in nearby Montana Territory in 1865, was Billy Bunton who was listed as second in command of the gang of highly-organized criminals known as "The Innocents."[13] Billy was the son of Elyaha Bunton who settled in 1860 near Coles Crossing on the Walla Walla River in Umatilla County.[14] Considering the unusualness of the name and the sparsity of settlers in this area, it could be assumed that Hank's companion was a brother of the errant Billy Bunton. Perhaps Dick Bunton was on his way to Cottonwood, Idaho Territory, to settle his brother's affairs.

Even though it was common knowledge that Hank had been associating with questionable characters like Bunton, from the moment Hank's family learned of his trial and sentence they began working to obtain a pardon. Like many others, they choose to believe that Hank had been working in Umatilla County when he fell in with a couple of stockmen who hired him to help drive some horses to Idaho Territory. Hank supposed they had bought the horses. The first night out after they camped and were asleep, he was wakened by gunfire. He saw through the darkness that men in the outlying brush were shooting up the camp and, without waiting to ask questions, he drew his gun and began firing. When the battle was over his supposed employers, who were rustlers, had made their escape and Hank was a prisoner of the sheriff's posse.[15]

Vaughan's father was in the army and did not learn of Hank's predicament until long after he was imprisoned. Aleck's unit had bivouacked on the Boise River until June 30 and then moved in a series of temporary camps along the plains of southwestern Idaho and adjacent Oregon. His company stayed near Silver City on the headwaters of Jordan Creek until August 31 and next moved to Camp Alvord and the desert region. After October 31, they embarked for Fort Harney to enter winter quarters, arriving there December 29, 1865.

Aleck was mustered out on April 14, 1866, after a tour of about fifteen months. During this period, his wife had taken her family back to their farm near Coburg. With Aleck home to lend support, Hank's family increased its efforts to have him pardoned.

Hank's case aroused considerable interest and the petition which circulated requesting his reprieve was signed by people as far away as Boise City, Idaho Territory. The son of one of the signers, Thomas Jefferson Monroe, said it was the only time his father ever signed a petition for reprieve or pardon.[16]

Being persuaded of Hank's innocence, Governor George S. Woods gave Vaughan a full pardon on February 22, 1870. Vaughan served four and a half years of his life sentence. In part, the pardon read:

> Know ye that having been petitioned by the citizens of the County of Baker, . . . and also by many citizens of the Counties of Union, Umatilla, Wasco, Lane, Linn, Marion and Grant, and also by many citizens of Boise City, Idaho Territory:
>
> Now therefore to the end that Justice may be done, I, George S. Woods, Governor of Oregon, do hereby give and grant unto him the said Henry C. Vaughn a full pardon . . .[17]

Many later accounts concluded it was unfortunate that Vaughan was ever sent to prison as they felt this was the cause of his later lawlessness. They thought he would not have embarked on an outlaw career had he not been thrown in prison with hardened criminals. William Parsons, a Pendleton lawyer who later had several dealings with Vaughan, wrote of the Maddock/Vaughan affair:

> It was the general opinion at the time that he was justified in shooting the sheriff. He was a mere boy . . . and the sheriff took it for granted that when he was called upon to throw [up] his hands he would do so without objection, but in this he was

> greatly mistaken. Hank was a boy but he had a large amount of nerve. When he came out of the penitentiary he was a hardened criminal with no respect for the laws of God or man.[18]

In all fairness to the Oregon State penal system, it can be said Hank Vaughan did not go into prison with much respect for the law either.

When Vaughan left the prison, he was given $16.50 to buy clothing. This allowance had been instigated a few years earlier by Warden Berry who said it was a shameful thing to turn the released men free with hardly a stitch of clothes. He allowed as how they had been brought to prison "with more or less clothing, but when they went out, their garments could not be found."

Of more consequence, Hank Vaughan left prison with a reputation. As an anonymous Boise valley cowboy later theorized:

> When Vaughn left the penitentiary he was a marked man. He knew it. In those days if you killed a man, no matter what the circumstances, you had a reputation whether you wanted it or not. Gunmen buckled on their six-guns and went on your trail. It would add to their own reputation if they got you.
>
> Vaughn knew all that: knew that from the moment he stepped through the gates of the penitentiary his life depended on the six little lead pellets in the chamber of his gun and his ability to shoot them exactly where he wanted them to go.[19]

This observation may seem overly dramatic, but events later proved it accurate as Hank did have to defend his reputation as a quick draw shootist on many occasions. Gaining this type of reputation was the most dangerous outcome of the Burnt River shootout. Four years of contact with Oregon's worst criminals introduced Hank to an association of lawless men and provided him an informal education into the tricks of their trade.

Acquiring an understanding of how the law operates was a positive outcome of his trial, incarceration and pardon. He learned how to use the law to his benefit. In his later career, although he would on occasion spend short periods of time in jail, he would never return to prison.

REFERENCES

Chapter 3

1. Holmes, Kenneth L. *Ewing Young: Master Trapper*. Portland: Binfords and Mort, 1967, 148.
2. Oregon *Journal*, April 4, 1938.
3. Pfeifer, William. "Men Who Wore The Oregon Boot," *Old West*, Winter 1966, 4.
4. Report of Superintendent and Commissioners of the State Penitentiary, Fifth Regular Session of the Oregon State Legislative Assembly, September 1868.
5. Oregon *Journal*, April 4, 1938.
6. Pfeifer, *op. cit.*, 2.

7. Report of Superintendent and Commissioners of the State Penitentiary, Senate Proceedings, Messages and Documents, 1866.

8. Salem *Statesman*, September 3, 1866.

9. Pfeifer, *op. cit.*, 6.

10. Report of Superintendent and Commissioners of the State Penitentiary, September 1868, *op. cit.*

11. The Great Register, Vol. 1, Oregon State Archives, Salem, 30. Roe was sentenced from Wasco County and was assigned Case 259 when he entered on December 20, 1867. He was 31 years old, 5 feet 10 inches tall, heavy set and dark complected. He had dark sandy hair, a broad face with hazel eyes. The only distinguishing mark was a foul anchor tattoo on the back of his left hand.

12. Works Progress Administration, General History 11, Inventory of Penitentiary, Petition No. 22, Oregon State Archives, Salem.

13. Gard, Wayne. *Frontier Justice.* Norman: University of Oklahoma Press, 1975, 182-3.

14. Gilbert, Frank T. *Historic Sketches of Walla Walla, Whitman, Columbia, and Garfield Counties in Washington Territory, and Umatilla County, Oregon.* Portland, 1882, 456.

15. Portland *Telegram*, June 30, 1926.

16. *Ibid.*

17. Governor's Executive Documents, Records of the Secretary of State, Oregon State Archives, Salem.

18. Parsons, William, and W.S. Shiach. *op. cit.*, 257.

19. Idaho *Statesman*, May 23, 1937.

IV.

A FRESH START IN NEVADA
(1870-1877)

Hank Vaughan was twenty-one years old in February 1870 when he was released from prison. As his family had moved from The Dalles back to Lane County, Hank was able to spend the remainder of the winter with them.[1] This was but a temporary arrangement giving him time to start the adjustment from being a prisoner to being a free man.

It can be certain he got considerable advice from his relatives as to what his next steps should be. They undoubtedly encouraged him to build on the training he had received in prison and perhaps work in the saddle and harness trade. It isn't likely he would have been interested in brick making. It was the belief of his descendants that after he was released from prison he went to Elko, Nevada, and became a successful farrier.[2] Closer investigation revealed he did go to Elko and he was successful, but not in a trade as physically demanding and unexciting as shoeing horses.

Hank started his second chance by throwing in his lot with another Vaughan cattle venture. During his early teens, he was involved with the family when they moved their surplus cattle over the mountains to supply the Oregon mining communities. This market no longer existed as during the past decade the mines were either played out or people in the mining towns were providing their own supplies. If the surplus Willamette Valley cattle were to be sold, markets had to be found further away.

The Vaughans had two possible options. One was to supply cattle to the booming mining towns in remote parts of Idaho Territory. Their second option was to take cattle into Nevada, to their closest contact with the new transcontinental railroad. When the Golden Spike was driven the previous year signalling the completion of the railroad which linked the settled eastern United States with the western United States, it opened the possibility for stockgrowers in the Pacific Northwest to capture a part of the market supplying beef to the large populations at either end of the line (fig. 9).

Just as earlier the Vaughans acted quickly to take advantage of the needs of developing Oregon mines, they now were among the first cattle raisers in the Willamette Valley to attempt to enter these far off markets in Nevada. It would be

(Courtesy Utah State Historical Society)

FIGURE 9—Construction scenes such as this were common while the Central Pacific Railroad tracks from California were being built across northeastern Nevada to join with the Union Pacific coming from Utah. Hank Vaughan took advantage of this kind of activity after his release from the Oregon prison.

a gamble considering the cattle would have to be taken across the unroaded wilderness of southeastern Oregon where feed and water could be scarce. This would be a high risk operation, but one that might prove extremely profitable and the Vaughans were ready to try their luck.

Grandpa Billy and Hank's father, Aleck, decided they would first trail their stock to the Silver City mining district in Idaho Territory. If that market was over supplied by the time they arrived, they would proceed to the Elko area and negotiate with buyers from either California or the eastern states. Their route would cross Oregon diagonally to the southwest corner of the state passing through some of the most arid parts of the northwest interior.

Most of the men were familiar with the part of the route between the Willamette Valley and central Oregon as they had helped with earlier cattle drives to Canyon City. Further along in the Owyhee River headwaters, Aleck and his father both had some knowledge of the country, but the section of the journey in to Silver City and to Elko, Nevada, would be over an unknown route.

The Vaughans accumulated extra cattle that spring through consignments from their neighbors until they had a herd numbering about 350. Hank was one of the cowboys needed to handle this number. Among the other drovers were various Vaughan uncles and cousins, including his fourteen-year-old cousin, Oren, the son of Thomas Jefferson Vaughan. One other person making the drive with the Vaughans was probably Billy Moody, Hank's friend from his Canyon City days.

By late June the herd was assembled, trail branded and ready to go once the Barlow Road was free of snow. Trailing the herd through the heavy timber on the west side of the mountain was slow and difficult; six or seven miles being a normal day's drive. Over the crest of the Cascade range, however, travel down the east slope through the more open pine timber was easier and feed was plentiful for the cattle.

From there, their route took them just south of the new village of Prineville, then southeast where they skirted the fringe of the desert, taking advantage of good grass and water on the foothills of the Blue Mountains. Following the tributaries of the Crooked River, they came out at Summit Prairie on the high desert sage-grass range with its scattered juniper overstory. Ahead of them lay Fort Harney near what would one day become the town of Burns. It was Hank's dad, Aleck, who was most familiar with these parts from his time spent with the Oregon volunteers. It had been twenty five years since Captain Billy, Hank's grandfather, and Uncle Bob Vaughan wandered across these grasslands with the Tetherow group. Later, the Applegate Trail traversed some of this same high desert land, but for now few people used the area and the grass was abundant for the cattle as they trailed slowly eastward.

After leaving Fort Harney on the Silvies River, the Vaughan party continued southeast between the headwaters of the Malheur River on the north and the Alvord Desert to the south. Scouting ahead, the party found that cattle prices were not good in Silver City, so they chose the route which would take them into Nevada. Picking up the southern forks of the Owyhee River they swung south past the present three-corners area east of Fort McDermott. They trailed south along the precipitous breaks of the Owyhee forks for nearly one hundred miles before turning southeast across the rolling uplands of the Owyhee plateau. Soon they were in sight of the Humboldt River divide near the Tuscarora mining camp and journey's end. East of the Independence Mountains, their unmarked trail crossed the old Oregon-California Trail between Fort Hall on the upper Snake and the Carson Sink in western Nevada.

Fifty miles down from the north fork basin of the Humboldt River they arrived at the tracks of the Central Pacific Railroad at Elko, Nevada. It had taken about three months to make the journey from Oregon. Now they must successfully negotiate a sale. The cattle were turned out on one of the nearby meadows to recruit while the men began looking for buyers. The iron locomotive was a new experience to the animals as it hauled its trailing cars over the rails along the Humboldt. The cattle, though nervous at first, soon became accustomed to the trains' smoke, whistle and clatter but the horse herd stampeded each day the train came by.

Even so, it only took a few cowhands to tend the Vaughan herd. This offered Hank and his partners a chance to investigate their new surroundings. Elko was the scene of much activity connected with mining as heavy equipment was being offloaded from the trains to supply mines in the surrounding area (fig. 10). The assortment of people drawn here was not unlike what Vaughan had seen in The Dalles a decade earlier.

By mid September, interested cattle buyers were located and the Vaughan cattle were sold for a good profit. While some family members left for Oregon immediately, Hank decided not to return. His prison record was too fresh in everyone's mind. Time would have to pass to dim the stigma he carried in Oregon as an ex-convict and a suspected man killer. Judging the opportunities created by the mining, railroad and settlement activity in this area, Hank was confident he could find work here. It is likely he choose to take part of his earnings from the cattle drive in animals rather than in cash. Drawing on his experience dealing with local butchers as a youth in Canyon City, he could make his own way quite profitably in Elko.

Although Hank, Oren and Moody would all leave this area for a period, eventually they all three returned to this Humboldt region. Oren, by mid 1870, came with a similar cattle drive and stayed to work in cattle camps about Elko. He would eventually have his own places, first in Lamoille and later in Star Valley ten miles southeast of Elko. Within a decade he married Jane Wines, the daughter of self-reliant Neomy Powell Wines, and settled down in Ruby Valley. Bill Moody established himself in Mound Valley, a place known as a refuge for stock rustlers.

Hank did find means to keep employed in the Nevada area and one of the places he lived was Toano, a town halfway between Kelton, Utah Territory where the Golden Spike was driven, and Elko. It was the supply point for the developing gold and silver mines in the White Pine-Pioche region of central and southeastern Nevada. Knowing Hank's ability to sell cattle and horses, it is likely he was involved in supplying these necessary products to this busy mining area which included Pioche, a much more exciting town than Toano if the following article from the Pioche *Daily Record* of December 29, 1872, is to be believed:

(Courtesy Northeastern Nevada Historical Society)

FIGURE 10—Railroad shops and a large business district proclaim Elko to be an important distribution center in the mid 1870s. In the background across the Humboldt River Valley is the Mose McBurney ranch which Vaughan bought in 1875.

> Pioche is perhaps entitled to the honor of being the wickedest place west of the Rocky Mountains. There are 36 places where wines and liquors are sold by the glass; there are also 16 faro banks, 3 keno games, 1 monte bank, 4 twenty-one games, 1 sluice dice game, 2 red-and-black games, 36 places where short cards are played either for money or drinks, 3 billiard saloons, 1 bagatelle table and 3 pigeon-hole games. All these institutions are supported by the honest miners of the district . . .

A young footloose buckeroo, such as Hank, would relish roaming through this area, savoring its exciting atmosphere as he wandered.

Assuming that Hank got involved peddling stolen livestock during this period, another reason he would have selected Toano is that its location afforded an excellent point from which to dodge the law. It was the closest town to the Utah, Idaho and Nevada borders. In a matter of one hour's fast ride, he could escape into Utah Territory or in about two hours he could be in Idaho. These strategic areas were convenient for persons handling livestock of questionable ownership.

Hank's father was also on the move during these years. After taking part in at least one more profitable cattle drive, Aleck was able to establish himself in the freighting business. By late 1872, he had acquired the Willow Creek Stage Station near Pearl about twenty-five miles northwest of Boise City in Idaho Territory. Here he put to use the experience he gained while working with quartermaster supply and hostelry in the army.

The Willow Creek stop was one of those typical stations located about every ten to fifteen miles along any stage or freighting route. After this travel interval, the working horses had to be changed for fresh animals. The passengers, too, needed a respite from the jostling and bouncing they received inside the carriages.

A travelling correspondent for the Boise *Tri-Weekly Statesman*, May 17, 1873, described a ride on a stage coach to Vaughan's Willow Creek Station:

> Six miles of sage brush and rolling hills brought us to the Willow Creek Station, kept by Mr. Vaughan. This, of course, is a desert looking place, and as no man's farm joins it, it is scarcely worth while to give the dimensions. Several men are said to have come here with nothing, and after keeping the place for a time, gone away poor. But this is not exactly the case with Mr. Vaughan. He says he came here with nothing, but he now has twenty-two head of cattle, and nine fine American horses, old and young, and 400 of this spring's chickens. He considers it the best place in the country for raising stock, for he has no one to molest him.

Early day travelers were accustomed to the rough conditions that went along with wagon freighting and did not expect to find genteel hospitality at these stations. According to the following account, because of Mrs. Vaughan's efforts, Vaughan's station may have been an exception to this rule. It was reported in the September 9, 1873, *Tri-Weekly Statesman*, that passengers stopping for supper at the Willow Creek Station were under obligation to A.H. Vaughan for a delicious meal of spring chickens. It was male chauvinism on the part of the writer that Mrs. Vaughan is not mentioned, for it is certain she and the older children were contributing much to the successful running of the station.

The Willow Creek Station was a stage stop along the Umatilla Road over which much of the commercial traffic from Pacific seaports had passed inland to Boise City and Idaho City during the preceding decade. Until the transcontinental railroads could haul heavy freight west from the manufacturers to the mines, the only viable freight transportation route was by ship around South America and thence up the Pacific coast to seaports such as Portland and from there up the Columbia River to Umatilla Landing. From here horse or oxen drawn wagons delivered the goods to the mines.

Once the Central Pacific and Union Pacific Railroads were completed the flow of freight from west to east along this route practically ceased. With the railroad lines stretched from eastern points of manufacture overland to the western settlements and mines, traffic up the Columbia River took on less importance. This slackening of business may have been why the former owners of Willow Creek Station had "gone away poor." Stage lines, too, changed hands. John Hailey, Sr., the man who kept a lynch mob from hanging Hank in Auburn, sold his interest in a freight service along this route to the newly organized Northwestern Stage Company for which Aleck now worked.

But until the railroads reached Boise Valley after 1884 horse freighting continued to play an important part linking the economy of that area with northern Utah Territory and Nevada, particularly from such rail towns as Kelton, Utah Territory, Elko and Winnemucca, Nevada. At these sites along the transcontinental railroad, supplies were unloaded to be transferred and freighted to the mining areas beyond Boise City.

Although the new rail connection resulted in less traffic from the west past Willow Creek Station it did increase traffic from the east. This was especially the case for passengers bound for the Pacific Northwest and for heavy freight coming from points of eastern manufacture. For example, The Idaho *Statesman* of April 28, 1874, reported that Aleck Vaughan had received by fast freight from Toano a new "fifty-hundred" freight wagon (2.5 tons) at his Willow Creek Station. This had undoubtedly been delivered by F.F. Marx, the forwarding agent in Toano, Nevada, whose fast freight was delivered by teams of twenty mules pulling three wagons.

Hank was in close contact with his family after they took charge of the Willow Creek Station. It would appear that he and his father had stumbled upon a good thing as per Aleck's boast he had come to the Willow Creek Station with nothing and now had twenty-two head of cattle and nine fine American horses. Five years after his release from prison, Hank had accumulated enough money to buy valuable land along the Humboldt River and was recognized at least by the local paper as being a well-known and popular citizen.

Several new people entered Hank's life during this period, people who were in trouble with the law. His sister married a man wanted in Idaho Territory and Hank himself married into the McCarty family which had come to Nevada to get away from problems in Utah Territory.

The first mention of Hank in Nevada newspapers was found in the Elko *Weekly Post*, March 2, 1875, in an account of a series of court cases in which Hank and William Joseph Butler were involved. The paper lists among the cases set for trial on "March 11th, State vs H.C. Vaughan—argued on demurrer and taken under advisement Thursday evening. The court then adjourned until 10:00 o'clock AM today." There is no record that this case ever came to trial, but demurrer statements indicate that Constable J.J. Billings was attempting to serve a writ of attachment issued from a Justice of Peace when Vaughan interfered. The defendant Vaughan was charged ". . . with the Crime of obstructing an officer in the service of a legal process, ..." The demurrer countered in Hank's defense that the indictment was in error on four counts, and that it exceeded the authority and jurisdiction of the Justice and court issuing it.

The case appears to have stemmed from an attempt to extradite Butler to stand trial in Idaho Territory where he was accused of assault with the intent to commit murder. Hank apparently stepped in to prevent Butler from being served the warrant. Although the court took no action at this time, the law had a long memory and the two men would face these same charges nearly a decade later.

It turns out that William Butler was married to Amanda Vaughan, Hank's eldest sister. Butler, who was reported to be a blacksmith, was an Eastern transplant who had left his home rather than become a Catholic priest as his parents fervently desired. It is possible that Amanda met Butler through Hank in Idaho Territory, but she married him in Elko in 1873. Amanda was not in Elko when the above case came to court. She had gone back to Idaho Territory in 1874 to be with her mother for the birth of her first child whom she named Henrietta after Hank. Amanda stayed on at the Willow Creek Station helping with the ranch work. Both she and her sisters were known to be excellent horsewomen, choosing to "fork" their animals rather than ride sidesaddle as most women did.[3]

The name of another of Hank Vaughan's Elko associates, William Moody, alias Billy Monty, appeared in Nevada papers about this time. He also was involved in a court case. The April 24, 1875, Elko *Weekly Post* showed Billy Moody being sued by C. Zimmerman.[4] This case was dismissed later with no record of cause, but the action was initiated by Zimmerman who claimed Moody had received $1,000 in gold coin as Zimmerman's agent and then refused to turn any of it over to Zimmerman. This could have been related to the possession of disputed property, probably cattle or horses, supposedly being shipped from the Toano or Elko stockyards but actually coming from Idaho Territory. Hank Vaughan, acting as a sage brush lawyer in a role that became typical of him in later years, probably gave Moody the legal advice he needed to beat the case.

About this time Hank first met Tom McCarty. It could have been that this contact was actually through Hank's former prison mate, J.C. McCarty. When J.C. was released from the Oregon penitentiary a few months before Hank, he apparently went straight to Nevada. Someone expected him to be there as the Pioche *Daily Record* of January 1, 1873 listed him among those having undelivered letters. His name appeared again on the 30th along with a Mrs. M. McCarty. Both were being notified of undelivered mail. Another McCarty in the area was William McCarty who was listed as a registered voter of the Pioche Precinct.

Tom McCarty was originally from the southern state of Kentucky where his father, Alexander McCarty, had served in the Confederate forces. In the late 1860s shortly after the Civil War, the family emigrated to Montana where they were involved in the business of trading horses and cattle. One part of this venture included an annual buying trip into Utah Territory where good quality cattle were bought from the Mormon farmers. The cattle were then trailed back to ranches on the plains of Montana where they brought handsome prices. By about 1870, after enduring several years of harsh Montana winters, the family moved their permanent headquarters into the warmer Grass Valley of central Utah Territory, north of what is now Antimony.[5]

While in Grass Valley, Tom and his brother, Billy, roamed in and out of the Bryce Canyon district, learning every secluded nook of this remote area. Their father showed them how they could be successful as legitimate stockmen, but they tended to prefer to make a "fast buck" and were attracted to the desperado types who infested the area.

These boys later became noted for the more serious crimes of bank and train robbery, but ironically their biggest trouble in Grass Valley arose over the theft of one of their own calves. The vengeful McCarty boys shot the three Navahoes who committed the transgression and thus precipitated an Indian uprising in 1874 which threatened the lives of many settlers. To appease the Navaho and to protect Mormon ranchers, the Avenging Angels of Brigham Young's band stepped in and forced the McCartys to pack up and leave the country. The McCartys showed up next in Nevada where because of like interests and temperaments they were drawn into a friendship and business partnership with Hank Vaughan.

It can be assumed that Hank participated in further profitable cattle drives either with Vaughan family members or probably on his own, possibly tapping into the Toano-Pioche supply route, because by 1875 he had accumulated enough money to buy property and stock it with cattle. That Hank had found a way to prosper was evidenced by an item in the Elko *Independent* of May 15, 1875, which reported:

> . . . Hank has purchased of Mose McBurney his river ranch for $1,500, upon which he has driven his stock, comprising some 600 head of cattle proposing to settle down and become a fixture in Elko township.

According to Elko County court records, Hank Vaughan purchased from McBurney 190 acres for $1,000 on May 13, 1875.[6] This tract was about three miles east of Elko on the floodplain meadows along the Humboldt River. Hank later bought two hundred acres of neighboring land from Woods Mayberry of Santa Clara, California, for $1,500.

A few months later, his father who apparently continued to prosper at the Willow Creek Station bought 410 acres of adjoining bottom land from J. O'Leary for $700. This gave the Vaughans control of about two miles of grazing land along the Humboldt River. The river bottom through this stretch is about one-quarter mile wide along the floor of the valley. Steep grass covered canyon walls rise to six hundred feet on the south side and 500 feet on the north side of the river before giving way to gentle rolling sagebrush and grass covered hills of public domain on the surrounding uplands.

It is interesting to speculate on why these two Vaughans decided to buy land and particularly why to buy adjoining land. They certainly recognized the increasing value of this bottom land as holding grounds for fattening cattle and, as Hank knew, it gave him a legitimate base from which to deal with both legally and illegally acquired cattle and horses. Perhaps the Vaughans also planned to assess a small toll for any cattle trailed across their property. It can be assumed that Hank had the greatest interest in the operation going on at the Humboldt River ranch. Although Aleck spent enough time around the area to be a registered voter, he was mostly occupied with the running of the Willow Creek Station in Idaho.

This "modus operandi" was the beginning of a pattern Hank followed the rest of his life. The pattern included setting up a legitimate front and becoming recognized as a well liked local resident. The legitimate front was one that could provide cover for stolen animals if necessary. Also a part of the pattern was for Hank to get noticed by the newspaper editors. Both he and his father were experts in exploiting the media to gain attention. Perhaps they did so to keep their compatriots informed of their activities.

(Courtesy Courtney DelCurto)

FIGURE 11—Lois J. McCarty may have been Hank Vaughan's first wife. She was a woman of strong character who raised and schooled their two sons with little assistance from Vaughan.

Hank's future in legitimate ranching in that location could have been secure if a later writer's description of Elko County were correct. According to the Elko *Weekly Post*, February 16, 1878:

> The grazing extent of country in this vicinity is large, and the hills are covered with nutritious bunch grass, affording splendid pasturage for cattle. The town of Elko . . . contains . . . inhabitants, who are alive to all great business enterprises. It has good schools, live newspaper men, energetic merchants, good hotels, and pretty women. . . .

Of the latter pretty women, one had entered Hank's life.[7] The announcement of their wedding appeared under the "Married" column in the Elko *Independent*, May 15, 1875: "In Elko, May 8th by Justice Taylor, H.C. Vaughan to Miss Louise [Lois] McCarty."

His bride was ninteen-year-old Lois J. McCarty (fig. 11), sister of Tom McCarty. Lois had recently arrived in Elko, moving there from Pioche, Nevada where she, her father, brothers and sisters had relocated after being forced to leave Utah Territory because of Tom and Billy's trouble with the Navahoes and the

(Courtesy Courtney DelCurto)

FIGURE 12—This portrait of Vaughan was taken in a San Francisco studio when he was twenty-six years old. The photograph was made in 1875, the year Hank married Lois McCarty.

Mormon Avenging Angels. Hank and Lois undoubtedly met through Hank's association with her brothers who had similar inclination to deal in matters outside the law.

Lois could easily have found Hank attractive (fig. 12). Descriptions of him said he had a neat appearance with well groomed hair and whiskers. He was an interesting speaker who had witty stories to tell. The two young people would have had much in common as Hank's background included cattle drives and wheeling and dealing in stock trading, the sort of life Lois knew with her family in the frontiers of Montana and Utah Territories. She probably did not know of his stay in the Oregon State Penitentiary, but even if she did, his misconduct as a young man so closely paralleled those of her own brothers she would not have been repelled by his behavior and its consequences.

Hank was not ungentlemanly or uncourteous unless he was under the influence of liquor. Drinking had precipitated his use of a gun to settle affairs with Headspot in Canyon City when he was only fifteen and it would continue to be a factor in his actions for the rest of his life. But as far as drinking affecting his relationship with Lois, she was probably never around when he was drinking. Married women were more-or-less protected from that kind of activity. The disposition Hank had to neglect his wife would cause Lois more trouble than his drinking, but that tendency wasn't apparent to her at first.

With the announcement of their marriage, another item in the Elko paper further indicated that Hank was by this time well-known to the area subscribers. He had become someone of note in the community and a person with whom the editor was on familiar terms:

> ANOTHER BENEDICT.—As will be seen by reference to the proper heading H.C. Vaughan, formerly of Toano, has reentered the ranks of the Benedicts, and the smile of calm satisfaction illuminating his manly countenance is in evidence that he's glad of it.

The words "reentered the ranks of the Benedicts" suggest that Vaughan had been married before. It can not be ruled out that he hadn't been married previously in view of the fact that little is known of his activities for the past several years. However, no record has been found of an earlier marriage. This same newspaper account also confirms that Hank at one time lived in Toano.

It could be that Vaughan was affluent enough to take his bride to California on their honeymoon as a portrait of him was taken by a San Francisco photographer at about this time (fig. 12). The trip could have been made comfortably by train from Elko. It is conceivable that Hank would have travelled as far away as San Francisco and perhaps he would have taken his bride there on a wedding trip.

The union of Hank and Lois soon bore fruit for on March 4, 1876, the *Weekly Independent* registered, "BORN.—In Elko, February 25, to the wife of H.C. Vaughn, a son—all boy, and weighs 10 1/4 pounds." This son was named Alexander after both his maternal and paternal grandfathers. The paternal grandfather Vaughan was in Elko as another news item that day told of the presence of three generations of Vaughans:

> SCORE ONE MORE.—The father of our townsman, H.C. Vaughan, and grandfather to the Inter arrival, dropped in upon us yesterday morning, and with an air of unalloyed satisfaction, announced the fact recorded under the head of "Born" in another column, generously invited the "devil" with the balance of the prints, to step out and moisten their clay at his expense, in honor of the happy event.

Listed among the nearly 350 registered voters for Elko County, State of Nevada, in the Elko *Weekly Post* on October 28, 1876, were Hank, his father, Aleck, and cousin Oren Vaughan. The Vaughans were registered, but none of the McCartys were.

The McCartys, with the exceptions of Lois and Tom, shortly left Elko for California. They later returned to Utah Territory and the area around Mount Pleasant. There they joined the Philander Maxwell and Thomas R. Ray families in a difficult trek to the LaSal Mountains where they hoped to find pasture for their cattle. These three families pioneered what is now San Juan County, Utah Territory, in 1877. In this beautiful isolated spot, they built up their cow herds on some of the most luxuriant grassland in Utah Territory.

While in Elko Tom McCarty made what was probably his first theft from a railroad when he held up the railroad agent at Halleck Station, about twelve miles out of Elko. He was caught shortly thereafter. His take may have included some cash, but he was tried and convicted on the charge of stealing railroad tickets only. This was a grand larceny offense for which he was sentenced to a year in prison. The Elko *Post*, July 28, 1877, printed the following:

> Taken to Carson.—In the absence of the editor of this paper, and knowing that being so far away no harm can come to us, we take the following from the *Silver State* [Winnemucca] of Monday [July 23]: "E.A. Littlefield of the Elko *Post* passed through last evening with Thomas McCarty, who was sentenced by Judge Flack to one year in the State Prison for larceny. Littlefield told the prisoner, who attempted to escape from the Elko jail, that he must behave and not attempt to escape, or he would advertise him, and this admonition had a very soothing effect

on the prisoner, who acted as if he understood its meaning, and kept quiet as a lamb."

Tom began serving this one-year sentence in the Nevada State Prison at Carson City on July 23, 1877.[8] He was not a cooperative prisoner and only the threat to make him available for extradition to Utah Territory to face Rockwell Porter and his Avenging Angels kept him under control.

With Tom in prison, the responsibility of keeping up their business contacts fell to Hank. It was perhaps for this reason he now did a great deal of traveling. In 1877 he appeared in Prescott, Arizona Territory, not far from where Tom McCarty was later known to have a ranch. Testimony taken in court once claimed that Vaughan was operating in that area.[9] He may well have been overseeing Tom's interests at the time.

The episode in Prescott was related in H.H. Bancroft's *Popular Tribunals*. It stated that in about October of 1877:

> Two noted desperadoes, Tullos and Vaughn entered Prescott and began amusing themselves by shooting dogs and presenting their loaded revolvers at the breasts of people, threatening to let daylight through them if they opened their mouths. Then mounting horses they rode down through Montezuma street at full gallop, yelling and shooting like demons. As a matter of course, the officers and citizens were obliged to put an end to such proceedings, and in doing so one of the ruffians was shot to death and the other nearly killed.[10]

Details of this affair were related in the Prescott *Weekly Arizona Miner* of October 19, 1877. Vaughan and Robert Tullos, were newcomers to Prescott, said to have recently come up from Texas and the Mexican border area. While in Jackson and Tompkin's Saloon, the two had accosted W.H. McCall, one using a drawn pistol and the other shouting abusive language.

McCall testified at the coroner's jury that he believed Vaughan recognized him as the only man in Prescott who could identify Vaughan as the man who had killed Robert Broddus on the Texas border. McCall continued that he (Vaughan) was known as a bad character.

After being intimidated and allegedly recognized in the saloon, McCall, fearful for his life, swore out a warrant for Vaughan's arrest. Constable Frank Murray went to the saloon where the two had been drinking and tried to serve the warrant. Thinking Murray was only concerned about the dog shooting episode, one of the pair drew his revolver on the constable and ordered him out of the place.

Murray withdrew to scout for reinforcements while both Vaughan and Tullos rode off at full tilt down main street to the edge of town, firing their pistols right and left as they went. Murray returned with Sheriff Ed F. Bowers, U.S. Marshal W.W. Standefer, a Mr. Earb and a Mr. McCall.

Marshal Standefer and McCall with shotguns at the ready drove a buggy down main street at a fast pace. Their plan was to surround the culprits and make them surrender. When well beyond Vaughan and Tullos, they stopped, tied up, and started back on foot. This would be Standefer's second encounter with Vaughan. It was Marshal Standefer who escorted Hank to the Oregon prison in 1865. Earb, armed with a rifle, went down the alley on foot until he was nearly opposite the staggering pair of desperados. At the time these three were coming into position, Sheriff Bower and Constable Murray rode up to within fifty feet of Vaughan and Tullos, brought up their revolvers and commanded them to surrender.

By now Vaughan at least, if not Tullos, too, must have realized that shooting dogs was not the only reason the law was interested in them. Presuming the involvement of only two officers, and both of them on horseback, it would be an even, if not easy, fight, so, according to the account in the Prescott *Weekly Arizona Miner* of October 19, 1877:

> Instead of surrendering they opened fire upon the officers, which seems to have been gallantly returned both by Bowers and Murray from one direction and Standefer and McCall from the other, and in the meantime Earb, who appears to have been playing a lone hand with a Winchester rifle was doing good service between the two fires.
>
> From this time to the close of the fight it seems to have been a busy season with all parties engaged. Each can tell what he did individually but had no time to observe the operations of his allies.
>
> The result was that when the fight was over Tullos lay dead near Granite Creek at Lucas' fence, with eight bullet and buck shot wounds in different parts of his body, and Wilson, alias Vaughn, was picked up by Noyes fence with a bullet hole in his head, of which it was thought he will die, but he had lived twenty-four hours, and may weather it through. Such men seem to be hard to kill.

Thus Hank survived another shootout and even though sorely wounded, he recovered.

How much Lois knew of her husband's injuries or the reasons for his many absences from home is not known. With Hank gone so much she would be busy keeping their own ranch running. By now she was pregnant again. On September 10, 1877, in Elko, a second son, Albert Irving, was born to Hank and Lois.[11]

Lois apparently realized her marriage to Hank was a mistake as in the winter of 1877 she abruptly left Elko taking her children with her. Whatever her immediate reasons were, she wasted no time in going. She next appeared in Douglas County in southern Oregon.

It would not have been an easy trip with two young children, one of them only a few months old. There was no direct route from Elko to southern Oregon. She could have gone via California, first joining her father and then proceeding north to relatives in southern Oregon or she could have travelled north by stagecoach through Idaho Territory. Perhaps she even stopped off with Elizabeth Vaughan at the Willow Creek Station. From there she would have had to go west to Portland, Oregon, and then south to her destination in southern Oregon.

J.C. McCarty may have been returning to his home in Coos County. He had been in trouble with the law in Nevada the past summer, being indicted in Elko for petty larceny. If J.C. were leaving then, she may have taken that opportunity to travel with him. But this resourceful young woman was able to make the relocation to Oregon and she took full responsibility from that time on for raising Hank's children.

Sometime after Lois and the boys left, Hank, too, moved out of Nevada. It had been eight years since he left the Oregon prison and he seems to have overcome any stigma that might have been attached to him as an ex-convict. During this period he was in close contact with his father. They had invested in land in Nevada, indicating that their stock trading ventures were quite successful. In those days, such rapid prosperity was usually accomplished by augmenting herds with stolen animals. There is evidence Hank was adding stock to his herds with the help of a loose network of thieves including both old and new friends.

Among Hank's new friends was his brother-in-law, Tom McCarty. It was while Hank ventured into Arizona Territory checking on Tom's affairs that he got involved in another shootout with the law. His injuries in this shooting did not slow him down. Traumatic experiences such as these were shrugged off by Hank. He comes out of each shooting incident, heals up and never looks back, neither does he shrink from a repeat performance.

REFERENCES

Chapter 4

1. Census, United States, Report of the Census Bureau, Oregon, 1870.
2. Personal interview, Mrs. Sophia Riede, Boise, Idaho, February 7, 1973.
3. Personal interview, Charles R. Ayers, Star, Idaho, February 28, 1974.
4. Elko County Circuit Court, Civil Case File No. 104, Elko, Nevada.
5. Kelly, Charles. *The Outlaw Trail.* New York: Bonanza Books, 1959, 15-20.
6. Elko County, Deeds, Grantee; Vaughan, Henry Clay and Alexander H.; Book 6, 365, 400 and 633, respectively. Elko County Courthouse, Elko, Nevada.
7. Elko County, Marriages, Book No. 1, 84, dated May 8, 1875, Elko, Nevada.
8. Biennial Report of the Warden of Nevada State Prison for the years 1877 and 1878. Vital statistics show: Thomas McCarty, age twenty-five, born New York, sent from Elko County, Crime, Grand Larceny, Term, one year, occupation. shoemaker. It must be noted that Tom was theatrical and an inveterate liar in later life. The authors believe Tom gave false information about his identification at the time of this trial.
9. Silver City *Idaho Avalanche*, September 27, 1879.
10. Bancroft, Hubert Howe. *Popular Tribunals*, Vol. 1. San Francisco: The History Company, 1887, 715.
11. Personal interview, Mrs. Laura Belle Rogers, Foster, Oregon, December 29, 1972. The Vaughan family bible is the possession of Mrs. Rogers.

V.

RELOCATING IN OREGON
(1878-1879)

When Hank started expanding his loosely run Nevada business dealings he relied on information from his father whose stage stop was strategically located along the route between Oregon and Idaho Territory. The information indicated someone with the experience and skills of Hank Vaughan could profitably take advantage of developments in Eastern Oregon if they acted quickly. The events that were occurring in the Pendleton area, where Hank next emerged, had been in the process of unfolding for several years. One event had to do with livestock. The other event had to do with Indians. Hank was familiar with both.

Pendleton was ten years old when Hank returned in the summer of 1878. The community served an area which had been a crossroads for man's activity since prehistoric times. The town was located between the Blue Mountains and the Columbia plains near the favored wintering quarters of the Cayuse Indians whose long lodges were seen by the white settlers as their wagon trains descended the mountains at Emigrant Hill from 1842 onward. These newcomers didn't linger but crossed the grass-clad foothills and after fording the Umatilla River just below the present Pendleton township continued on their journey to the valley of the Willamette.

A few miles above here, in 1846, the black-robed fathers of the Catholic Church opened St. Ann's Mission to administer Christianity to the roving Cayuse. In the early 1850s, Dr. William McKay built a trading post nearby and by 1852 Green Arnold brought the first cattle back from the Willamette Valley to the rangelands of the Eastern Oregon Territory.

For the next decade development was slow. In the early 1860s mining activity brought miners and their equipment up the Columbia River to Umatilla Landing where they proceeded by foot and wagon train to the inland gold fields. Even with this increase in traffic, there was little in the way of settlement here until in 1864 Moses Goodwin built a bridge over the Umatilla River. This structure became the main crossing for mining parties and freight bound for the mountains. In 1865, when Marshal Standefer escorted Hank through here after his trial in Auburn, only a few shops and a livery station had been built near the bridge, but Pendleton grew up from that beginning.

When Vaughan returned in 1878, Pendleton was thriving because the livestock industry in the Northwest had finally begun to prosper. For twenty years, beef herds had been multiplying. It seemed there was no limit to this growth as native pasture lands appeared to extend forever. Cattle numbers continued to increase even after some devastating winters killed off thousands of animals. With no large population centers nearby, the lack of markets was a problem. Cattle surpluses coupled with the general depression afflicting the whole United States during the 1870s caused prices to plunge. In Walla Walla, a cow and calf that sold for $40 to $45 in 1871 were selling for only $10 a pair in March of 1874.

This made it economical for buyers from as far away as Nevada and California to buy what were considered superior quality breeding stock.[1] Thus the markets opened for Oregon cattle and the exodus of cattle began. In June 1875, the Walla Walla *Union* reported that:

> A number of bands of cattle left the [Walla Walla] valley within the last few days. Dan Drumhiller [sic] has taken one band of 1000 head over to Grande Ronde, where they will remain until they are joined by four or five hundred more being brought up here, when all will be taken to Nevada. A number of other bands are now making up and will start in a few days. Those who have come over the mountains lately, say that there seems to be almost a string of cattle from this valley across the Blue Mountains . . . .

By November, 1876, The Dalles *Mountaineer* said no fewer than 36,000 head of cattle had ". . . been driven from Eastern Oregon and Eastern Washington down towards the Pacific Railroad." The Vaughans had participated early on in this movement, except they used the southeastern Oregon route to take cattle to the railhead in Nevada. The northeastern route through Pendleton had become the most popular trail of cattle drives when Hank returned, a factor that was causing this community to prosper.

Hank was not so much interested in the cattle market as he was in the market these drives opened up for horses. Cattle buyers and trail drivers were paying premium prices for horses as they needed them to move their herds. The Great Plains were now mostly cleared of buffalo and the cattle barons who were stocking their ranches wanted cattle and horses. It was relatively easy for Hank and his partners to hide a few stolen horses amongst a band furnished to these outlets. Not many questions were asked in this freewheeling market as horses gathered in Oregon were moved out along the trails to points east.

Another market for horses was along railroad routes as these were being built. Thousands of horses were needed to pull and skid the fresnoes and scrapers used in the construction of not only the big transcontinental lines but for each spur road developing from them.

The other event playing itself out in the Pendleton area at the time Hank chose to return had to do with Indians and their continued protest against the encroachment upon their lands by the white settlers. After Custer's defeat in the Little Bighorn Valley, the army hastily started herding several scattered tribes onto allotted reservations. Some like the Nez Perces in Eastern Oregon refused to go, thus precipitating the pursuit and defeat of that band in 1877. Many tribes who did go peacefully to reservations were later abused or denied promised benefits. Such was the case of the Bannocks of the Fort Hall area in Idaho Territory, but they chose not to accept this treatment passively.

After their Camas Prairie Reservation was mistakenly opened for settlement in the spring of 1878, the Bannocks went on the warpath. They crossed southern Idaho in an attempt to combine forces with the Malheur branch of the northern Paiute tribe. Their plan was to escape through Oregon and Washington Territory into Canada, recruiting other Indians as they passed through their reservations. They stole horses, guns and ammunition to increase their capability for warfare; they also plundered for food and took a few white scalps wherever the opportunity was presented.

The Bannock Chief, Buffalo Horn, was killed during an engagement with white volunteer troops near Silver City before the band left Idaho Territory. Then Chief Egan of the Paiutes became war chief. With the addition of some Shoshones and renegade Snake Indians, the group of hostiles swelled to nearly two thousand with almost half the force being capable warriors. Their path was broad through the Steens and Harney Valleys and most ranchers abandoned their stock and headed for the safety of Fort Harney.

Some who were working stock on the range were caught by surprise and had to flee for their lives. Two such stockmen were Peter French and A.H. Robie. Robie had sold his Diamond Ranch and cattle to French in 1877 and they were gathering Robie's horses off the ranch when the Indians attacked. The stockmen first raced to the P Ranch for fresh horses and then they fled to Fort Harney. Several weeks later, as a result of exhaustion and complications from this desperate ride, Robie succumbed and died, but before he did, he placed a $1000 reward for the head of Chief Egan. These events and Robie's demise later played a significant role in the future activities of Hank Vaughan.

Hoping to cross the Columbia River near Umatilla Landing, the warring Indians turned north into the Blue Mountains passing near John Day in late June. Army forces and volunteers managed to engage them at Willow Springs (Battle Mountain) twenty-five miles south of Pendleton and turn their column east back into the Blue Mountains. The warring Paiutes and Bannocks were unsuccessful in convincing the Umatilla Reservation Indians to join them and, in fact, the Umatillas chose to assist the army and betrayed and murdered Chief Egan.

Hank's return to Eastern Oregon coincided with this period of extreme uneasiness around Pendleton. The danger to the settlers was very real, as before the Indians were defeated, there were several dozen casualties among ranchers, regulars and volunteer troops. This was the period when George Coggans, a traveler en route from La Grande to Pendleton, and four teamsters were killed at what became known as Deadman's Pass.

While these bands of Paiute and Bannock Indians were actively raiding along the foothills of the Blue Mountains in early June of 1878, settlers abandoned their ranches and herds, fleeing to Pendleton in fear of the renegades. With the settlers temporarily away and their stock unprotected, some Indians and white rustlers began taking advantage of the situation. An incident reported by early-day Pendleton resident, J.L. Sharon, said:

> One such party, under the leadership of "Rattlesnake Jake," passed through Pendleton and on east over the Blue Mountains, and as reported after the Indian troubles were settled, these twenty-five outlaws landed in Wyoming with over three hundred stolen horses.[2]

Hank was probably not involved with "Rattlesnake Jake" but he, too, was taking advantage of horses abandoned by their frightened owners. On one of his roundups he was caught red-handed. He and his partner, Billy Moody, had reined in at the deserted way station on Battle Mountain late one afternoon. They were in the process of corralling some loose horses when they were surprised by a posse. The rancher posse was scouting for horse thieves who were cleaning up on settler stock in the wake of the Indian scares.

When surprised, Vaughan and Moody got separated from their mounts at the front of the station and made a dash for the barn. Although the posse fired a barrage of shots into the barn, the horse thieves successfully held off the posse until nightfall. During the night a couple of loose stage horses wandered into the barn lot. These horses had never been ridden before, but the rustlers caught and rigged them up as saddle horses. What followed was a furious bucking show which the posse only heard and because of darkness could not see. The suspected thieves escaped in the night. Later, when the barn was checked, it was found to be shot so full of holes it seemed impossible that they had escaped without injury.[3]

The clue that Hank had returned to Oregon was buried in the Pendleton *East Oregonian* of August 1878. The newspaper noted that a general delivery letter was waiting at the post office for H.C. Vaughan. As was seen earlier in Nevada, printing the names of people who had unclaimed mail was a service extended by early day newspapers. This letter for Hank indicated someone expected he had returned to Umatilla County.

Vaughan's first public business venture in Eastern Oregon started when he, Still Heulet, and Billy Moody brought a band of horses to Umatilla County ". . . and sold them for a handsome sum."[4] By coming to the area with horses to sell, he appeared to the locals as a legitimate stock trader and thus continued the pattern which he repeated as he moved into new areas.

Other pieces in this pattern of establishment in new locations included developing an appearance of permanence and respectability. Shortly after his arrival in Pendleton, Hank accomplished this by getting married. He wed Louisa Jane Ditty after what had to be the briefest of courtships. They were married on August 31, 1878.[5] She was about twenty-seven and Vaughan was twenty-nine years old. Louisa, her sister and brother-in-law, Sarah and David Howdeyshell, had come only recently from the Midwest. They would have had little knowledge of Hank's background and certainly no inkling that he already had a wife and a family.

Immediately after their marriage the couple moved to a log cabin at the head of Wildhorse Creek in the Blue Mountains just north of the Umatilla Reservation. According to Louisa's brother-in-law, the cabin was situated ". . . in a lonesome place a long distance from any neighbors. . . ."[6] The closest settlement was Centerville about halfway to Pendleton. The *East Oregonian* of August 24, 1878, described that fast growing hamlet:

> Centerville.—This is the name of a flourishing little village just started on Wildhorse near what was formerly known as Richard's station. The town site was selected, surveyed and plotted only a few months ago. Then not a house was here, now there is a large Agricultural Hall, one beef market, one drug-store, one grocery store, one hotel, one livery stable, one harness shop, one school house and a number of other buildings and residences, and still they continue to improve. The village is in the heart of good farming country and if it continues as it has begun, will soon be quite a town.

Having set up his legitimate front, Hank began to concentrate on setting up his other operation. One of the facilities he needed was a strategic collection point where stolen stock could be cached until arrangements were made for their sale. Since much of what he did required secrecy and seclusion, he prevailed upon the local Indians to allow him to operate from the reservation.

Vaughan, with the help of his Cayuse friends, built a substantial set of corrals where Sumac Creek enters McKay Creek (fig. 13). These corrals were used by Hank and the Indians when they prepared a band of horses for sale. Since this was within the original boundaries of the Umatilla Indian Reservation it was surrounded by an unlimited holding pasture not frequented by white men.

Vaughan's corrals were a half day's ride south from the Wildhorse cabin where Louisa stayed. They were about six miles northeast of the settlement of Pilot Rock which in 1879 was a sleepy little cow town of some 150 people. The town took its name from the huge basalt bluff which was a landmark to drovers taking cattle back along the Oregon Trail headed for Cheyenne and other eastern points (fig. 14).

As he entered the business world in Eastern Oregon, Vaughan began his routine hanging around the saloons of Pilot Rock. He would play poker, drink and socialize with prospective horse buyers at the same time keeping tabs on the departure of the big cattle herds. Drovers with these bands had great difficulty when they tried to haze their animals up the slopes of the Blue Mountains. Cattle used to the flat prairie lands of the Columbia Basin were not cooperative when attempts were made to trail them up the rocky hillside.

About mid day as these tired, sore-footed cattle reached the forest, some of the cows would quit the herd and head into the brush. There was not much a half dozen drovers could do immediately about gathering these strays. They would have to wait until the main herd reached Starkey Prairie at the end of the next trail day. Once there, while the herd laid over, some of the drovers would return to search the timber for the strays.

To take advantage of this situation, Vaughan built a cabin and another corral on McKay Creek at the mouth of Wood Hollow just north of Rocky Ridge. Hank and his Indian riders could be one jump ahead of the herders, gathering the strays of the Cheyenne herds into his Wood Hollow corral. The next day they could move them to the far side of Cabbage Hill and scatter them among the grazing Indian cattle on the reservation.

One day Hank picked up some strays from a herd in which many of the stock had come from nearby Pendleton. What resulted has become part of the folklore of Pilot Rock.[7] Cowboys whose own cattle were on consignment in the herd had been helping get the cattle started on the trail up Rocky Ridge. As the strays broke

FIGURE 13—The site of the Hank Vaughan horse corrals at the forks of Sumac and McKay Creek on the Umatilla Indian Reservation. It was from this remote spot in the Blue Mountain foothills that Hank and his Indian friends started many a band of horses on the eastward trail in the late 1870s and 1880s.

FIGURE 14—Pilot Rock as viewed from the center of the historic stock driveway. From here cattle began their climb over the Blue Mountains on the route which eventually took them as far as Cheyenne, Wyoming. The bluffs beyond town are where Hank made his legendary leap while evading a posse.

away from the herd, the locals who knew the country tracked them to Hank's corral. It did not take long for them to figure out Hank's game and four of the local stockmen attempted to catch and punish him.

The men soon confronted Vaughan at the poker table in a Pilot Rock saloon. Denying any knowledge of the corral or of the strays, he picked up his chips and strolled away from the group that surrounded the table. He headed for the bar, riffling his chips as he went. Three feet from the bar he dropped the chips, whirled, and leveled his revolver on the quartet, all before any of the chips hit the floor. Poker players fell away from the table and the stockmen's hands went straight in the air. They all knew Hank's reputation as a quick draw expert and one who would not hesitate to shoot. They figured it would be suicide for at least two of the four if they went for their pistols. Hank had them drop their gun belts and march out and up the street as he mounted his sleek bay gelding tied to the hitching rack in front of the saloon. Instead of heading for the timber and familiar haunts, he headed south out of town up the dry gulch on the trail to Heppner.

The deputy had been warned earlier by the stockmen that there might be trouble. He took only a few minutes to organize a posse. Hank's dust had not settled before the stockmen and posse were hot on his heels. About two miles out of town he turned north up a draw that led to the flat open ridge that formed the bluff overlooking Pilot Rock. Gaining the top, Hank spurred his horse east back toward town. The posse saw him duck up the draw and took several random shots as he disappeared from their view. They lost ground gaining the ridge top and he was well out of range when they topped out on the flat.

Seeing that Vaughan was headed right for the bluff, the posse fanned out with the lead riders blocking his escape trail north toward Pendleton. The locals expected Hank would have to jump through a fence in order to get around the thirty-foot bluff. By then they planned to have him surrounded. What the posse did not know was that Hank had earlier taken full measure of his escape route and had calculated the effect of jumping his horse off Pilot Rock. He was confident that his mount would not even falter as he had been off similar rims with him before.

As Hank approached the bluff, he reined in the gelding, letting the posse close to a distance of about an eighth of a mile. Then without hesitation, he spurred the bay over the rim disappearing from view of the flabbergasted posse as they closed in to the point of the rock. All were dumfounded to see this vanishing act and fully expected to find horse and rider in a mangled heap among the rubble at the base of the first rim or perhaps tumbling over the second or third lesser rims.

Vaughan's mount hit the steep slope below the top rim with his hind feet gathered under him in perfect position to take the subsequent lesser rims and they were on the flat just west of town when the posse was in a position to see what had happened. As the posse converged with pistols drawn, ready to pick off what might be left of Vaughan after the wreck, they pulled up their steeds to witness his demise. Vaughan emerged from the cloud of dust and cantered up main street heading for the bar from which he had speedily departed only twenty minutes before. Vaughan rode straight into the bar and ordered the bartender to get a double shot for him and one for his horse. He made the keeper pay off the poker winnings he had dropped on the floor and told him to go to the brewery for a bucket of beer for the posse that would be coming along very soon.

In the meantime, pandemonium broke out on the rock—milling horses were nickering and frustrated riders were cursing, shouting orders, and shooting pistols in the air. Some of the posse tried to gather courage to follow Vaughan's style off the rock, others were heading for the fence jacks at the sides of the bluff, and still others were just milling about in the cloud of mushrooming dust. Several horses had collided and other horses were pawing the air refusing to jump. By this time, a cluster of townspeople gathered on the street to watch the commotion. Vaughan was among them. After downing his drinks and also the one for his horse, he mounted and headed for McKay Creek and the tall timber of the reservation.

He continued replenishing his herds by poaching stray horses from the surrounding stockmen, but a big source of horses was always available from ponies belonging to the Cayuse Indians. In 1875, the Umatilla Reservation was known to have eight thousand horses.[8] The *East Oregonian*, September 7, 1878, noted:

> Bill Switzler bought over 500 head of horses from the Indians since the first of July, and has sold a great portion of them. He knows all about Cayuses. Those in want of gentle ponies give him a call.

According to Starkey pioneer Obediah Burnett, the Switzlers kept a crew of fifteen Indian cowboys breaking horses most of the summer at their Cold Springs range headquarters.

In the fall when the valley stockmen brought their herds off summer range they often joined forces with neighboring ranchers to gather and sort the animals. Unbranded horses or cows called "slick ears" or "slicks" were fair game for whoever caught them first. In Vaughan's business it was his practice to be the first to pluck off as many of these strays as possible.

But when Vaughan ventured off the reservation, it was risky as the stockmen were constantly on the lookout for suspected rustlers. His respectable reputation didn't fool many of the ranchers. On one occasion, Vaughan was spotted on Bill Matlock's open hill range directing a small band of horses toward the mountains. A company of men attempted to capture him. Range rider-rancher, Ted Stickler, of Tutuilla, related how his father, along with an eight-man posse, then ran Hank from East Birch Creek south of Pilot Rock onto the reservation and up McKay Creek into the mountains.

According to Stickler's father, instead of just attempting to outrun the posse, Vaughan reigned his horse back upon entering the draws and washes or when rounding bends in the trail. He would then take a couple of well-aimed shots at his pursuers, sending them scrambling for cover. Taking advantage of the posse's confusion, Hank would again spur his pony away. After a few repeats of this, Vaughan outdistanced the other riders and made a successful escape back into the reservation.

This kind of action was an expression of the dramatic flair for which Hank was to become known. Stickler said it was the combination of this tactic plus the fast horse he was on that saved Hank's neck. He said it was known that Hank only stole good horses and then kept the pick of the lot for himself.

Hank usually escaped to the reservation but the reservation was not always a sanctuary for those who stole horses. The following advertisement appeared in the *East Oregonian*, August 16, 1879:

NOTICE

> If persons who have horses gone will send me a description of them, with authority to get them up, I will do so at a reasonable charge. I am on the range often and know of many strange horses now on the reservation. Address, Wm. Lishaw, Pendleton, Oregon.

When it was appropriate to sell horses Hank and his crew rounded up their ponies from the reservation land and drove them to Vaughan's corrals where the herd mares and young colts could be cut back from those meant for sale. This gathering and sorting was a period of much deliberation as the Indians selected which horses to sell and settled the problems arising over ownership or unbranded animals. The whole process of gathering, sorting, and branding took two to three weeks.

Since much of Hank's operation depended on stolen horses, it was necessary that the animals he sold be marketed far from where they were acquired. To accomplish this, Vaughan disposed of his herds through his contacts in Idaho Territory. As a small band of horses was ready for sale, one of his cohorts with several Indian wranglers would take them via the less travelled routes through the mountains. Such trips could be accomplished in about a week's time and the frequency of the ventures were limited only by the ambition and hardiness of the riders.

The *East Oregonian* of September 13, 1879, described the prevalence of such undertakings in remote sections of the Blue Mountains. John Starkey's ranch, where the following was observed, was only a day's ride from Vaughan's corrals:

> There is scarce a day passes but what the discerning eye will see some suspicious looking characters passing through these mountains. The last we noticed was about two weeks ago with a band of NN horses, . . . They came to this place early in the morning. The horses evidently got away from someone. In a short time two men came for breakfast. They seemed very anxious about the horses but did not undertake to drive them away. They left soon after breakfast, and two more men came along and inquired about the stock. Mr. Starkey did not give them any information as to which way the horses went, but those enterprising young men took the trail and soon found them, and slyly drove them away.

While Hank was hustling business between Oregon and Idaho Territory, Louisa was left alone, sometimes for a month at a time, without any arrangements made for her care and comfort. Perhaps Vaughan felt she would be helped by the Howdeyshells who weren't far away. David Howdeyshell said on occasion when he and his wife visited Louisa they found her without any wood or provisions. He had seen Louisa ". . . go out into snow three feet deep and dig for wood to make a fire." As with Lois before, Hank appeared to feel Louisa should be able to take care of herself.

The cabin on Wildhorse was Louisa's only home but it was just a hangout for Hank as he set up his new base of operation. He had chosen Pendleton because it was a center of livestock trading activities. The pattern that emerged there was similar to his Nevada operations. Whereas he had his own ranch in Elko as a holding ground for stolen stock, in Oregon through his rapport with the Indians he would have a refuge on the Umatilla Indian Reservation. He entered the Northeastern Oregon scene with assets, a band of horses. He acquired a wife and a cabin and gave the appearance of settling down in the community. That accomplished, he proceeded to use his organizational skills to parlay stolen horses into a way to make a living.

REFERENCES

Chapter 5

1. Oliphant, J. Orin. *On the Cattle Ranges of the Oregon Country*. Seattle: University of Washington Press, 1968, 139.
2. Sharon, Julian L. "Pendleton-Umatilla County and the Oregon Country." Manuscript, Umatilla County Library, Pendleton, 25.
3. Personal interview, F.G. "Whit" Whitney, Ukiah, Oregon, June 23, 1967.
4. Tucker, Gerald J. "Hank Vaughn's Fatal Ride," *Frontier Times*. April-May, 1966, 43, 65, 66. Also Obituary, *East Oregonian*, June 16, 1893.
5. Umatilla County Court, Book of Marriages, Page dated August 31, 1878, Pendleton.
6. Umatilla County Circuit Court, Divorce Case No. 191-30, Louisa J. Vaughan vs. H.E. (sic) Vaughan, awarded June 22, 1883. Umatilla County, Pendleton.
7. Personal interview, Ray Strack, Starkey, Oregon, June 16, 1974. Mr. Strack retold the story as he had heard it from Dave Horn who claimed to have been an eye witness.
8. Umatilla County Tax Rolls, Secretary of State Biennial Reports 1870-1877, Archives Division, Oregon State Library, Salem.

VI.

APPEARANCES IN IDAHO TERRITORY (1879)

Hank's business endeavors in Eastern Oregon were closely tied to Idaho Territory and in the following years he was frequently in Boise Valley. He was most often there because of his own interests, but on one noticeable occasion he was called into court as a witness involving his brother-in-law, William Butler. Little has come to light about this case. The family has revealed nothing. No information is available in existing Ada County court records and the newspapers of that period carried few details of the court action.

Charges were lodged against Butler on April 15, 1879 for an assault that happened five days previously. The trial got underway on April 27 with Hank Vaughan and Jesse Wailey sworn in as witnesses for the defence. However, on April 29, the Idaho *Statesman* reported "The People vs. Wm. Butler discontinued." There was no other explanation. Hank had gotten Butler out of the grips of the law several years earlier in Elko. Perhaps he was again able to suggest action that enabled Butler to avoid prosecution. But Butler could only delay court action. Eventually he did stand trial for this assault.

A short time after this appearance in court Hank showed up at his father's ranch where he reportedly was involved in a rather minor accident, but one that resulted in a painful injury. Details of this incident were related in the Boise *Tri-Weekly Statesman* of May 6, 1879:

> A Painful Accident.—Mr. A.H. Vaughn was in town [Boise City] yesterday after medicine for his son Henry Vaughn. He says they had been hunting stock for some time, and on Friday last when Henry was in the act of hitching his horse the horse jumped back, and having hold of the rope it threw Henry on the ground, though the horse did not touch him. He got up and did not think he was hurt much and walked up Willow Creek a short distance towards the old ranch, his father followed soon after and found Henry flat on his back in the most excruciating pain in his back, perfectly helpless. His father went to the house and got the wagon to take him home. He suffered great pain and came near having the lockjaw. So much so that they had to pry his mouth open two different times. They have had a doctor, and his pain is somewhat alleviated, but he is still perfectly helpless. The injury is in the backbone.

This news item made it appear that an accident had physically incapacitated Hank. The report may have been a ruse to give Hank an alibi. Whether there was any truth in the story, it did show that Hank and his father were well known by the local press and received publicity if they wanted it.

Vaughan was seen so frequently in Idaho Territory during this period that newspapers of the time considered him a resident of Boise City. In those days, Boise City was no metropolis. The census of 1880 fixed its population at only 1,899. The community was growing, however, due to its location as a convenient supply point for those mining the rich mineral deposits in the mountains to the north. Several competing stage lines linked the city and the mining camps with the transcontinental railroad which was several hundred miles south in Nevada. All of these activities required horses and supplying these horses was the business Hank was getting into.

He divided his time between the Pendleton-Blue Mountain area and the Boise Valley in the summer of 1879; at least Louisa wasn't yet claiming he had deserted her. He was making contacts and moving stock between Northeastern Oregon and southwestern Idaho Territory where the rest of his gang were operating. In mid-June, one of his partners, Still Heulet, who was now handling the Elko area and holdings, ran afoul of the law. The following item in the Boise *Tri-Weekly Statesman*, July 17, 1879, tells of his arrest and hints at the illegal nature of their business:

> Arrested on a Telegram.—Wednesday afternoon officer Weaver [Tuscarora, Nevada] received telegram from Sheriff Finch, instructing him to arrest Stil Huling [Still Huelet], who was on his way north with a lot of stock, and to take possession of and hold the animals. Mr. Weaver started out immediately and yesterday he arrested Mr. Huling on Bull Run Creek. He brought the prisoner to town last evening and is holding him here subject to orders from Elko. The telegram did not state what offense was charged against Huling.—*Times Review.*

This was the first mention of the telegram, an efficient new communication system which reached the west following the arrival of the railroads. By using the telegram, law enforcement agents were able to quickly alert their associates to suspected criminals headed into their territory.

About two months after one of his partners got into trouble in Nevada, Hank showed up in southwestern Idaho. According to the Silver City *Avalanche* of September 27, 1879:

> H.C. Vaughn of Boise City spent several days here recently and made a host of friends among our best citizens all of whom will be pleased to see him among us again.

Hank's visit to Silver City undoubtedly had something to do with the arrest a few weeks earlier of Charles McDermett. The *Avalanche* of September 13, 1879, had given these details of the McDermett case:

> A Variety of Misdemeanors.—Justice Wickersham has been quite busy during the past week in disposing of cases that came before him. Charles McDermett was up

> on Wednesday for grand larceny. Charles is a bad egg. He stole three mares from Hank and Scott nearly three months ago. They deputized Milt Polk to hunt him up, and the latter, with the aid of the Sheriff of Cassia County, succeeded in getting possession of the delinquent a few days ago at Goose Creek [160 miles southeast of Silver City near the Utah line]. He was brought here and lodged in jail. The justice placed him under bonds to the amount of $1,500 to appear before the next grand jury.

McDermett may have been a defecting member of Hank's operation and someone Hank wasn't interested in protecting from the charges. McDermett did stand trial for the above horse theft and after he began serving a two-year sentence in the territorial penitentiary, the *Avalanche*, of November 15, quoted him as having confessed:

> . . . that he was one of a gang of lawless men whose operations covered a large section of the Pacific Coast, extending into Utah, New Mexico, and other points. There was a large number of these depredators, and many of them are still at large. McDermett states that Hank Vaughan, late of Boise City, was one of the leaders of the band, and that the safe robbery in the store of Schwabacher and Co. was planned nine months ago [March 1879].

The La Grande, Oregon, *Gazette* of November 22, summarized the McDermett case and passed the word to residents in Eastern Oregon that Hank Vaughan had been named ring leader of a band of horse thieves operating throughout the Pacific Northwest and down into the Southwest. Law enforcement officers would have been delighted to try Hank on these charges, but apparently there was not sufficient evidence to bring him to justice.

The Schwabacher robbery which McDermett referred to took place in Boise City, October 9, 1879. Hank Vaughan was in Boise City at that time but his activities appeared to be unrelated to the robbery. Boise City was one of the popular horse racing centers of those times and because of Hank's growing affinity to gamble, he had attended a series of horse races that were held between a popular local horse named Sleepy Dave and a touted four-year old bay stallion from Kentucky. It can be assumed that Hank was in attendance at the race and if his money was on the winning Red Boy, he would soon have been at the bar in the Overland Hotel offering drinks all around in celebration.

The proceeds from those races were not deposited in a bank, but in a safe belonging to Schwabacher and Co. Early Thursday morning, the safe was forcibly opened. The thieves had entered the mercantile company through the alley, gaining access to an inner room where the three thousand pound safe was located. With the help of crowbars and drill, the robbers methodically opened the outer and inner doors of the safe. At this point, for some unknown reason, they left their work in haste, leaving behind most of the safe's contents. It was estimated that only $3,500 was taken and Mr. Schwabacher immediately offered a reward of $250 plus 10 percent of any money recovered for the arrest and conviction of the criminals.

To add to the excitement generated by the horse race and the safe robbery, a shooting affray occurred in the middle of town that evening. The Idaho *Statesman* of October 11, 1879, had the following to say about the shooting in which Hank was a principal participant:

> An altercation took place about dusk Thursday on the sidewalk in front of the Stage and express office, between H.C. Vaughan and Pitt Smith. Some sharp words were exchanged, when Smith drew a pistol and fired at Vaughan, missing him, when the latter also fired a pistol at Smith; the ball taking effect in Smith's hip, inflicting a painful though not fatal wound. Vaughan was before Judge Curtis yesterday for an examination, when it being proved that Smith was the assailant and that he fired the first shot, Vaughan was discharged.

Why did Pitt Smith accost Hank? The *Avalanche* in Silver City indicated there had been past troubles between the two:

> Latest News.—Special to the *Avalanche*—Pitt Smith and Hank Vaughn had a shooting affray last night at 8 o'clock in front of the stage office. Smith was dangerously wounded in the hip. He is easy this morning. There is great excitement over the affair, which is the result of an old quarrel.

It is tempting to try and link this shooting with the Schwabacker robbery which McDermett claimed Hank had masterminded but in later years a friend claimed the shooting was a direct result of Hank being forced to defend his reputation as a shootist. As the friend recalled:

> . . . His gun fight with Pitt Smith was a direct outgrowth of it. Smith was a quick tempered proud fellow. He was jealous of his reputation with a gun. He had made open declaration of his intention to "get" Vaughan. They met one day right on the corner of what is now Main and Eighth Street, directly in front of the old Overland Hotel. Of this encounter Vaughan's cowpuncher pardner says "I didn't see the gun play but Pitt was on the ground when I happened along right afterward. We carried him into a nearby drug store and they began to probe for the bullet then and there."[1]

Although this gunfight was a traumatic affair for Vaughan and Smith, local newspapers made no more mention of the episode, devoting their attention instead to the Schwabacher case. One of the earliest arrests in connection with the robbery was J.C. Alexander, an associate of Hank's. The *Idaho Statesman*, October 23, reported the arrest of more of those suspected of carrying out the safe robbery. The paper claimed that one of the robbers, Frank Trullinger, alias Frank Johnson, upset that he received only $2.50 of the take, had turned state's evidence. Because of information he gave, William Davis, Stephen Walsh and John Wilson had been apprehended. Shortly after their arrest, these three accused robbers escaped from the Boise jail. According to the *Idaho Statesman*, November 20, 1879, they were soon recaptured.

Davis was the most notorious of the gang. According to the *Idaho Avalanche* of October 18, 1879:

> . . . the man Davis, accused of complicity in the recent safe robbery at Boise City, was brought in from the vicinity of Banner, to which point he was fleeing with a view to escaping arrest. District Attorney Hawley and Deputy Sheriff McClintock

> captured the man and had him forwarded to Boise City, where he is now safely lodged in jail. Davis worked as a miner on Shaw's mountain last summer, but has every appearance of being an expert in the robbing business.

Davis had been in trouble with the law in Elko during the period when Hank was there. The Elko *Post*, February 15, 1878, said he had been acquitted of murder, but according to other sources, Davis acting as a "special policeman" had deliberately murdered Louis Ash at Virginia City on October 8, 1877.[2]

After his arrest, the *Idaho Statesman*, October 14, 1879, found that Davis had been under arrest in Boise City once before on a charge of stealing horses in Oregon but that he had been discharged before the requisition from the Governor of Oregon caught up with him. The *Statesman* of December 4 further claimed that Davis was wanted in San Francisco for burglary where he went under the aliases of Wm. Meade and Charles Prop.

The trial for the Schwabacher robbery ended on January 13, 1880, with Davis, Walsh and Wilson receiving sentences of seven years each in the penitentiary. Alexander was acquitted of the charge.

The confession of McDermett that Hank had masterminded the robbery a full nine months earlier, the fact that Davis had been in Elko with Hank and was wanted in Oregon for stealing horses, and Hank's friendship with J.C. Alexander tend to link him as more than a casual observer to this robbery. If Hank planned the robbery, he had been careful enough to keep that involvement from the men who were convicted of the crime as he was not mentioned by them during their trial. Hank would often be accused of playing the inside man for similar undertakings, but as in this affair, he was never brought to trial. James F. Johnson, a deputy in Umatilla County in the 1880s, said:

> He [Vaughan] would hang around town and keep watch on where the sheriff and other peace officers were, while the cattle thieves operated. We never could get evidence to connect him up with the night riders, but there is no doubt he was cooperating with them and headed one of the bands.[3]

Perhaps there was a connection with this strategy of Vaughan's and the fact that the chief law enforcement officer of Boise City, Marshal Chase, was out of town when Schwabachers was robbed. The Idaho *Avalanche* of October 11, 1879, quoted the following from the Walla Walla *Statesman*:

> A Carpet Bagger.—Marshal Chase and wife, of Boise City, arrived in town [Walla Walla] recently with his own 2:40 team, having left the "Damascus of the Plains" last Sunday. He confirms the opinion given elsewhere, that the recent raid on the Weiser was the work of white men. He is of the opinion that the thieves are an organized band and will run the stolen animals off to Nevada. He had just returned from a chase and capture of thieves that will ever be memorable for strategy, pluck and perseverance. After riding 50 hours without rest, he got ahead of the robbers who committed the recent depredations in the Boise Valley. He says that he knows that the celebrated James brothers, of Missouri, are in Idaho, although they have not been seen. It will be well for our citizens to keep a good look out now, for the country is full of desperadoes of every description.

Marshal Chase was describing just such a band of horse thieves as Hank headed. But Hank was not one of those he captured. Marshal Chase was out of Boise City at the very time of the Schwabacker robbery. While he bragged about his heroic exploits to the citizens of Walla Walla, the residents of Boise wondered where he was when they needed him.

Author Robert Ballou who interviewed a friend of Hank's said:

> Old timers, in on the know, asserted that he was the master mind for many years behind a gang that were guilty of all kinds of law violations from petit larceny to highway robbery. Hank himself did not take an active part, but was alleged to have made the plans and directed activities. His part being to furnish bail, defense and advice for all members of his gang who ran afoul of the law. On the other hand he became a man of considerable prominence and acquired the confidence of many reputable citizens.[4]

Hank's latest shootout and the public accusations that he was the leader of a gang of lawless men brought him considerable renown. But he didn't go into seclusion on account of the notoriety he gained. He appeared to have complete confidence in being able to outdo any challenges to his shooting ability and no concern about allegations of his lawlessness.

REFERENCES

Chapter 6

1. The *Idaho Statesman*, May 23, 1937.
2. Angel, Myron. *History of Nevada.* Oakland: Thompson and West, 1881, 353.
3. Kelly, John W. "Hank Vaughan: A Story of the Old West." *Oregon Motorist*. September 1930. 12-13.
4. Ballou, Robert. *Early Klickitat Valley Days*. Goldendale: The Goldendale Sentinel, Printers, 1938, 61.

VII.
MOVING INTO WASHINGTON TERRITORY
(1880-1881)

Vaughan's most recent stay in Idaho Territory included a violent shoot out on a downtown Boise City street and accusations that he not only headed a band of horse thieves but that he had helped plan a safe robbery for which some of his friends were now awaiting trial. News of this preceded his return to Eastern Oregon as local papers carried versions of the episode reported in Idaho Territory papers. One wonders how his wife, Louisa, was affected by the notoriety of her husband. Perhaps because her cabin was in such a remote spot and since Hank so infrequently spent time with her, few people associated her with him.

He couldn't have spent much time with Louisa in the Wildhorse area that winter because within 2 1/2 months of the Boise City shooting, he was on the move again headed north checking out the markets for products he and his syndicate could deliver. He touched base in Eastern Oregon long enough to put together a band of sale horses to finance an exploratory trip into Washington Territory.

On this first business venture into Washington Territory, he again encountered the lawman, Frank Maddock. Their confrontation fifteen years previously had been a violent event in the lives of both men. This was when Maddock attempted to arrest Vaughan near the Express Ranch in Baker County. Maddock bore a permanent facial disfigurement after this meeting and he would never forget the loss of his deputy, John Hart. Vaughan, too, lost a companion in the affray and was injured by a bullet, plus he served nearly five years in prison after that episode.

Maddock, his wife, Lucy, and their four children were now an established ranching family near Stansberry Flat (later Heppner). But during this period in 1880, he was a deputy sheriff serving the area which later became Morrow County. The *East Oregonian* of January 3, 1880, reported:

> Frank Maddock passed through town on the 27th . . . in hot pursuit of a man who was getting out of the state with a lot of horses on which no taxes had been paid, and no clear bill of sale had been given.

On January 10, 1880, a further communication in the *East Oregonian* revealed that Maddock and Vaughan had finally come face to face. The article said:

> Frank Maddock just returned from Palouse country, says he collected his bills, got his horses and made a perpetual treaty of peace with Henry Vaughn who he met at Dayton.

Ever since Vaughan was first seen back in the country two years previously, there had been the possibility of a confrontation between the two men. Everyone knew it was inevitable that they meet. Their encounter finally occurred in the town of Dayton. This community, twenty miles northeast of Walla Walla, lay in the center of the rich prairie grasslands which were once the home of the Palouse Indians and their fine horses. Most people living here were involved in the potpourri of businesses that make up a county seat. Since Dayton was neutral territory for both men, perhaps few bystanders on that cold winter day even recognized the deputy and the outlaw or knew of their earlier contact.

Maddock was a brave lawman who had learned through bitter experience that calm and reasonableness were the most prudent ways to approach men whether they were law abiding or lawless. Hank was reasonable when he wasn't drinking and he must have been sober on this occasion. We can only assume that after some preliminary formalities these two advanced to a cautious exchange which resulted in their perpetual peace pact.

Hank could have been in possession of the herd of horses Maddock was following. If he were, he was prepared to pay off the taxes Maddock was after and thus avoid any charges that might bring him to court. When he moved horses along well established routes, he carried bills of sale or some type of papers to identify the horses as legitimately his. He wasn't so careful to provide proof of purchase when he took the less travelled trails.

Dayton was along the route Hank would use as he became involved in the new markets in Washington Territory. These markets would later include providing horses for the construction of Henry Villard's Northern Pacific Railroad but presently there appeared to be more immediate need for horses to help move cattle eastward to stock the ranches in Montana Territory.

Apart from the initial gold strikes at places such as Virginia City and Bannock, Montana Territory had provided more prospecting than prosperity. That the real wealth of her lands lay in the endless prairie and mountain pastures was just now beginning to be appreciated. As the rich ranching land of central and eastern Montana was being opened up, there was a scramble to locate cattle to put on the ranges. Ranchers preferred the hardy shorthorn cattle of the Pacific Northwest. Experience had shown that Texas longhorns used earlier to stock the Wyoming ranges could not withstand the bitter winters of the northern plains.

In these days everything was touted as "Oregon"—Oregon cattle, Oregon fruit, Oregon lumber. Washington Territory and its products were comparatively unknown.[1] But many of the cattle which would go to Montana Territory would come from Washington Territory. Montana ranchers were paying about as much for Washington Territory cattle as the ranchers in Colorado and Wyoming were paying for so-called Oregon cattle.

Hank knew of the demand for cattle in Montana Territory and his reconnoiter into the Spokane Falls area showed him that stock from northern Washington could be in Montana Territory much sooner than stock moving on the more southerly route through Pendleton, Boise City, American Falls and northward over Monida or Targhee Passes. The route from Spokane Falls was over the Mullan Trail which stretched from Wallula on the Columbia River to Fort Benton on the Missouri River in Montana Territory.

Although accounts were not documented, an informed source reported 26,000 head of cattle were moved into Montana Territory from Oregon and Washington Territory in 1880 and 60,000 in 1881.[2] Reports on the sale of horses estimated 3,000 to 6,000 were driven to Montana Territory during the same years.

Large numbers of these animals were driven over the Mullan Road. The area around Spokane Falls became the center of activity for this eastward movement of Washington cattle and horses. Here, before the road entered forested mountain terrain, stock could be collected and gathered into trail herds.

Hank first appeared in Spokane Falls early in 1880. Recognizing the opportunity here he began to establish himself in what was a typical scenario for him. He arrived in town with money in his pocket, made himself known to the local newspaper editors, set up a home base, and made friends with important local people.

Spokane lore has it that Hank's town headquarters was in a cabin built in 1879 on the corner of Main and Bernard (fig. 15). After Vaughan moved on, the cabin was used as a carpenter shop. It was later purchased by the Catholic Church and it is said that the first mass in Spokane Falls was celebrated in 1881 in Hank Vaughan's cabin.[3]

Vaughan spent the next few months setting up the route and system he would use bringing horses from eastern Oregon to Spokane Falls. The most important post was at Peone Prairie, a vast meadow about ten miles north of the Spokane River where cattle herds were assembled before their trek to Montana Territory. According to local legend, Hank lived on a ranch there in the early 1880s.[4] This ranch may have been run by his cousin, Harry N. Vaughan.

In the spring of 1880, Hank and Harry, along with Indian friends from the Umatilla and Colville Reservations, set up their stock corrals and camp in a timbered glade at the edge of Peone Prairie. Here Hank and company could assemble horse herds which would either be sold directly to the drovers taking cattle to Montana Territory or be driven to Helena for sale to the railroad construction builders.

A profitable side operation for Hank's group would develop through picking up stray cattle from the herds being assembled on Peone Prairie. These were furtively transferred to safe refuge on the Spokane Reservation until they could be sold at less risk.

During the course of the construction of this outpost, Hank and Harry purchased some of their supplies on credit from the local merchants. Although he would be in and out of Spokane Falls for the next few years, it would take these merchants several years to collect their bills from Hank Vaughan.

Between the corrals on Peone Prairie and the gathering point on the Umatilla Indian Reservation, Hank's gang would have need for some kind of secluded night

(Sketch from West Shore by Kirk Skovlin)

FIGURE 15—This cabin located at the corner of Main and Bernard Streets south of the falls of the Spokane River was known as Hank Vaughan's cabin. It later served as the first Catholic Church in Spokane Falls.

camp every thirty to forty miles, the distance that could be covered by a band of horses in a day. The usual route followed old Indian trails.

Not many luxuries were associated with driving horses. There were no chuck wagons or cooks to prepare meals as was common with the slower moving cattle drives. More than likely Vaughan's horse drovers were accompanied by a camp tender and his string of pack animals which would include three or four stout horses each with a pair of light alforja-type saddlebags lashed tightly to sawbuck saddles. One horse packed the food consisting of essentials like coffee, bacon, sour dough start and a sack of flour. A second carried pots, pans and iron skillets along with horseshoeing gear and extra carbine rifles. A third horse carried the cowboys' bedrolls.

In conducting his business, Vaughan not only utilized the knowledge and experience of his Indian friends, but of his relatives as well. It is not known that Hank Vaughan's relatives were active in his syndicate, but he depended upon them and imposed on their strategic locations as he made his rounds lining up buyers and contacting his suppliers. He appeared to mix his business trips with social family calls, staying a few days with relatives, checking on happenings in the nearby towns, and then moving on.

For the most part these relatives were respected ranchers of long standing in the territories. Being well informed on local events, they were invaluable sources of information and helped Hank keep his finger on the pulse of local affairs throughout the interior. He used and sometimes abused his relatives in carrying out his business affairs.

His uncle, John Quincy Vaughan, lived near Goldendale which would become the county seat of Klickitat County, Washington. John had farmed in the Klickitat valley since 1869. In Ellensburg and Yakima were cousins, John and Bill. His uncle, William Vaughan, settled along the foothills of the Blue Mountains eight miles east of Walla Walla in 1875.

Vaughan also had relatives scattered about in Idaho Territory whom he did not hesitate to call upon. One of those was William B. Vaughan, a cousin who lived in Albion, Cassia County, Nevada, the territory where the convicted horse thief, McDermett, operated. It is likely William ran a livery stable there. He later moved to Baker City, Oregon, and was a partner in The Red Barn livery stable which ran a successful horse trading operation.

Although nothing has ever come to light that would incriminate any of Hank's uncles, many of his cousins were not above directly assisting him in his far flung horse trading enterprise. Some of Hank's generation and those younger than he found it exhilarating to be involved with a man of his notoriety. Tragedy would be connected with at least one such nephew.

Hank was not able to run his operations on a cash basis. There were times after a sale of a herd of horses when he would have money. But for those other times, he took advantage of his quick wit and ability to find ways for others to finance him. Many of the horses he sold were on consignment, loose arrangements where he might or might not be called upon to account for transactions. Possibly it was through just such a horse sale that Hank came to owe some money to J.C. Davis. Davis later testified that Vaughan offered to give him his cook stove as "he (Hank) was going to sell every dam thing there was and leave the country." According to Davis, Vaughan claimed:

> . . . [He] had no money to pay me but he would give me a bill of sale of the woman and that was the only show I had to get my money. I asked him what he meant if he was going to leave his wife, he said he was. I asked him why and he said "I'll be God dammed if I want to live with a woman." I told him he had better not sell the stove but leave it with the woman if he was going to leave her he said "I do not give a God dam she can go to her folks to live."[5]

This outburst could have followed an argument with Louisa at a time when Hank had no ready cash, but it more than likely was the way Hank chose to avoid paying Davis.

By fall, Hank came back to Louisa and persuaded her to move with him into the Grande Ronde Valley of Union County. This move from the Wildhorse cabin across the Blue Mountains deeper into eastern Oregon was connected with the necessity of refining operations out of Pendleton. Population expansion and pressure from the law and local stockmen were making it more difficult for horse thieves to operate along their normal routes.

Near the end of the decade of the 1870s, settlers occupied nearly all of the land along the foothills and had begun homesteading fertile mountain valleys. Their new presence disrupted traffic in several ways. First, the settlers were in a position to view and report the presence of strangers or unusual happenings in remote locations. Moreover, to protect their crops from loose stock, the settlers fenced and in so doing they blocked former stock trails. At first just the occasional field was fenced with split rails but by 1880 entire homesteads were being enclosed by the newly invented barbed wire. This wire was often called "the Devil's hatband" and horses unfamiliar with its sharp barbs suffered serious cuts when they became entangled in it.

In order to adapt his operations to these changing times, Hank realized the need for both new routes on which to move his stolen stock as well as a more secluded horse-holding ground. While locating these new areas, Hank and Louisa would live in the Grande Ronde Valley for about one year. This was an area much admired by travelers of the Oregon Trail, some of whom returned after finding the Willamette Valley not to their liking. By 1880, several thousand people lived in and around the towns of Union, La Grande, Summerville and Forest Cove. Most of the settlement was along the elevated parts of the valley as large areas of the valley floor were flooded each spring by the Grande Ronde River.

Hank was not as visible setting up in Union County as he had been in Spokane Falls, although he did bring Louisa which gave him a degree of respectability and aura of permanence. For a time they lived on a small ranch near Union, the bustling county seat.

One incident which occurred while Hank and Louisa lived out of Union involved the disputed ownership of a horse. The matter was never seriously contested after the first owner became aware of Hank's reputation. In the spring of 1881, William J. "Bill" Knight was freighting between La Grande and Alkali Flat (later Enterprise) in Wallowa Valley. A filly he bought in the Grande Ronde Valley the fall before ran away when Bill stayed over night with friends on Cricket Flat. When he reached Summerville, he asked the filly's former owner to watch for her.

The filly never appeared at her former home, but several weeks later, Bill heard she had been seen near Union. On his next weekly trip to Union, Bill saw the horse in a pasture on a ranch where Vaughan and Louisa were living. Upon being questioned about the horse, Hank Vaughan was friendly and cooperative, even suggesting they go to where she stood so the young horse could be identified.

Upon getting a closer look, Bill told Vaughan that this was, in fact, his horse and he would be glad to take her off Vaughan's hands. Bill caught up the filly, inquired if he owed anything for her keep, and started to lead her out of the lot. With that, Vaughan pulled his gun, motioned at Bill and said for him to "leave her be." Furthermore he added, it was not Bill's horse and that could be proven and Bill was to leave the place immediately.

Bill was properly intimidated and left. He said Vaughan whom he did not recognize at the time was just matter of fact and not belligerent. Bill did not know how Vaughan had come by the horse, but because he wanted to get her back, he contacted the former owner who was willing to testify to the brand and provide a bill of sale. When Bill went back through Union to press charges, he found that

Vaughan was no longer around. After learning more about Hank, Bill decided that it was just as well it ended that way.[6]

Louisa was not in good health during their stay in Union County and she complained that even when she was sick, Hank went off for two or three weeks at a time without leaving anyone to take care of her.

During these absences, Hank was looking for a new hideaway. The obscure spot he chose was on the upper reaches of the remote Minam River at what is now known as the Horse Ranch. Hank had learned of the area from his Indian friends. No miners were working there as precious minerals had never been found in the western Wallowa Mountains and stockmen had not moved into the area. The range was considered too rough for cattle. It would be the late 1880s before Jake Sturgill first brought his flocks of sheep into this high mountain land (fig. 16).

To get better access to the area of the Horse Ranch, Hank moved Louisa from Union to a cabin on the upper end of Indian Creek just over the mountain rim above the Minam River. Indian Creek emptied into the Grande Ronde River about two miles upstream from the community that would become Elgin. Hank's cabin was about twelve miles up this drainage along the route to the Horse Ranch.

Time-wise this location was nearly midway between the Umatilla Reservation and the Horse Ranch. Horses started at day break near Wildhorse could be driven over Black Mountain, passing near the Ruckel Springs Stage Stop, then down into the valley north of the Grande Ronde River crossing and up Indian Creek to Vaughan's cabin and corrals in one day. From there, the seclusion of the Minam was but one-half day's easy drive.

Those driving stolen horses in and out of the Columbia Basin area began taking this route rather than the much travelled Meacham Road or the Starkey or Daley

(Courtesy Gerald Strickler)

FIGURE 16—Sturgill Basin was named after Jake Sturgill who first brought sheep here, but it was used in earlier years as a holding ground for stolen horses.

route which was congested with herds of cattle and drovers from early May through July.

It wasn't long before horse thieves were moving small bunches of horses into the Minam River hideout. Here the horses were held until a large, economically profitable herd was ready to be pushed across the mountains in whatever direction the markets lay. Vaughan and his cohorts would gather and sort through the horses, branding when necessary.

Those that required special care were driven even further up country where they could be kept all summer if necessary. About fifteen miles above the Horse Ranch at the 7,000-foot level, the broad grassy slopes of what is now known as Sturgill Basin could feed a lot of horses.

Vaughan's special holding ground was adjacent to Sturgill Basin. Now listed as Vaughn Basin, this mile-long glaciated cul-de-sac had steep canyon walls and a headrim (fig. 17). Scattered timber along the creek bottom and luxuriant open bunchgrass slopes provided excellent feed. The lower entrance of the U-shaped basin where it narrowed to join Sturgill Creek was heavily timbered with lodgepole pine and could easily be fenced. It was the pick of the secluded mountain pastures.

About one-half mile above the mouth of Vaughn Creek, where Sturgill basin opens out into a large treeless subalpine park, Vaughan and his friends built another corral. As late as 1960 the remains could still be found of this corral where stolen horses were worked over with running irons, rebranded and then turned out to fatten while their new brands healed. By fall, Vaughan's cohorts would have a new band of valuable horses ready to be sold with a minimum amount of risk that the legal owners could ever again prove ownership.

Early residents of Northeastern Oregon were aware that this Horse Ranch area was frequented by an outlaw element and avoided it unless they had a compelling reason to pass through.[7] Many of the names given the geographic features in the close vicinity reflect this early outlaw use: Horseheaven, Horse Basin, Whoopee and Cache Creeks, Buckaroo and Horseshoe Springs, Horse Meadow, Deadhorse Flat and Thief Valley.

It was during this period of stay in Union County that Hank and Louisa separated for the last time. Her bad health and Hank's frequent absences contributed to Louisa's unhappiness, but even more distressing to her was the interest Hank showed in the local girls. She was particularly indignant about one Nancy Tucker who would sometimes visit their cabin. When she caught her husband kissing Nancy, she protested that this was not a proper way to treat a wife in her own home.

Her disapproval didn't stop Hank's philandering nor did the affair stop with a friendly kiss. Louisa testified later that on several occasions she saw Hank lying on the bed with his arm around Miss Tucker. He only laughed at Louisa when she reprimanded him for this action, saying it was none of her business.

But it proved too much for Louisa when Hank took Nancy into the bedroom, locked the door and remained there with her for over an hour. Louisa told Hank she could not live with him any more, and, in September 1881, she took the stage to Weston. This time Hank did give her some money, but only enough to pay her stage fare one way.[8]

FIGURE 17—Vaughn Basin is a glaciated pocket high in the Wallowa Mountains. Its steep canyon walls and grassy slopes provided an excellent hiding place for Vaughan's selected horses.

REFERENCES

Chapter 7

1. Lewis, William S. *The Story of Early Days in the Big Bend Country.* Spokane: W.D. Allen, Publisher, 1926, 35.
2. Oliphant, *op. cit.*, 178.
3. The *Spokesman Review*, January 29, 1911.
4. Becher, Edmund T. *Spokane Corona, Eras and Empires.* Spokane: C.W. Hill Printers, 1974, 314.
5. Umatilla County Circuit Court Case No. 191-30, *op. cit.*
6. Personal interview, William J. "Bill" Knight, Sr., La Grande, Oregon, February 2, 1967.
7. Tucker, Gerald J., Personal correspondence, Imnaha, Oregon, March 14, 1974.
8. Umatilla County Circuit Court Case No. 191-30, *op. cit.*

VIII.

DEVELOPING CHARACTER

During the past three years, Hank extended his horse trading interests from northeastern Nevada through southern Idaho Territory and northeastern Oregon into eastern Washington Territory. In the process he set up an operation which earned him the reputation of boss horse thief of the interior Northwest. He no longer found it necessary to operate directly with the small time horse thieves as he had in Nevada and eastern Oregon. He had a well-trained corps of key men leading the grass roots operations and these men reported to him from their home locations. If there was trouble in the ranks, Hank was quick to sort things out. If there was pressure from area ranchers or the local law, Vaughan did the headwork to neutralize these efforts or laid plans to avoid showdowns with the law. His legitimate front allowed him to move openly wherever he chose.

There is no record that Hank ever frequented the famous outlaw hideouts in places like Robber's Roost in Utah Territory, Brown's Hole in Colorado and Hole-in-the-Wall in Wyoming. Horse thieves and outlaws, particularly in the inter mountain states, often assembled in remote areas like these while planning new jobs or when winter curtailed their activities.

Ideal areas for these encampments were close to state lines where a half day's fast riding would place a man clear of the jurisdiction of the local authorities. Sheriff posses and even vigilantes were fearful of entering these strongholds of lawlessness in the belief that those who used these refuges were desperate men who would not hesitate to take another man's life.

The outlaw winter quarters closest to Hank was in northeastern Washington Territory near the British line. The Walla Walla *Statesman* of December 17, 1881, described this area and the activities of the thieves who camped there:

HORSE THIEVING EXTRAORDINARY
Military Assistance Asked to Capture
The Robbers Who Are Encamped Near The British Line.

An organized gang of horse thieves has for some time been operating in Eastern Washington, their depredations having been principally confined to the Yakima and Klickitat sections, from which during the past year over 1500 horses have been

> stolen, Mr. Ben Snipes of The Dalles, being one of the principal losers. . . . The usual course taken by these thieves in driving their plunder to market, is, it has been ascertained, to travel up north through the Kootenai country and cross the line into the British possessions, where they can pursue their course as far east as they please unmolested. The sheriff of Yakima county has received information that a band of these thieves, some twenty in number, is encamped in a valley in the Kootenai region, and near the British line, where they are wintering some 300 of the stolen horses. They are all desperate characters and frequent the town of Ventnor, where they indulge themselves in cutting and shooting affrays.

An energetic person like Hank was not apt to hole up in this type of hideout for any period of time. In winter he would more likely be found in a place like The Dalles making business deals and enjoying his new affluence.

Winter brought an end to much of the outdoor life in Eastern Oregon. Travel halted when the mountain passes became choked with snow. Cold weather plus the biting winds kept people indoors. It was a sociable time for the men to gather in the saloons, sharing news and retelling stories, while drinking the products of the local breweries.

The winter of 1880-1881 was perhaps the first winter he was able to afford to return to The Dalles. For cattle buyers, sellers, gamblers, and the likes, The Dalles in the early 1880s was the place to be. It was once again the hub of activity for the bunchgrass interior as it had been during the roaring 1860s when Hank lived there as a boy (fig. 18). Mining activity was the economic impetus in those days. The building of Henry Villard's railroad was the driving force now.

Villard had bought the Oregon Rail and Navigation Company (OR&N) which until now had operated the boats on the Columbia River and the portage railroads around the rapids in the river. He paid $4,000,000 for property which started out worth only $175,000. Then he began building a railroad up the Oregon bank of the Columbia, intending to join it with the Union Pacific which was being built westward across southern Idaho.

But the Union Pacific would not agree to join their line with the line Villard was building, so Villard hit upon one of the wildest plans in all the history of American railroads. He borrowed money from his rich friends in the eastern United States and Europe and bought control of the Northern Pacific Railroad which was being built across northern Idaho. He then proceeded to link his Oregon line with the Northern Pacific line via a deviation across Washington Territory.

Because of the railroad, two decades after the mining boom, The Dalles was again the scene of considerable activity. The main shops of Villard's OR&N were here and even during the winter layoff the place was alive and humming. The town flourished because of the magnitude of funds that circulated around the building of the railroads. It is recorded that Villard spent $30,000,000 in Oregon on railroads.[1]

In reporting construction of the line up river from The Dalles, the *East Oregonian*, March 13, 1880, said:

> Over eight hundred men are now on the works and there is a call for more. Teams are scarce. 40 horses were sent up only a few days ago from Portland. . . . Grading is going on along the line and we may expect that the road will be completed as far as Umatilla by the first of September.

(Courtesy Oregon Historical Society)

FIGURE 18—This 1884 picture of Second Street in The Dalles shows striking improvement in the heart of the city since the days twenty years earlier when supplying the mines was the main enterprise.

There is no doubt that Hank Vaughan would learn of this shortage of horses and come to arrange to deliver them from his own sources in eastern Oregon. Hank's ride out of The Dalles twenty years before was as a young prisoner in custody of the law. When he returned in the winter of 1881, he came roaring into town only to be greeted by a new city marshall by the name of Adam Croasman. Adam related:

> During the time I was city marshall [of The Dalles, Oregon, 1881-82] I got word that a cowboy from the east of the mountains had come to paint the town red. I saw him coming down the street as hard as his horse could run. I stepped out into the middle of the street and held up my hands for him to stop. He pulled his horse on his haunches to see what I wanted. I said "We have a racetrack out at the edge of town. If you want to do any racing, go out there. We don't permit it in town."
>
> He said, "My name is Hank Vaughn."
>
> I said, "All right, Hank, you can go out to the racetrack and do your racing, or go to the livery stable and put your horse up."
>
> He went to the livery stable and put his horse up. About an hour later I dropped into George Allen's saloon. He said, "Have you got your gun on you, Adam?"
>
> I said, "You know I never carry a gun."
>
> He said, "You better get one. Hank Vaughn is looking for you."
>
> When I went to Tim Baldwin's saloon, Tim said, "Have you got your gun, Adam? If you haven't take mine. Hank Vaughn is looking for you."

> I said, "Keep your gun, Tim, and tell Hank Vaughn when you see him that he can find me on the street any time he wants."
>
> A few minutes later I dropped into another saloon and, standing in front of the bar, I watched in the mirror at the back of the bar to see who came in at the door. I saw Hank come in. Everybody in the saloon stopped talking. I didn't turn around, but I watched in the mirror every move he made. The minute he pulled his gun I was going to knock him out. He stepped up to me and tapped me on the shoulder. I turned around and he said, "I want to shake hands with you."
>
> I put out my hand and said, "It won't cost you anything to shake hands with me, Hank."
>
> He shook hands and said, "You are the whitest police officer I ever met in my life."
>
> Turning to the men at the tables and to the others standing around, he said, "Come on up, everybody. The drinks are on me." When he had paid for the drinks, he said, "Come on outside. I want to speak to you." When we got outside he said, "Where is the best gents' furnishings store in town?" I took him into a clothing store and he plunked down a $20 gold piece. "I want to buy the best hat you've got in your store for the city marshal here." The proprietor bought out a high silk hat, for which Hank paid $15. Then Hank asked me to take him to the best jewelry store in town. He said to the proprietor, "I want you to give Adam Croasman here the best cane you have in stock." He picked out an ebony cane with a gold head, for which he paid $25, and handed it to me. He said, "I like you. I like your nerve. I like your grit. I like your style. I'll never give you any trouble."[2]

Finding that he could not intimidate the marshall, Hank must have considered that flattery and gifts would be well invested if he planned on using The Dalles as a winter quarters.

As his self assurance grew and his financial situation improved, Hank began to develop a city demeanor (fig. 19). Up until now, he had mostly operated in the field or on the road so to speak. He had made his presence known in Elko during the period he lived in Nevada, but since that time he had been on the move setting up his operations along the lesser travelled parts of the country. This winter would be a period of testing his acceptance in The Dalles. His reputation as a horse thief had, of course, preceded him as well as the knowledge of the Pitt Smith shooting in Boise City last fall. The fact that he had been pardoned for his part in the shooting of Deputy Hart seemed to give him an aura of folk hero. Those who frequented the bars soon found him an entertaining companion and he quickly became popular and a familiar figure in The Dalles.

Historian Noah Brown, who worked in the Umatilla House in The Dalles and later in the Villard Hotel in Pendleton, provides a vivid description of Hank during this period. His account which follows also reveals that Hank's behavior was greatly affected by his consumption of alcohol:

> He weighed about 165 pounds, erect and straight as an Indian and had peculiar blue gray eyes that held you in a grip as it were, when thinking seriously in contemplation or after imbibing a few drinks. He wore his hair and whiskers well groomed. They were of a brown, red cast. A broad rim hat, fashioned after the cowboy's style, high heeled boots, a well fitting suit of clothes of the Prince Albert style and invariably of a snuff colored cloth composed his makeup. When Vaughan was not under the influence of liquor he was possessed of not an ungentlemanly or

(Courtesy Sophia Riede)

FIGURE 19—At about 30 years of age (ca. 1880), Hank Vaughan posed for this studio portrait in his town garb, complete with plug hat.

uncourteous manner. He was quite charitable, and usually pleasant. He was an interesting talker, and an entertainer, as a witty story teller, a quick thinker and judge of human nature. He did not seem to know the word fear and when in a state of intoxication or in a bad mood nothing daunted him.[3]

Writing of Vaughan and describing The Dalles during this period, Brown further recalled:

The first time I saw Hank Vaughan was in the Umatilla House (fig. 20) in The Dalles, Oregon, in 1881, when I was employed by Handley and Sinnott as night clerk in that noted hostlery. Immigration was pouring into that section from the east.

The machine shops of the Northern Pacific were being established. There were large forces of wharf, boat and steamboat men, barges loaded with wood and lumber, for fuel and building, pile driving and tunnel crews, immense freight wagons drawn by six and eight span of horses, passenger stage lines arriving and departing for Yakima, Ellensburg, Goldendale, Antelope, Prineville and other places. There were stock raisers and eastern stock buyers, with their rough and ready cow boys, bawdy houses and dance halls, with roulette wheels, faro, poker and other games of gambling devices, with an added bunch of real expert gun men, who would flash a six shooter from his hip pocket when roused to action as quickly and as readily as a bunchgrass buckaroo would rope a wild steer. These things made it in every sense of the word a typical "wild and wooly west" town and an ideal rendezvous for the type of men with hot blood in their veins, searching for

(Courtesy Oregon Historical Society)

FIGURE 20—Since 1865, the Umatilla House in The Dalles had been a popular spot for traveling men. During his career, Vaughan spent many nights there drinking and playing cards.

adventure, excitement and action. Such was the type and character of Hank Vaughan.[4]

In the same article, Brown described a celebration in The Dalles which Vaughan attended. This spree was put on by Lang and Ryan, an eastern cow outfit well known in The Dalles as they had been involved in moving Oregon cattle to points in Wyoming for several years. Being a good sport and of a jolly spirit, Ryan decided to promote a full night's entertainment for his men. Brown related this narrative of the activities:

> . . . Conditions will scarcely permit of the giving of the names of the half dozen leading prominent characters of the town, who took an active part on this occasion, with the exception of Hank Vaughan, who dropped in at a later hour . . . On entering the saloon the drinks were ordered for the house. Needless to say a crowd ambled up to the mahogany and foot rail in the sampling of Old Crow until the room was full to overflowing. It was not a great while until nearly every individual was in the same fix . . . A shot fired from a six shooter in a frolicsome way pierced a hole through a back bar mirror. Tabs were kept on all drinks, damage to furniture, incidental expenses added and by the next evening those typical early day western trail blazers and pioneer characters dug down in their belt and paid . . . the full lucre, for their gentlemanly tete-a-tete of their own liking in the year of 1881.[5]

The Lang and Ryan company's operation had been described the year before in the *East Oregonian*, March 13, 1880, which noted:

> Messrs. Lang and Ryan have purchased their cattle. Forty men have just arrived by steamer to help drive. They will divide their cattle into seven bands, having 1,000 in each band. Will leave Wasco and the Western portion of this county as soon as the grass is good.

Traditionally, once conditions were right, Lang and Ryan started across the Blue Mountains with their herds, but shortly, in 1881, according to reports in the *East Oregonian*, the big drover, M. [Mike] Ryan Jr., was returned to Pendleton from Union County by the sheriff to face a charge of larceny of a horse.

There was no question that he was headed east on a stolen horse, but after preliminary hearings, Ryan convinced the court it was a simple matter of mistaken identity and he was prepared to make full restitution. Charges were dropped as authorities were not wont to prosecute a man from an outfit which regularly left thousands of dollars in the hands of local ranchers.

It is noteworthy that Vaughan had been supplying horses to Lang and Ryan and it could have been one of Hank's animals that later got Ryan into trouble. That Ryan didn't hold this mistake against him was shown by Hank's inclusion in the party in 1881.

From the description of that riotous party thrown by the Lang and Ryan outfit in The Dalles, high-spirited, destructive activity such as this was not unusual during that period of time, and indeed was rather expected. Hank was a star when it came to related pastimes, most of which would not be tolerated today. One of his favorite pranks was to demonstrate his marksmanship by shooting at local landmarks. While in Boise City, R.E. Rogers recalled:

> He was a crack shot . . . and when braced by dynamic fluid he was prone to show off a little.
>
> On the south east corner of what is now Eighth and Main Streets there used to be a one story hardware store owned by Frank Coffin. On the roof of the store there was an iron coffee pot (fig. 21). Vaughan liked to shoot at that coffee pot. He'd go into the saloon across the street and get a drink and then come out and shoot at it. He'd do that until blinded from within, and then when finally he'd miss he'd turn to the spectators and grumble, "Aw, I guess I'm getting old."[6]

Hank displayed another rather peculiar talent while in Boise City according to writer Rogers:

> Personally, he was a quiet and unassuming fellow to meet. There was nothing of the braggart about him. He wasn't quick tempered and he wasn't quarrelsome. Sober, he had the moral and physical courage to defend his human rights; drunk, he was reckless and daring. . . . Drunk or sober he was an expert horseman. One of his favorite stunts was to chase dogs on his horse and lift them from the ground without leaving the saddle.[7].

(Sketch from West Shore by Kay Woodman)

FIGURE 21—The coffee pot atop Coffin's Hardware Store in Boise City, Idaho Territory, was Hank's favorite target after he had indulged in drinks at the Overland Hotel bar in the building under the flag pole. It was also at this corner where Vaughan shot Pitt Smith.

On another occasion in Boise City, Vaughan and a couple of his cronies initiated a prank that was guaranteed to attract attention. He was in company with Bill Moody and J.C. Alexander, a couple of toughs who followed him. The information provided by pioneer John J. Curtis describes the incident which resulted in a dramatic confrontation between them and Ada County Sheriff J.B. Oldham. This event which probably happened in the summer of 1881 had a humiliating finale for Hank and his buddies.

> On the evening in question Vaughan and his two swaggering companions, noticeably under the influence of liquor, rode into Boise City for the purpose of shooting up the town and incidentally killing the city marshal, Fred Hines, for whom Vaughan entertained a feeling of bitter enmity. Forewarned the city marshal went into hiding.[8]

Vaughan paused long enough from his galloping about town to direct a practice of the city volunteer fire company. Hank was making them pull their hose about squirting people and property when the sheriff who had been summoned arrived at the scene. Curtis said that Sheriff Oldham, like Maddock, White and others:

> . . . was the most fearless and courageous man who ever held in the early days the office of sheriff of Ada county, Idaho Territory. Singular to say he seldom carried a gun except when on the trail of an outlaw.
>
> A rawboned man 6 feet 4 inches in height in his stocking feet Sheriff Oldham was a fine looking fellow, cultured, always immaculately dressed, a genial, affable gentleman who enjoyed a wide circle of friends among the best element of south Idaho.

Of this confrontation Curtis said:

> . . . The sheriff, unmounted, unarmed and coatless, approached Vaughan who whipped out his gun. In his usual calm, persuasive manner Oldham invited Vaughan and his companions to accompany him to the Overland hotel bar a block away for a drink.

Though Vaughan's companions advised strongly against it, Vaughan thought a drink or two on the sheriff would be a pleasant experience:

> Lining up at the bar Vaughan . . . was on the sheriff's left. On his right were the surly Moody and Alexander. After indulging in several rounds of drinks the sheriff reached down, pulled Vaughan's gun from its holster, at the same time quickly swinging the desperado around so that he could be used as a shield.
>
> "Drop your guns," calmly ordered Sheriff Oldham of Moody and Alexander, "and be very quick about it."
>
> This was all done so swiftly and quietly that only a few patrons in the barroom realized that anything unusual was taking place.
>
> At a low command the officer followed the trio, apparently stunned by the suddenness of the turn of affairs, to the sidewalks on the Main street side of the hotel. The bad men from Dry creek swung into the saddles of their horses at the hitching rack.

"I'm serving notice on you Hank Vaughan," declared Sheriff Oldham in a determined tone of voice, "that Idaho Territory isn't large enough for you and me. I'll give you fellows just 48 hours to clear out. If you have not left at the end of that time we are coming together."

The crestfallen Vaughan was as meek as a whipped cur, but it was freely predicted that John Oldham was a marked man. However, he did not seem in the least perturbed. . . .

Before daylight at the expiration of the time imposed Sheriff Oldham with a small posse, quietly rode out of Boise City in the direction of the Robie ranch. He returned before noon with the satisfaction that his order had been obeyed. The western bad man of those days instinctively knew the difference between official gunplay and quiet, determined command from one who meant exactly what he said.

Humiliating as it may have been to have Sheriff Oldham get the better of him, Vaughan chose to back away and avoid a showdown. For business reasons he couldn't risk provoking the authorities to the point where they would have halted his operations on Dry Creek. That Hank could convince his rough neck companions that this was the wisest action showed his control over the gang.

In Hank's search for excitement and action, he could often be found at the gambling tables. A trait he shared with many a venturesome soul was a compulsion to gamble. He was addicted to games of chance. Clark Wood, the journalist from Weston, said, "He was an inveterate gambler and played for high stakes. A good amateur, he could not match the skill of Pendleton professionals of those days."[9]

John Sims, a northwest gambler of note, agreed with Wood about Hank's mediocre ability with cards. Sims said, "I . . . was considered one of the best poker players in the country, and had been up against Hank Vaughn . . . and a dozen others a trifle less notorious, but some of them better players."[10]

Whatever Hank lacked in skill, he attempted to make up in frequent and fearless play. This foolhardiness made him a favorite of the professional gamblers. Most of the gambling tables from The Dalles to Boise City knew him. On occasion he was in Portland where he lodged at the Gilman House on First and Alder Street and frequented the gambling rooms in that vicinity.[11]

An anonymous writer gave his impressions of Vaughan on one of those occurrences:

It was on the occasion of one of Vaughn's semiperiodical visits to Portland, in 1881, that the writer saw him first. Hank and a group of congenial spirits had taken possession of the large public room of the old Cosmopolitan hotel and were deep in a stiff game of poker which would have delighted Bret Harte to sketch. They played $2.50 ante, with red chips at $10 and blues at $50, and "pots" of $1000 or $2000 came along with interesting frequency. Literally "the floor it was strewed like the leaves on the strand" with cards that Hank had rejected. "Give us a new deck," he would call out, and suiting the action to the word, he would raise his hand above his head and scatter the old deck with a vigorous flip that filled the smoke charged atmosphere with 52 flying cards.[12]

While Vaughan was in Portland in 1881, it was reported by the *Weekly Standard* of December 23:

> He spent several weeks in this city a short time since and is reported to have lost and squandered some $8,000, a well-known gambler here having won $2,000 from him at one sitting. Vaughn who is known to his associates as "Hank Vaughn" or "Bunch Grass" is said to be a daring fellow, and when in funds free hearted and generous, but when drinking a quarrelsome and a dangerous man.

From the sound of the large sums that Hank was purported to be wagering, it would appear he had come into possession of considerable money. His lack of judgement while gambling would lead one to believe he had arrived in town with the small fortune and not that he had won it there. It was unlikely he had won the money from the big city gamblers.

If indeed he had lost several thousand dollars to these professional gamblers, it might partially explain his malevolent behavior a few weeks later when he had his famous encounter with the unpretentious cowpoke, Charlie Long.

REFERENCES

Chapter 8

1. Villard, Henry. *The Early History of Transportation in Oregon*. Eugene: University of Oregon Press, 1944, 96.
2. Lockley, *op. cit.*, 222-224.
3. Wenatchee *Daily World*, December 18, 1922.
4. *Ibid.*
5. *Ibid.*
6. Idaho *Statesman*, May 23, 1937.
7. *Ibid.*
8. Curtis, John T., *Idaho Daily Statesman*, November 26, 1933, sec. 2, p. 4, *from* Thomas Teakle Collection, "Pacific Northwestern Transcripts," Vol. 72, Idaho Vigilantism, 169-172, Penrose Library, Whitman College, Walla Walla, Washington.
9. *East Oregonian*, March 27, 1948.
10. Parsons and Shiach, *op. cit.*
11. Kelly, John, *op. cit.*
12. *Spokesman Review*, August 16, 1913.

IX.

SHOOTOUT AT PRINEVILLE
(DECEMBER 1881)

December was a slow time of the year for the stock business. During this slack period Hank got into the habit of visiting the big cities looking for excitement while searching out business deals. In 1881, his journeys took him west through The Dalles and on to Portland. At some point along the way, he decided to investigate a situation which was developing on the sagebrush plains of central Oregon, something that might impinge on his trading activities.

The focus of this was in the cattle town of Prineville (fig. 22) where excellent pasture along the Crooked River had attracted early day cattlemen. When rangeland was wide open and free for the taking, Prineville became the cow capitol of central Oregon.

Walter Meacham, pioneer historian, told of the establishment of Prineville and the clientele it attracted:

> Barney Prine, with gold from the mines of southern Idaho in his pockets, was looking for new worlds to conquer. The wide-open range appealed to him so he filed on a land claim at the junction of the Crooked River and Ochoco Creek. There he opened a store, saloon, blacksmith shop, all under one roof, and laid out a race-track nearby. It wasn't long before Prine's establishment became the nucleus of a frontier town, known in 1871 as Prine. The following year the "ville" was added to it. Prineville was typical of its time, a place for the hard-riding, hard-drinking, straight-shooting cowboys to go to drink, gamble, fight, and otherwise sluff off their surplus cash and energy. There were shooting and hanging, range wars and feuds until the law moved in to stay.[1]

These feuds and range wars Meacham referred to were caused by a conflict building between two rival groups of stockmen. On the one side were about fifteen cattlemen with big investments in stock. These men, along with Col. William Thompson, an influential business man, John Luckey, deputy sheriff, Judge Powell, justice of the peace, and a lawyer were alleged to head the local vigilante committee.

The other faction was composed of ordinary citizens and many of the smaller stockmen of the territory. Jim Blakely, leader of this opposition, quite likely had known Hank from childhood when they lived on homesteads only a few miles apart

(Courtesy Crook County Historical Society)

FIGURE 22—At the far end of this lane across Hangman's Bridge is the main street of Prineville as it appeared in the mid 1880s shortly after Hank and Charlie Long had their famous gun fight.

in the Willamette Valley. Blakely and other cattlemen found themselves being intimidated by the vigilantes.

The vigilante committee was concerned that a considerable amount of cattle rustling had been going on in the area, some perhaps with the sanction of the local bosses. Within a few months after Vaughan's visit, the committee exterminated a rancher and several suspected rustlers. In its hasty processing of justice, an innocent half-blood Indian was hung from the Crooked River bridge. It was not until after Crook County was separated from Wasco County in 1884 and Blakely was elected sheriff that the former city syndicate scattered to the four winds.

That Vaughan had no ulterior motive for visiting Prineville except to confront Charlie Long is open to question. It is more likely he had come to Prineville to look into the treatment of certain rustlers there for whatever bearing this might have on his own operations. The popularly accepted reason was that Vaughan was spoiling for a fight, but this idea is not in keeping with his calculating nature.

Charlie Long was thought to have been one of the cowboy toughs who worked for the vigilante factions as he was on occasion on the payrolls of Colonel Thompson and Ben Snipes. Unless Long represented some rival cause or had previously wronged him, Vaughan would not have singled him out. Certainly it was unwise for him to confront another gunman in unfamiliar surroundings outside his own territory.

There are more accounts of the encounter between Vaughan and Long than any other duel in the bunchgrass territory. Nearly every newspaper in the northwest immediately carried accounts of the action. Many old timers later related their personal recollections. Though all of these accounts vary a great deal in detail, the general theme is the same. The following story is a synthesis of at least eight accounts of the happening as reported in newspapers or by eye witnesses to the event.

Hank rode into Prineville on a winter afternoon in December 1881. His outdoor attire would have been modified some to protect him from the cold, but even so he was an imposing figure. It is reported that he usually wore a huge white hat with a rattlesnake band, a Mexican sash, and chaps.[2] His six gun and cartridge belt were always much in evidence. His horse would have been an impressive sight, also, as Hank always rode the very best of the horses he handled.

The next morning as he made himself known in the barrooms about town, he came across Charlie Long who was drinking in his regular hang-out at Dick Graham's saloon. Long knew all about Hank and seemed to be glad to have him come along, not having anything else on his mind just then.

Hank was looking for a card game. That was his favorite method of inaugurating the practical jokes he so much enjoyed. When Long suggested a game of 7-Up, Hank readily complied. Drawing out a pack of cards Hank sat down on the floor and Long camped right there with him. Both obviously had several drinks under their belts and were open to some unorthodox methods of play.

Taking his Bowie knife from its sheath Long calmly thrust the long, keen blade through Hank's new buckskin trouser leg, pinning him to the floor. Hank followed suit, pinning Long to the floor through the leg of his leather chaps. Prudent bystanders began to edge toward the door. This was an excellent thing to do. Nobody had ever before taken such liberties with Hank. It looked like a good bet on the subsequent burial of Long to everybody except Long himself. Charlie was small and quiet, and slow to be provoked. But once he was angered, he had all the combative energies of a crate of wildcats. He never looked for trouble and, also, he never looked the other way when trouble looked for him.

Charlie didn't seem to have any better sense than to beat with aces full over the kings hand that came Hank's way. Then the crowd got another surprise. Hank pulled the knives out of the floor, disentangled himself and went outdoors. The bunch began to wonder if this man who had faced more gunplay than he had fingers and toes had lost his nerve. It looked that way.

Hank hunted up one of the Matlock boys and bought a fast horse from him. He gave Matlock $50 to hold the saddle horse at a corner near the Singer Saloon. He said he had a killing on and might have occasion to leave in a hurry. In about an hour, he went into Til Glaze's saloon where he found Long leaning quietly against the bar with his face to the door. He seemed to be half expecting something, although wholly indifferent to what it might be.

Hank walked straight up to him and said, "You'd make a good sheepherder, Long."

A quicker way of getting gunpowder out of a cowboy than calling him a sheepherder was never invented. And the two understood each other and the situation perfectly.

"You'd make a good cannonader in hell, Vaughan," Long answered.

This appeared to suggest arid possibilities to Hank. "Drink with me like a gentlemen," he invited. Long made no motion or response.

"Which is it, peace or war?" Vaughan demanded when he put down his glass.

"They both sound alike to me," Long answered.

At that Hank pulled off his bandanna and with his left hand offered the end to Charlie for the "Missouri Duel."

There is considerable divergence of opinion as to what took place next, possibly because few cared to stick around close to the shooting. One report said only two men remained in the room with the combatants—one of them hidden behind a screen, and the other lying on the floor dead drunk.

Both gripped the bandanna with their left hands. With a whoop and a leap to one side, Vaughan led the draw but held his fire. Hank let Charlie take the first shot. Long let go with his .44 and cut a streak across Hank's scalp. Hank fell back against a card table and Long waited.

Hank came back on his feet with a jump, brushed the blood out of his eyes and cut loose. Long returned shot for shot, but he was shy on gun fight judgment. He hadn't been up against the game as often as Hank and at first he stood still while Hank leaped from side to side. In consequence, Long stopped every bullet, while he hit Hank only twice. But both of those shots came close to Hank's heart and were about all he needed. In the final seconds, Long came to grips with Vaughan, pressing his revolver to Hank's head but the hammer fell on a defective cartridge and the bullet misfired.

Long got a bullet in the hand that coursed up his arm, another through the body over the heart, one through the abdomen and the last through the right arm.

Both men walked to the back door, covered with blood and bleeding freely. They were taken to Graham's saloon where there was a bed in the back room. Sitting down on the bed, Hank spoke to Jim Blakely, who helped him get there. "Jim, I wish you'd pull my boots off. My old father always said I would die with them on, and I want to fool him."

Jim pulled his boots off and sent for old Doc Whittacker. The doctor said, "Meat doesn't spoil in the mountains," and he was right, for both Hank and Charley recovered from the effects of their "friendly" shooting match, without a decision as to who was the better man.

After the doctors did what they could, Vaughan was taken to Cy Hodges' livery stable to convalesce.[3] At Cy's, Hank was protected from the local residents whose sympathies were strongly with Long. Suspected of being a gun slinger who had come spoiling for a fight, Vaughan was none too popular following the shootout. Hodges who was noted for his generosity and fairness was one of the few men in Prineville who could harbor Vaughan without bringing retaliation upon himself.

Til Glaze was another who was liberal minded enough to take Vaughan in even though the majority of citizens resented this intruder who had shot up one of their own. Hank's pain may have been blunted by medication from pharmaceutical mixtures delivered from the stock in Til's saloon. Glaze was not a stranger to violence such as that acted out between Vaughan and Long. The Portland *Standard* of December 23, 1881, reported:

> Til Glaze, in whose saloon the quarrel occurred, will be remembered as a saloon keeper at Dallas, Polk County, [Oregon] who was implicated in the killing of Whitney [Whitley] some years since.

After being acquitted of the shooting death of the two Whitley brothers, Glaze came to Prineville where he bought the Singer Saloon which he operated until about 1882 (fig. 23). Glaze himself met a violent death a few years later. He died in the Tex Saloon in Burns defending the results of a race run that day by his horse, Wasco. Aided by strong drink, Til and his friend, Loren (John) Parker, were goaded into a gunfight by Bud Howard. Glaze and Howard were killed in the exchange of shots. Parker was convicted of shooting Howard and served seven and a half years in the penitentiary for his effort.[4]

For the rest of his life, Vaughan carried a visible reminder of his encounter with Long. Later pictures of him show a prominent scar in the hairline near the center of his forehead. This was from Charlie's first shot and it came close to being the last one fired in the duel.

This kind of gunplay was discouraged by the law and, when their health

(Photo Courtesy Frances Juris)

FIGURE 23—Til Glaze, on the left, and central Oregon's first brass band pose in front of his noted Singer Saloon. It was here in 1881 Hank Vaughan and Charlie Long had their bloody shootout.

permitted, the two warriors were hauled into court.

Since Prineville was in Wasco County at that time, the trial was held in The Dalles. Adam Croasman who was the city marshal told how he got involved with the case. Croasman had a run in with Hank a few months earlier but they had reached an amicable settlement. When Hank came for the trial, Croasman recalled:

> . . . I went to him and said, "Hank, a lot of your friends have come to The Dalles, and also some of your enemies. Pass the word around that I won't have any gun play or any trouble."
>
> He said, "All right, Adam. I once gave you my word that I would make you no trouble, and that goes."
>
> The mayor came to me and said, "There are some men at the Cosmopolis Hotel who want to see you."
>
> I knocked on their door and I heard them pull a chest of drawers and some chairs from in front of the door, unlock the door, and open it a crack. I stepped in and said, "I am the city marshal. What do you want?"
>
> They said, "We are the witnesses against Hank Vaughn, and we want protection."
>
> I pointed to the rifles leaning against the wall and to their six-shooters on the table and said, "Did you figure you were going to fight an army? It don't look to me as if you needed any protection. Hank Vaughn isn't carrying any gun, and I won't allow you to carry guns, either. You'll have to turn them over to me till the trial is over."
>
> Hank was acquitted and no trouble occurred.[5]

Although Hank recovered rapidly from his wounds, some local papers mistakenly reported he had been killed. They proceeded to relate uncomplimentary obituaries such as this in the Walla Walla *Statesman* of December 24, 1881:

> Few, if any regret Vaughn's departure, for all feared and dreaded him as a man to keep away from. There are many in this community, who are now married and settled down to whom in an earlier day a fight would have been a matter of course; but for now, in justice to their growing families it is a thing to be avoided. Vaughan knew this and insulted many good citizens, who could have whipped him out of his boots were it not for the shame and disgrace which would attach to them in after life by killing such a man.

The Boise *Tri-Weekly Statesman* of December 24, 1881, was somewhat more guarded in its assessment of Vaughan's character since there seemed to be a question as to whether he actually died. It reported, "Hank Vaughn, a desperado well known here, met his match at Prineville, Wasco County, Oregon, a short time since."

The Pendleton *East Oregonian* of December 23, 1881, was not exceptionally blunt, but editorial writer John P. Wager, closed his account in this fashion:

> Latest advice say both are dead. Vaughn was a well known desperado and has had a checkered career on this coast. But when a boy he shot Frank Maddock, then sheriff of this county, through the jaw and killed one of his deputies who were trying to arrest him for horse stealing. If it is true that he turned his moccasins up to the sun there will be but few to mourn his loss.

According to Russell Blankenship, a historical writer from Idaho:

The report was slightly inaccurate and distinctly premature. . . . By way of correcting the gross inaccuracy and rebuking Wager's editorial carelessness . . .Hank rode to Pendleton, descended on the *East Oregonian* office waving a gun, and sent editor, reporters, printers, and printer's devils skipping into the street.[6]

According to John V. Webber, who was once a guard at the Walla Walla Penitentiary, Hank didn't stop at chasing the Pendleton editor and staff into the street. Webber claims Vaughan visited the newspaper office and dictated an editorial which he ordered to be printed without change or he would "blow a hole right through [the editor]." The following is the editorial as Webber remembered it:

To Whom It May Concern

Whereas this putrid imitation of a newspaper, in the course of its weekly wandering through the town garbage cans, printed a news item to the effect that Hank Vaughn, prominent and respected citizen of this section of Oregon, was in the hospital in Prineville suffering from bullet wounds that would undoubtedly prove fatal, and, whereas, this alleged news item carried the further statement and comment to this effect, viz., that the aforementioned Hank had guzzled his last guzzle of whiskey, and cheated in his last game of poker, and was about to be measured for a suit of wool clothing, and, whereas the same item further mendaciously stated that the same event and prospects were an occasion of joy and hallelujah in Pendleton and ought to be celebrated with bonfires and the explosion of gunpowder. And, whereas, these statements have proved wholly and totally erroneous. And, whereas, the editor of this sheet always was, is now and always will be an unmitigated liar, who is a stranger to the truth, he acknowledges the aforementioned Hank Vaughn is not dead and never has been dead, but is now as always a citizen of fine character and unblemished reputation, a genial, kind-hearted individual, responsive to every noble impulse and a credit to the name of American citizenship that the aforementioned Hank Vaughn has taken over the guardianship of this newspaper and anyone hereafter finding fault with anything published in its pages or with anything connected with its operation is asked to make due complaint to him and he will see that apology is made. The aforementioned Hank Vaughn makes this statement with totally unbiased mind, because he knows the editor is a being without courage and states further that he is a louse, a worm, a snake in the grass who deserves to be stamped and trodden under foot. Signed: The Editor.[7]

At the conclusion of the above dictation, Webber claimed Hank arose, walked over to the marble block on which the type for next week's paper was setting. With gusto, he shoved all the frames containing type off on the floor and announced that was a sample of what could be looked forward to if that editorial was not printed word for word.

The *East Oregonian* wasn't the only newspaper to feel Vaughan's indignation. He proceeded on to Walla Walla, arriving on February 13, 1882, where he paid a visit to Col. Frank Parker, editor of the Walla Walla *Statesman*. About 11 o'clock

Monday morning the editor strolled into the copy room to notice three strangers composing something at the table. According to the *Statesman* of February 18:

> . . . he went up to them and all at once recognized as one of the trio the noted Hank Vaughan. Vaughan appeared in a good temper and shook hands with a very hearty manner and after a little jocular talk he directed the editor's attention to the writing and said he wanted it published . . . and that he intended to make it hot for those who had said anything about him when he was supposed to be dead. Commenting on the writing Vaughan then began a torrent of abuse on the editors who stated the public expression of opinion, . . . adding with an oath, "G-d d—n you, I'll make you put it in."

Editor Parker objected to such dictatorial terms and refused to insert anything of the kind in his paper. According to him, "Vaughan then suddenly struck out and caught the editor on the upper lip inflicting a nasty cut on the inside." During the commotion, someone summoned the law and Vaughan was taken before Judge Lucy who fined him $25 and cost. A warrant was also issued against Vaughan for the threats he had made on Parker's life, but to avoid further problems with Hank, the *Statesman* added:

> This is the challenge to our citizens which we refused to publish and which caused the cowardly attack:
>
> Walla Walla, Feb. 13, 1882
>
> Hank Vaughan arrived in the city.
> A donkey can kick at a dead lyon
> The lyon is not dead
> The donkey's had better not kick.
>
> Hank Vaughan's brother-in-law
> fighting member of Vaughan's family.
> Dick Alexander.

In the "Local Jottings" column on the same page, the *Statesman* took pot shots at competitors by saying:

> The morning paper's account of the Vaughan-Parker affair is so grossly inaccurate that we prefer to let it stand as an ever-living monument of the fellow's ability as a liar.
>
> A coward that is so ready to eat dirt as the editor of the *Union* is, need never be afraid of placing anyone under bonds; he can be made to eat his words only too easily.
>
> The *Statesman* holds the proud pre-eminence of being the only Walla Walla newspaper that is not to be dictated unto by desperadoes.

Vaughan was required to post a bond against breach of the peace probably on Colonel Parker's complaint. The *Statesman* of February 18, 1882, records:

> Bound Over.—On Tuesday morning Hank Vaughan was brought up before Justice Laman, who after hearing the evidence, made very short work of it by binding him over in the sum of $500, to keep the peace.

Listed with Hank's bondsmen was W.H. Bender, a saloon keeper in the city of Walla Walla. Hank could usually count on the local gamblers and saloon keepers to bail him out of temporary financial crisis. In his early days, these were the men he counted as friends, but later he realized the value of having friends in higher places and he went out of his way to court their favor.

A year later, Vaughan was making friendly overtures to Editor Parker as the *Statesman* of March 17, 1883, related:

> Hank Vaughn has presented the editor of the *Statesman* with a handsome and very curiously twisted silver mounted walking cane, and the donor can rest assured that it will be sacredly preserved as a memorial.

REFERENCE

Chapter 9

1. Meacham, Walter. Manuscript, Property of James H. Sturgis, Curator and Historian, Blue Mountain College Museum, Pendleton, Oregon, no date, 1.
2. *East Oregonian*, March 27, 1948.
3. Personal interview, John O'Kelly, Prineville, Oregon, July 28, 1974.
4. Ballou, *op. cit.*, 91-92.
5. Oregon *Journal*, March 17, 1926.
6. Blankenship, Russell. *And There Were Men.* New York: Alfred A. Knopf, 1942, 228.
7. The *Sunday Oregonian*, January 15, 1933.

X.

COVERING THE TERRITORY
(1882)

Vaughan, displaying his remarkable physical ability to heal, was able to travel within two months of receiving the injuries in the shootout in Prineville. He headed up country through eastern Oregon, stopping in Pendleton only long enough to chastise the editors of the local papers. He continued on to Idaho Territory via Union County where he took care of some domestic matters.

On March 4, 1882, at Keating in Baker County, he posted a letter back to Louisa in Weston:

> Dear Wife
>
> I will write to you for the last time. I have come after my things and will send your things to you. I am well and hope this will find you well.
>
> I am living in Boise Valley, Idaho, Ter. but I will not stay there very long. I am going to Wood River. I wish you would send Fanney's picture to me.
>
> H.E. Vaughan[1]

This note is quite brief. He does not communicate much to his wife and, as will be seen later, this is probably their last correspondence before Louisa begins divorce proceedings. The reason he chose to use the middle initial "E" in his signature is not known but it was related to his marital identity. His license to marry Louisa Ditty in 1879 shows his name as H.E. Vaughan as do all later documents pertaining to this union. His intentions were obviously to have ambiguous records in order to conceal his plural condition in wives as he was not yet divorced from Lois McCarty.

When Vaughan wrote that he was going to Wood River, he was referring to the mining district at Hailey one hundred miles east of Star, Idaho Territory. This region had only recently come into prominence as a silver producing center. In 1882, the Oregon Shortline Railroad was pushing to complete a branch up the Wood River to serve the area. Mining and railroads needed horses and Vaughan and his partners had undoubtedly tapped into this market supplying horses to the Oregon Shortline Railroad all along its various routes.

Five days after he wrote to Louisa, Vaughan sent another letter. This one was mailed from Star where his parents were now living. They had moved onto the Spring Creek ranch just east of Star in early 1880 after selling the Willow Creek Station on the Umatilla Stage Road. Aleck had advertised it "for sale or trade for liberal terms" in the Boise *Statesman*, October 12, 1879.

Hank was laying over at the family ranch when he wrote the following letter to Mr. Tucker of Union County. It reveals more details about the matter of his and Louisa's property.

Star, Ada Co. I.T.
March the 9 1882

Mr. Tucker Sir

I received your of the 4 it found me on my pins I have got a letter from there last month stating that you had writen to hur and wanted to know what to do with the things and know I will tell you what to do with them I left them in your cear if she wants them let hur come to me and if I demand you to send them on the next stage for that is my property and if you do not want eny thing to do with my affairs you send them to me and I will settle my own business and you have the money to pay the freight on them I do not want to give you eny truble but if I dont get them they will be truble some where and you can keep out if by sending them to me and I will sent you a clear receipt for them you can write to hur and tell hur my address they outfit has beet me out of plenty to pay all claims aganst me oblige me with sending them and save your self from farther truble I will be down in May to Union I will hie there on the first day of cort This will lurn hur not to sleep with other men no more this time and if you are not going to send them wright on reciving this letter and I will proceed for them and I will get them before long.

H.E. Vaughan
Star Ada Co. I.T.[2]

This letter was to Gardner Tucker, the postmaster at Elk Flat, in Union County. Elk Flat was the closest post office to the Indian Creek cabin where Hank and Louisa had recently lived. Mr. Tucker was also the father of Nancy whose name would be mentioned in Hank and Louisa's divorce proceedings.

It seems Hank and Louisa's belongings had been left in Mr. Tucker's care. With both parties claiming the property, Mr. Tucker found himself in an uncomfortable position. Hank's letter to Tucker was particularly threatening. It hinted at other problems with the "outfit which had beet him out of plenty to pay the claims against him." This could refer to Louisa and her relatives, the Howdeyshells, who may have entered the picture in order to protect Louisa. It seemed unchivalrous of Hank to refer to infidelities on Louisa's part to Mr. Tucker, but this may have been the issue he would use in the divorce case to reduce his responsibility to her.

Whether Hank came back to Union for the "first day of cort" is not known, but, according to Louisa, he did go through eastern Oregon later in March. She claimed at that time he sold all their household furniture, most of which she declared had been hers before their marriage. According to Louisa, he sold everything that had belonged to them including clothes and Louisa never received anything as Hank kept all the proceeds himself.

On returning to Oregon, Hank went on to The Dalles. The Baker City *Reveille* of March 22, 1882, reported:

> The latest we had on Hank Vaughn, the leadbasket, is that he is in The Dalles. We humbly hope that he and the *Mountaineer* man will let us pass through unmolested. We promise not to be naughty any more.

Word had undoubtedly gotten around that Vaughan was calling for retractions from editors of the newspapers that had given him poor obituary billings.

Hank's reason for going to The Dalles would have been the occasion of the trial over his public disturbance with Long. One wonders why since he had gotten as far away as Idaho Territory he would return to face a trial in Wasco County. Several reasons can be advanced for this. For one, he undoubtedly had competent legal advice that assured him he could beat an assault case with Long since he could prove Long shot first. Other reasons to keep clean with the law had to do with his need to operate openly in The Dalles as it was a key point for mingling with prospective stock buyers.

Hank did go back to The Dalles for the trial as Marshal Croasman recalled and he was acquitted. Croasman also related that Hank's friends and enemies gathered there at the same time, possibly to try to influence events.

He had earlier ingratiated himself with Marshal Croasman. While in The Dalles for his trial, Vaughan was further credited with aiding the law when he helped a Marshal Kline in the arrest of some railroad men and scow hands. The Dalles *Sun* of April 15, 1882, claimed "Vaughn drew his revolver in support of the law! In a row he is a good man to have on the right side." No explanation was given for Hank's participation in the marshal's behalf but this behavior indicated he could see some benefit in being on the good side of the law.

When Hank travelled back for the trial, he passed through the Powder Valley along the route taken by the great herds of cattle which were annually driven from the ranchlands of the Pacific Northwest to the nearest transcontinental railheads. This eastward movement of cattle had dropped off slightly in 1882 partially as a result of the long cold winter of 1880-1881 when thousands of cattle, sheep and horses died. Witnesses claim the landscape was strewn with carcasses come spring. Ranchers were trying to build up their herds and owners of marketable cattle were not as eager to sell. This brought prices up. In Umatilla County, sellers paid $20 to $30 a head. The buyers had to work hard to find animals to fill their quotas and in some cases they began substituting sheep and horses.

Powder Valley in Baker County had become an important holding place for animals before they were gathered up for the big drives. Buyers preferred to wait here while sellers brought their animals over the timbered mountains (fig. 24). The eastern buyers didn't want the responsibility of trailing stock over the forested Blue Mountains where passes were often choked with snow until June. By taking delivery in Powder Valley, the buyers shifted more risk onto the Oregon "bush poppers."

Hank's trips through the area this year were in early March and April when spring was just beginning to return and the grass was still dormant from the long

(Photo Courtesy McCord Collection)

FIGURE 24—Baker City was an important town where stockmen, buyers and herders met to make the final preparation for moving stock from Oregon ranges to eastern markets. A group of these men are shown in front of John Palmer's saddlery in the spring of 1880.

cold winter. However, by June the Powder Valley would be a sea of rich meadow grass where what weight loss cattle had suffered in crossing the Blue Mountains could be regained as they were sorted and branded in preparation for their long trek to market (fig. 25). All these preparations created much activity which was duly reported in the local newspapers. The Baker City *Reveille* of March 29, 1882, noted:

> Mr. Hastings, who had been here for some months past buying cattle for driving to the East, is preparing to brand at Perkin's Ranch, near this place. Several cords of wood have been delivered at the ranch to be used in branding.

The Baker City *Bedrock Democrat* of April 12, 1882, added that the Hastings men would receive 12,500 head on Willow Creek [northeast of Baker City]. After trail branding they would go out in five bands with ten men to a band. On the 19th the *Democrat* observed that the Hastings cowboys began branding on the Gettis Ranch several miles north of town. Other mention was made that Johnson's outfit began branding on Finlayson's ranch east of town and that Clay Carn had just returned from Boise City with two horse team loads of saddles for the Johnson cowboys.

John Rollinson's excellent account of trail driving from Oregon to Wyoming vividly depicts the local stock industry of that day. Rollinson quoted trail driver Frank Murphy concerning a large drive:

(Photo Courtesy Utah Historical Society)

Figure 25.—Each spring, beginning in the mid 1870s, thousands of Oregon cattle were delivered to buyers in the Powder River Valley of eastern Oregon. Cowboys counted, sorted and branded before the herds began their arduous walk to market.

In the spring of 1882 I left the N-bar cow ranch on the Running Water in western Nebraska, along with forty cowboys, to go to Oregon to receive 15,000 head of cattle for Zeke Newman of El Paso, Texas. The cattle were to be driven from Oregon in five separate herds.

These five herds of cattle were to leave from five different valleys; some with Jim Dahlman, who was the foreman, and who later became the Mayor of Omaha for many terms. This herd was to leave Baker Valley after they had been branded.[3]

In 1885, cow puncher Jack Porter had just arrived from Wyoming by stage with orders to join a group of drovers at the Whipple Ranch in the Powder Valley. His portrayal of the local scene provides a particularly good description of the trade in horses Hank Vaughan and his cronies on the Minam River knew so well:

Our long stage journey was now at an end, and we took our saddles and bedrolls off the boot of the stage and left them in the stage company's barn while we walked about, stretched our legs, and had our first look at Baker City, Oregon.

We were delighted with our first glimpse of this busy city in far-away eastern Oregon. There was much to see and much to do, and though I was in and around Baker City for several weeks, I was always interested in the place and its nice kindly people, and never outgrew a feeling of contentment while there. There was much activity in and around Baker City. . . . It was . . . the center of the Western horse business, and hundreds of animals from the Northwest were trailed to the

> vicinity of Baker City and there ranged until sold, when they were put into trail herds of horses bound for eastern ranges, farms and cities.
>
> These Oregon horses weighed from 1,000 to 1,150 pounds, and a few weighed 1,200 pounds. They were as active as mustangs, had wonderful feet, and hard, well-shaped, small hoofs. For the most part they had good dispositions, and after a few days of riding, all made fine saddle horses. Some became very good rope horses, and a few turned out to be splendid cut animals.[4]

There is no doubt many of the horses offered for sale here were brought up off the secluded holding grounds on the Minam River by Hank's cowboys. Clever horse thieves could sell their stolen stock quite easily to buyers looking for large bands of horses. Once the horses were on the trail, their drovers had to be on constant watch for other thieves. It was common practice for thieves to follow bands like this and stampede the herds in the night, driving off and capturing as many animals as possible.

While Hank's buddies on the Minam River would be actively participating in providing horses for these drives, the Spokane Falls *Chronicle*, July 11, 1882, reported Hank himself left for Montana Territory over the Mullan Trail with a band of horses. The story continued that he was going by way of Coeur d'Alene with a "big outfit." The paper neglected to say that Hank had raised some hell in Spokane Falls while he was there, but that is a later story.

Since horses travelled much faster than cattle, he probably reached his delivery point in early August and headed home. "Home" was a rather nebulous place by this time. After seeing Louisa off on the stage to Weston, and having since sold their household belongings, Hank was in need of establishing a new home base. It would soon be obvious that he had something in mind.

When Hank once told Louisa after one of his long absences that he had been away prospecting, he was not referring to mining. During one of his trips into the Boise City area he was proving up on and developing his friendship with Martha Craig Robie, the widow of a wealthy rancher and a neighbor of his parents in Star Valley. Over a period of years this relationship between Hank and Martha firmed into a lasting partnership which continued the rest of Hank's life.

Martha was the daughter of William Craig, the famous mountain man and Idaho pioneer. Her mother was Isabel, daughter of Chief James of the Nez Perces. In 1860, when Martha was about fifteen, she married A.H. Robie who had worked with her father during the Indian troubles of the mid 1850s.[5] Robie came from England as a young man, arriving in the Pacific Northwest with a survey party headed by his uncle, I.I. Stevens who later became the first governor of Washington territory.

Robie was next a freighter and then a successful stockman with connections throughout eastern Oregon and central Idaho Territory. He first ran cattle in the Harney Basin of Oregon and in 1871 under the Swamp Act obtained the 42,300-acre Diamond Ranch which he later sold to Peter French, the eastern Oregon cattle king.[6]

Robie and French had been gathering the Robie horses off that ranch when they were caught in the advance of the Bannock Indians as they rampaged through southeastern Oregon in 1878. As a consequence of this strenuous flight ahead of the warriors, Robie died.

After Robie's death in 1878, Martha continued to live with her five children on their ranch on the Boise River. This ranch was about ten miles west of Boise City near the present town of Star. Hank's parent's lived on a nearby foothill ranch. It is likely that both Hank and his family knew the Robies as early as 1872 when Aleck ran the Willow Creek Station.

The Portland *Standard*, December 23, 1881, suggested, "A little over a year ago he (Hank) married the widow of a man named Ruby [Robie] who was killed in the Nez Perce [Bannock-Paiute] outbreak." The facts in the newspaper's story were fuzzy, but they showed that as early as 1881 Hank was known to be associated with Martha.

That Hank spent a lot of time in Idaho Territory is evident from a description of Idaho desperados by Idaho historian, M.D. Beal, who claimed Hank was operating from a base in the Spring Creek-Dry Creek area. Beal did not indicate dates or give references to sources, but one can assume the period was generally throughout the 1880s. His report said:

> A trio of unsavory rustlers, who operated in this region [southern Idaho], was Hank Vaughan, Billy Moody, and Jim Alexander. One of their places of rendezvous was the Robie Ranch on Dry Creek, near Boise. From that base they and their confederates were disposed to ride into the territorial capitol and terrorize the citizens.[7]

An interesting discovery concerning two of the men in the above threesome surfaced in a search of the Ada County "Book of Marriage Intentions."[8] This record showed that in 1879, Clara R. Robie, oldest daughter of A.H. and Martha Robie, married Charles I. Thews. Less than a year later, on April 5, 1880, Clara, then nineteen married J.C. Alexander. She was married next in 1882 to William P. Moody after his wife, Sarah Greathouse, died. Clara took over the care of his two young sons.[9]

Clara's marital history reveals the close association of the Robies with Hank and his gang. Nothing is known of Clara's first husband but her second husband, Alexander, was a suspect in the Schwabacker safe job which Hank had been accused of masterminding. In that case, Alexander stood trial, but was acquitted. William P. Moody was the same Moody Hank had known from childhood and had associated with in Elko. After he and Hank took a band of horses to sell in Pendleton in 1878, it can be assumed Moody continued to be Vaughan's chief lieutenant and contact in Nevada and Idaho Territory. He had been living in Silver City, Idaho Territory, when he and Clara were married. In 1886 Clara moved with her children to the Umatilla Reservation. Although she listed herself as a widow after 1891[10], Billy showed up again in Mound Valley near Elko in 1896.

It would be several years before Martha and Hank formalized their union. Later events proved, however, the two had reached a satisfactory living arrangement. Both brought complementary resources to the partnership. Martha had financial assets through the estate she had inherited from her husband. She was also eligible to claim land on the Umatilla Indian Reservation. Hank, although he had few tangible assets, was a skillful manager of people and capable of taking advantage of any and all situations he encountered. Their partnership would involve them in much of the historic development of eastern Oregon and particularly the Umatilla Indian Reservation.

REFERENCES

Chapter 10

1. Umatilla County Divorce Case, No. 191-30. This letter is on file with the divorce papers of Louisa J. Vaughan vs. H.E. Vaughan. The picture Hank requested was probably of his sister, Fannie Vaughan, who married William J. Dement at Middleton, Idaho Territory, December 1881, and moved to Wallowa Valley in Oregon.
2. *Ibid.*
3. Rollinson, John K. *Wyoming Cattle Trails.* Caldwell: Idaho, Caxton Printers, Ltd., 1948, 114-115.
4. *Ibid.*, 68-73.
5. Josephy, Alvin M., Jr. *The Nez Perce Indians and the Opening of the Northwest.* New Haven: Yale University Press, 1965, 370-372.
6. Brimlow, George Francis. *Harney County, Oregon, and Its Range Land.* Portland: Binfords and Mort, 1951, 78, 90.
7. Beal, Merril D. "Rustlers and Robbers," Idaho *Yesterdays*, 7:1 (Spring, 1963), 24-28.
8. Ada County Book of Marriage Intentions, Book 1. Vol. 2., 183, 209.
9. Statistics of Idaho, Silver City, Owyhee County, L.D.S. Genealogical Library, La Grande. Oregon. Billy Moody married Sarah Greathouse, August 9, 1874 at Silver City. They and their two sons, Willy and Louis, lived there until the late 1870s.
10. National Archives, Office of Indian Affairs, Census of Mixed Bloods of the Umatilla (Confederated) Tribe of Indians, Umatilla Agency, Oregon, June 30, 1891, Washington, D.C.

XI.

ROLLING STOCK AND RUNNING STOCK

(1882-1883)

Hank Vaughan was closely associated with railroads in the northwest. As a youth, he rode on the very first railroad line in Oregon. This was the tiny line which portaged freight and passengers around the falls on the Columbia River. He later trailed cattle from the Willamette Valley to Nevada to ship on the first transcontinental railroad across the United States.

The year he returned to Oregon from Nevada Doc. Baker was selling his "rawhide" railroad to the Oregon Steam Navigation Company whose owners had ambitious plans for expansion and development. The efforts of Oregonians to link with a transcontinental railroad which would take Oregon products to the large eastern markets were close to fruition as the railroad baron, Henry Villard, exerted his considerable energies to their cause. Villard was pouring money into connecting the route along the south side of the Columbia River in Oregon across Washington Territory through Spokane Falls to connect with the Northern Pacific Railroad now being built across Montana Territory.

Hank's involvement with the railroads now turned to supplying horses for the construction crews working at either end of these tracks. Demand was high for horses as thousands were needed to move the men and equipment working toward completion of the lines. The Dalles *Times Mountaineer* of January 6, 1882, noted the progress of construction on the Northern Pacific Railroad across Montana Territory during the previous year:

> Three hundred and twenty-five [miles] finished in the Yellowstone valley . . . and 125 miles up the valley of the Clark's fork of the Columbia, in Idaho and Montana. . . . In addition to these there have been 200 miles of grades. The gap between the two ends of the track in Montana is now 280, nearly all being in the old settled portion of the territory between Bozeman and Missoula, where the gold mines attracted considerable population as early as 1862.
>
> The total mileage of the finished main line now operated by the company is 1564. So far advanced is the work of the uncompleted section that the opening of the entire line to the Pacific Coast is regarded as certain to take place next summer.

Along the old Indian trails, across the prairies and mountain ranges, the railroad approached the Pacific Northwest. Working from both east and west, the lines were fit together rail by rail until one sunny day in September 1883, the transcontinental Northern Pacific Railroad was completed. At the dedication ceremonies in western Montana, President Villard addressed the gathered crowd to tell them of his hopes that this great work of man would stand forever, bringing immortal honor to its builders, permanent pride and profit to its owners, and, most of all, an everlasting blessing to man.[1]

It is doubtful Hank Vaughan had any such grandiose feelings but he did benefit with the advent of the railroad's progress. He had horses for sale and horses were needed by the crews that pushed construction of the line. Demand for his horses did not end with completion of the main lines on the Northern Pacific and OR&N, as, in this heyday of railroad construction, local spur lines continued to be built to serve nearby communities.

Vaughan prospered during this period and, with this prosperity, he emerged with a new identity. When his range operations were at a standstill in the winter, he began spending idle time in The Dalles. He had money to put on the gambling tables and contacts to be made with cattle and horse buyers in the saloons and hotels. The Dalles provided plenty of excitement for the free-spending cowboys, miners and railroad hands.

Hank and his cronies had long been familiar figures in this freewheeling western town, but by the winter of 1881-82, he was seen with a new companion—Martha Robie. From Lulu Crandall, The Dalles historian, it is learned:

> They lived at the old Jackson Hotel. They had all evidences of wealth. Mrs. Roby-Vaughn wore diamonds of the finest water, and "Hank" had a pocket full of gold twenty-dollar pieces that he won shuffling cards.[2]

Hank and Martha would soon become a familiar pair everywhere along Hank's haunts as Martha often travelled with him especially during his winter trips. When passenger service became available on the railway, they traveled by rail, finding it a more comfortable means of transportation than either horseback or carriage.

One of their frequent destinations was Spokane Falls, a trip that usually began at Ainsworth on the Washington side of the Snake River. Here, until a bridge was built in 1883, the cars and engine of the train crossed the river on ferries. It was not uncommon for passengers to wait at Ainsworth for a full day while this transfer took place. On several occasions, Hank got into trouble while he waited.

During these years when Hank and Martha traveled by train, he earned a reputation for frustrating train robbers. One incident occurred as they were on their way to Spokane Falls on the Northern Pacific Railroad. It was probably in 1882 when a holdup was attempted a few miles out of Sprague. Vaughan had been dozing when three men entered the front of the coach and announced their intentions of relieving every passenger of their belongings. They demanded everyone stand with their hands high. While two thieves stationed themselves at either end of the coach the third went down the aisle collecting the passengers' valuables in a grain sack.

Martha was in such a position that when Hank gave her a signal she moved his gun belt around so he could drop his hand and grab his revolver. When the gun was in his hand, Hank started shooting. The holdup men lost their nerve and departed from the train, leaving the loot behind. Hank explained to the other passengers that it wasn't right for a whole carload of men to let a handful of bandits take advantage of them.[3]

Another episode when Vaughan intervened for the railroad was told by Lue Vernon:

> . . . I remember one time two men undertook to ride between Ritzville and Sprague without paying fare, and they were as tough as I ever saw. Both had Colt's guns and swore they would ride or hurt some one. It was in the summer time and Hank was trying to take a "snooze," as he called it. When the conductor came through collecting fares the two bad men refused to pay. The conductor tried to explain that it was his duty to collect the fare and if they did not pay he would put them off. This was the conductor's mistake. The bad men swore by all that was holy that all the Northern Pacific employees from St. Paul to Tacoma could not make them pay fare or put them off. They flourished their guns and the passengers on the car were terror-stricken.
>
> When Hank saw that the conductor was getting the worst of it, he took a good stretch, yawned several times and quick as a flash struck the largest fellow over the head with his own silverplated gun, took him to the platform of the car and kicked him off. Everyone expected the other desperado to kill Hank, but he began to beg for mercy, but Hank took him by the collar and—well, I never saw a bad man get the drubbing that this fellow received. Hank was the hero of the hour and every one wanted to be the first to shake his hand. Hank kept the two guns as mementoes of the occasion.[4]

H.W. Fairweather, the superintendent for western division of the Northern Pacific Railroad, told of another time when Hank aided the company:

> Hank also prevented the railroad pay wagon, with about $200,000 on it, from being robbed between Spokane and Pend Oreille. Fairweather received an anonymous warning that Hank himself had planned the holdup, but he showed Hank the warning and engaged him to guard the wagon for $50 a day. There was no symptom of a robbery. To put Hank on his honor was to win his allegiance.[5]

For these displays of virtue, Henry Villard was said to have given Vaughan a lifetime pass to travel any time on the Northern Pacific. Many in Umatilla County claimed this gave him easier access to the scene of his depredations. Less grateful uttering were that he only broke up the train robbery because of the boldness which the robbers showed in poaching within his territory.

Hank was never a hand to hire out to do someone else's dirty work, but he probably came the closest to being a hired gun slinger during this period. It was said while under the employment of Fairweather in Spokane, Hank once rode his horse into a saloon on Riverside Avenue after a man named Florence and urged him out of town by means of bullets.[6]

As a regular visitor to Spokane Falls, Hank had seen a thriving town emerge on the site where only a few cabins existed when he first came. The main part of town had built up between the railroad track and the south side of the river where the Spokane River cascades through a series of basalt dikes. Streets had been laid out and leveled atop the gravel beds along the river bank. Most of the buildings were wooden and of temporary quality. There were not as yet any structures worthy of particular notice, with the exception of a fine residence or two, a couple of hotels, and a mercantile house.

The town was mostly dependent on the neighboring farming district and railroad activity, but the potential of the river to produce power was expected to attract "thousands of factories and mills." There were several churches. The number was conspicuous, mused a *Democrat State Journal* writer, as there were so many; the number of school houses was also conspicuous, because there were so few.

Hank's disruptive influence was felt even in the schools. The first school in Spokane Falls was located on the main street next to a saloon with only a clapboard partition between the two. The building front was but a layer of warped board and batten which let the winter winds howl through while pupils huddled around the stove. The first school mistress lamented the hardships of providing education under such adverse conditions:

> . . . even more disconcerting than the prospect of physical discomfort was what Miss Mattie [Mattie Hyde] learned about her pupils: two were pals of the bibulous Hank Vaughn and occupied themselves at night dealing faro bank.[7]

Speaking further of the period when Vaughan frequented Spokane Falls, author Lucile Fargo had more to say in describing Hank and his activities:

> Hank Vaughn was a character unpleasantly known in most of the Inland Empire. He had a well established reputation as horse thief and desperado, and after a drinking bout his favorite pastime was to ride his horse into the nearest hostelry. Just how the proprietor [Bill Gray] of the California House met the situation on the two or three occasions when Hank appeared there is uncertain, but, each time, the overenthusiastic horseman was persuaded to cease and desist without recourse either to the law or to firearms.
>
> Once in a while some other rampaging or trigger happy individual had to be escorted from the premises. Hank Vaughn's local crony, saloon keeper Bob Knox, was one such. Everyone in town could tell how Vaughn and Knox had once settled a temporary misunderstanding with a shooting bout conducted from opposite sides of the street.[8]

Spokane Falls was one of the towns where Hank chose to show off his considerable riding skills. According to Clark Wood:

> He always rode the finest horse he could get and right here in Spokane he has displayed his horsemanship by picking up coins on the street from the saddle with his horse on the gallop.[9]

Hank gained a reputation as a hell raiser on his visits to Spokane Falls. Accounts of two episodes came from recollections in the History of Spokane County:

> John Glover and Lane Gilliam had their livery stable on the spot now occupied by the Windsor block. Hank Vaughn, the noted western character, . . . paid Spokane Falls a visit one time and hired a hack from Glover and Gilliam and started out for a drive. About the first thing he did was to try to drive into Al. Jones' saloon, but the only damage he did to the saloon was to knock down the posts of the awning. It looked as if the whole building would come down for a while. Hank was famous for his fast drives all over the western country. But he always paid for what he destroyed and nothing was ever said about it.[10]

The second account, related by a newspaper reporter, fills in some details:

> Somewhere around Spokane are the relics of the first pretentious carriage brought to the town, a barouche, for public hire. Frank Dallam, who founded the *Spokesman Review*, recalls a lively ride in it by Hank:
>
> During the winter Hank favored Spokane with a visit, and while here gave no exhibition of shooting up fellow citizens, because no one was inclined to doubt his ability, he gave the town a touch of high life that made history on Howard street. He had to have a ride in that barouche, and proposed to do the driving. The fit took him at a time when his discretion was somewhat at fault, and he attempted to drive into a barroom under the old Star lodging house. As the walk was a couple of feet above the road and the horses going at some speed, the body and wheels of the hack parted company. Hank and the team were lined up at the bar, but in such confusion that the "barkeep" was at a loss to fill the order.[11]

His reason for coming to Spokane Falls was for the opportunity to do business with the railroad. Much of this was through his contact with Fairweather, the superintendent on the Northern Pacific. On at least one occasion, however, Fairweather and Vaughan met under different circumstances than railroad business:

> Fairweather . . . went into a room in Walla Walla one day [probably the Stine House] and found Vaughn with a gun in his hand and Congressman John Hailey on the other side of the table, unarmed, inviting Hank to commit murder. Hailey was administrator of the Robie estate. Hank married Mrs. Robie after her husband had been killed in the Snake Indian uprising. Of the $80,000 left her Hank had invested about $10,000 in his own fashion and felt that he needed more. He was trying to convince the administrator of that fact when Fairweather interfered.[12]

Somehow, Fairweather had chanced upon Vaughan trying to intimidate John Hailey, Sr., over the settlement of the Robie estate. When this estate was probated, the Boise *Tri-Weekly Statesman* of April 13, 1882, listed among the holdings a ranch on Dry Creek, a farm on Spring Creek, and considerable real estate in Boise City. It stated that $13,150 had already been divided between Mrs. Robie and the five children with another $14,000 to be released as a settlement from a bond security. This was considerably less than the $80,000 cash Fairweather spoke about, but by the time Hank accosted Hailey, the real estate may have been sold for cash.

It was perhaps this final matter Vaughan was attempting to settle with Hailey, the same man who had defended him against a lynch mob in the mining town of Auburn some twenty-two years earlier. It was evident that Hailey had lost none of his courage, and his good judgement now told him Vaughan had no intention of doing him bodily harm. As administrator of the Robie estate, Hailey was aware of the cash settlement that had already been made. This same cash may have been what financed Hank and Martha's conspicuous wealth and free spending in The Dalles.

For the next few years, Hank's railroad activities took all forms, from riding guard on pay wagons for his friend Fairweather to using the tracks as a means of escaping the law. One instance of the latter kind took place near Pendleton in 1883 when a branch of the OR&N was being put across the reservation to the crest of the Blue Mountains. A friend of the family recalled that Hank was being chased by a posse when he chose to escape by using a railway bridge which was under construction:

> In order to elude his pursuers, Vaughan was said to have jumped his horse off a steep cut bank onto an unfinished railroad grade. He ran the horse a short distance to the newly completed bridge crossing the Umatilla River. At this point, he fearlessly spurred his horse across the bridge on the narrow planking that would later hold the ties. One misstep and horse and rider would have plunged to the water and boulders below. Those of the posse who dared ride their horses down the steep bank were stopped at the bridge crossing and the chase was abandoned.[13]

Railroad towns were the settings for two more of the gunfights in which Hank was involved. Few details have surfaced about one of the fights, but the second one followed the scenario of the Missouri Duel with the combatants holding opposite ends of a bandanna.

An item in the Boise *Tri-Weekly Statesman* of April 12, 1883, quoted the Walla Walla *Statesman* that rumor was common in town last week that Vaughan had been in a gun fight in the railroad town of Ainsworth. Copies of the daily Walla Walla papers of that period are lost but a note from the "Ainsworth Budget" column of the Boise *Tri-Weekly Statesman*, April 12, 1883, did mentioned that, "Hank Vaughn has been in town several days."

The rumored gun fight in Ainsworth may have been caused by foolhardiness brought on by liquor, but in the railroad town of Sprague when Hank challenged Bill Singleton it was to test who was the best gunfighter:

> Singleton was not more quarrelsome naturally than Hank, but he had a reputation as a fighter to maintain and there was always more or less speculation, which both Bill and Hank were conscious of, as to what would be the outcome should the two chance to come together.
>
> It happened one night over cards at Pat Dillon's saloon at Sprague. The eyes of the crowd were upon them. Each appreciated fully the nature of public expectation that enveloped them. A dispute started that otherwise might have passed unnoticed, and both men were on their feet. Every voice in the saloon instantly ceased. "How do you want it?" Vaughan asked. "Make it over a handkerchief if you like," Singleton replied.
>
> "Your style suits me" was Vaughn's assent.
>
> Each took hold of an end of the handkerchief and stretched it tight. Their other hand went to their guns. With that the crowd came to life in a stampede for the open country and knocked over the lamps. They separated Hank and Bill in the rush and when the riot had simmered again the two were cooled off and became the best of friends afterwards.[14]

Although working closely with Fairweather and the Northern Pacific Railroad might have given Vaughan an air of respectability, folks still considered him a desperado. In reminiscing of the times, Oliver White, Hank's former prison guard, said Vaughan spent some time in Dayton supposedly working with a band of horse thieves although no real proof was found.[15] The suspicion was true that he was working with thieves, but he was successful in appearing open and legitimate in his operations. He even advertised in the 1883 Eastern Washington Directory as a horse trader with a residence on Fourth Street, between Main and Alder [Walla Walla].[16]

Most of the spring of 1883, he assembled horses along the foothills between Pendleton, Oregon, and Lewiston, Idaho Territory, which included the area around Dayton. On March 2, 1883, the Dayton *State Democratic Journal* quoted from the *Washingtonian:*

> Hank Vaughn & Co., have about 320 head of horses on the Blalock ranch [present site of the town of College Place], besides about thirty or forty valuable animals stabled in this city. Before driving to Missoula in April this firm expect to have about 600 head.

If Vaughan and company were able to accumulate and deliver the 600 horses as planned, they would collect a sizeable sum as the March 3, 1883 *Journal*, reported:

> HORSES IN DEMAND.—Quite a number of buyers from the east are here purchasing horses to be taken east of the mountains to Montana and other more eastern markets. We hear of one band that $50 a piece was offered for the lot; but $55 was asked. The buyer shortly after proceeded to Grande Ronde valley where he expects to purchase his complement on more reasonable terms than was offered here.

The same column of the *Journal* contained an obituary telling of the unfortunate death of Hank's cousin, Joseph Smith, Jr., age twenty-two, who had committed suicide in the Columbia Hotel in Walla Walla. The principal source of this news was from the *Statesman* which said:

> It seems the deceased arrived here a day or two ago and commenced hunting for Hank Vaughn who is a nephew to Mr. Smith, his father. He was in an impecunious state, and made himself notably conspicuous by his frequent importunes for money. Vaughn assisted him several times and on each occasion he squandered the money at billiards and pool. This became monotonous, and his benefactor got tired of his oft repeated requests for money. In the meantime it seems he procured a room at the Columbia, where he so successfully ended his earthly career.

It appeared that Smith had been trying to copy the antics of and attach himself to his cousin Hank without success. In despondence, the young man used strychnine to accomplish his self destruction. He rallied slightly under the effects of antidotes administered by doctors, but "expressed himself as displeased at their interference, and said he did not want to live." Smith's parents had been ranching in the Dayton area for years but shortly after their son's death they relocated along the Imnaha River in northeastern Oregon.

About a month later, it could have been that Vaughan and his men were gleefully anticipating the trip to Montana with the herd of horses. They chose to repeat the type of celebration made famous earlier in The Dalles by the big cattle buyers Lang and Ryan. At any rate, the *Statesman* of April 17 noted Hank was settling up for some mischief he'd been into while in on a recent evening spree:

> ACTED SQUARE.—Hank Vaughn and his companion promptly paid all the damages caused by the runaway night before last, which amounted to something like $75. He left last night with his horses for the Umatilla reservation and will shortly drive them to Montana.

About ten days after this latest horseplay, Hank and his boys came back to town and again, according to the *Statesman*, April 28, they livened up Walla Walla:

Taking the Town

> Main street, on Saturday evening, was the scene of an excitement that would have reflected credit upon Tombstone, in Arizona, which is the boss cow boy town in the country. One of Hank Vaughn's stock men rode around cursing, and defied every attempt of officer Ames to arrest him and chief Hank stood in with his man. For a long time things looked dubious, but the officer, finding things getting troublesome, took the money offered by Vaughn for his appearance and the man rode off. He afterwards allowed himself to be taken before the judge who fined him $10. Our officers may just as well let cowboys have a little fun when they come to town for they are bound to have it any way.

The Dayton *State Democratic Journal* was outraged at such uncivilized carryings on and was critical of lax law enforcement in its report of April 27, 1883:

> COW-BOYS.—Hank Vaughn and a gang of his cowboys made it lively for the citizens of Walla Walla the other day. Shouting, swearing and running horses through the streets seems to have been the amusement, for which only one arrest was made and a fine of $10 imposed. Such leniency only gives encouragement for a repetition of such scandalous proceedings.

This was easy criticism to level at a neighboring town's attempt at crime prevention twenty-five miles away, but Marshal Ames had been at close range and to arrest Vaughan when he was drinking would have been unhealthy. Ames would be just as dead had the fine been $100. Moreover, both Judges Lucy and Whitman had encountered Vaughan on previous occasions and they fully expected him to come back to town to "make things right." Many years later, a first hand account of this Walla Walla drama was told by John V. Webber who recalled with amazing detail, much embellished by passing time, how the local citizenry was beginning to tire of this rambunctious breaking of the peace:

> They determined to rid themselves of Hank and his pestiferous gang, so they elected a saloon keeper named Robinson as mayor. He knew Hank and wasn't afraid of him. He didn't hunt the job, but he said gang riding in that town must

stop. He picked a marshal who wasn't afraid of anyone and an assistant marshal, but the stock of nerve ran out before they reached him.

Of course, Hank heard the news, and it classed as a number one specimen of humor for him. He rounded up his gang and they came romping to town to the tune of hoofbeats and revolver shots. With the first warning the assistant marshal was told to go out and bring them in. He hied himself to a conspicuous corner where there was a large tree. And he kept behind the tree while the gang went roaring past. But it happened there was a straggler whose horse had gone lame and who couldn't keep up. The assistant marshal saw the chance and he came out brandishing his gun. He told the straggler he was under arrest. The straggler hollered for Hank.

The marshal had his eye on the whole proceeding, and he now showed up with a double barreled shotgun. Both barrels were loaded and the triggers raised. As the whooping crowd came up. the marshal raised his gun and said: "Hank Vaughn, you are under arrest."

Hank thought it a good joke, but the marshal didn't crack a smile. He ordered his nervous assistant to take what loose guns he could find, and with their hands in the air he marched the crowd to the justice's office. The justice was so nervous that he had a hard time getting the gang docketed. This done, he rubbed his hands sociably and said: "And now what can I do for you?" "I want you to fine them and fine them plenty," roared the marshal. The justice managed to levy an assessment of $10 each. No one of them but Hank had any money, and he didn't have enough. "Well," said the justice, trying to be agreeable, "maybe you can pay the next time you come to town!"

"Not much!" shouted the marshal. "Pay it right now or the whole caboodle goes to jail!"

Hank, growing milder all the time. After a little talk the marshal escorted him to the bank, where it turned out he had some credit. During the visit the bank officials were about as visibly agitated as was the justice. The fine paid, Hank asked to have his guns back, and was accommodated when the release was accomplished, the justice continually prompted by the marshal.

The marshal then stood up and made an oration. He said there might still be towns in the great west where it was considered proper to use kerosene lights as targets for pistol practice and cause citizens to dance to the jig tune of a .32, but this sort of music was out of date in Walla Walla. The town had advanced in the social scale. The Star-Spangled Banner and *e pluribus unum* were now functioning, and let each ye and all ye beware. No more monkey business. When you come to town behave like white men and keep out of jail.

When the talk was done Hank and his satellites walked out as from the presence of a solemn experience. There was some muttered talk as they mounted their horses, but no whiskers on the promptness with which they ambled out of town. Word filtered back that these particular bad men had boycotted Walla Walla. A town that wasn't keen enough to see the point of a little joke as it was intended needn't expect any trade from Hank Vaughn and his gang.

But Walla Walla didn't hang out any symbols of mourning—no black crepe over the doorway. And they took turns slapping the marshal on the back and tendering congratulations. In due time Hank returned. He drank and gambled as before, but there were no more forced loans, no more shooting out lights, no more strangers made to dance to the jig time of a .32.[17]

Vaughan no longer took part in stealing horses. He wasn't even risking his own local cronies, finding it more advantageous to direct the work of the professional horse thief. These outside pros could put their illegal stock in with Hank's legitimate band when it was time to head for the market. If a local rancher ever recognized his own brand on any of these animals, Hank's drovers could produce proof of purchase.

The Walla Walla *Statesman* of April 27, 1883, carried a front page article about some horse thieves who had eluded a posse and were at large in the immediate territory. Although there is no direct link to Vaughan, the recent travels of the gang, their mode of operation and place of discovery suggests that they may well have been local suppliers to the Vaughan enterprise:

HUNTING THEM DOWN
Horse Thieves Driven to the Mountain And Hotly Pursued—
A Description of the Scoundrels.

From Hon. P.J. Kelly, of Cottonwood, we gather the following latest particulars respecting the chase of two horse thieves who have recently been depredating in the country north of Snake river and Walla Walla and Umatilla counties. The farmers near this city have known for some time that the men were gathering horses, and had in their possession ten or fifteen head, and that they were professional thieves; steps were at once taken to arrest them, but having friends the thieves were informed of the intentions.

Phillips, the constable, at once raised a squad of men and started in pursuit from the farm of the late Tom Branson, to the Lewey mountains and there discovered them. The thieves immediately struck out for a canyon where they had a large band of horses secreted. They then tacked and returned to the Branson farm and occupied a washout where they had natural breastworks. The thieves being well armed with repeating rifles and revolvers the party in pursuit decided to leave them until morning when it was discovered that they had escaped. Pursuit was again made up Birch creek, but as it had been raining hard all night they could not be followed.

One of the men is Warren Drake, who escaped from Union county jail last fall, and for whom a reward of $800 is offered by the authorities. [The thieves] abandoned two pack horses in which were novels purchased very recently at Sprague. They had with them one black mare branded on the left hip with H, which belongs to the Warren family, in Spokane county, also one light grey horse, one brown, a two or three year old stallion colt and one bay horse with two or three white feet. The thieves cannot be far away from this city and every farmer and officer should be on the lookout for them.

Just as these horse thieves were being closed in upon, Hank's operations were becoming increasingly restricted. The civilian population was growing as the railroads linked these remote areas with the rest of the world. Local promoters even spoke of mills and factories. Law abiding citizens, increasing in numbers, were stiffening their resistance to being cheated and bullied by roughnecks. The lawless breed was becoming a smaller minority.

Characteristically, Vaughan adjusted to the changing times and turned his attention to other pursuits. This new endeavor was farming; location, Umatilla Indian Reservation. It must have been a skeptical public that read in the June 1, 1883, *Statesman:*

The *Examiner* Centerville says Hank Vaughn has turned granger and is tilling the soil in the neighborhood of Centerville.

REFERENCES

Chapter 11

1. *West Shore*, September 1883, 237-8.
2. The Dalles *Chronicle*, July 22, 1926.
3. Blankenship, *op. cit.*, 232.
4. The *Spokesman Review*, February 5, 1899.
5. The *Spokesman Review*, January 29, 1911.
6. *Ibid.*
7. Fargo, Lucile F. *Spokane Story*. New York: Columbia University Press, 1950, 132.
8. *Ibid.*, 123-4.
9. *East Oregonian*, March 27, 1948.
10. Edwards, Jonathan. *An Illustrated History of Spokane County*. Spokane: W. H. Lever Co., 1900. 300-301.
11. The *Spokesman Review*, August 16, 1913.
12. The *Spokesman Review*, January 29. 1911.
13. Personal interview, Charles R. Ayers, Star, Idaho, February 28, 1974. Mr. Ayers had worked for Hank's father at Star and was a friend of Hank's brother, Marion.
14. The *Spokesman Review*, January 29, 1911.
15. The Dalles *Chronicle*, September 23, 1926.
16. *Eastern Washington Directory*, compiled by D. Allen Miller, Walla Walla: Harris, The Printer, 1883, 105.
17. The Portland *Oregonian*, January 15, 1933.

XII.

BREAKING NEW GROUND

(1883-1885)

During the next decade Hank Vaughan would participate in a period of great change in the American West. Dramatic developments were taking place in the character of land ownership. These developments would adversely affect his horse thieving activities.

In Umatilla County where he based his operations, it had not been unusual in the past for one man to claim an entire township where his stock grazed freely on thousands of acres of land. Now the countryside was being deeded into quarter sections and blocked out into 160-acre parcels. The open range was being fenced and plowed by ever increasing numbers of farmers. Many of these had been enticed here by the railroad's campaign to increase economic activity at the far western end of its transcontinental lines.

As the rural areas became more populated, the towns began to prosper and law and order arrived. The *West Shore* of January 1885 described this phenomenon:

> Formerly about the only business which men came here to pursue was that of stock raising, for which nearly the whole of this county was excellently adapted. It was a hardy, healthful, yet not a very hard-working sort of a life, and if properly pursued could hardly fail of success. But the plow has driven the flocks and herds almost entirely from some portions of the county, and greatly restricted them in others; and though the stock raising interests will always be large, this is even now, and will be still more so henceforth, an agricultural county. Scores of townships, which four years ago were uninhabited except by roaming herds of stock, are now transversed by wire fences and dotted with settlers' cabins. Many, indeed most, of these people who intend to pursue farming as a business are poor. They are obliged to go in debt, consequently, the plentiful and "flush" times of years ago are no longer with us.

The county seat and chief commercial center of Umatilla County was Pendleton [fig. 26], a town of 1,800 inhabitants in 1885. It was ideally situated on the western verge of the reservation and surrounded by superb agricultural lands. It was connected with the rest of the country by good roads and railroads. The Baker City Branch of the OR&N line passed through town, placing it on the recently completed through route to the East by way of the Oregon Short Line.

Pendleton boasted of having a national bank, five large general merchandise stores plus the usual number of hotels and shops. The cheap wooden buildings that had been erected in former years were gradually being supplanted by more permanent and commodious brick ones. The semi-weekly *East Oregonian* was published there by J.P. Wager, editor, and C.S. Jackson, business manager. This was the leading newspaper of that region.

Several smaller towns were appearing to the north of Pendleton. The hamlet of Adams (fig. 27) had been laid out in 1883. It now had a population of three hundred and was thriving as a trade center for the surrounding farming area.

Five miles northeast of Adams, and adjacent to the corner of the reservation, was the town of Centerville (fig. 28), population about four hundred. It lay in the very heart of the wheat lands which were making Umatilla County famous. Centerville was on the line of the railroad to Walla Walla, but the line was not yet operational. The next town serving this wheat belt was Weston, three miles northeast of Centerville. It too was a flourishing business point, although a severe fire in late 1884 had set back its development hopes.

Wheatlands which nourished these communities extended into the Umatilla Indian Reservation and after settlers had worked up all the surrounding land they turned their attention to encroaching onto the Indian land. This was a development followed closely by Vaughan.

(Photo Courtesy Howdeyshell Studio)

FIGURE 26—Pendleton by mid 1880 was a thriving metropolis. In two decades it had sprung from a desolate ford on the Umatilla River to a major center of commerce. Vaughan frequented the Villard House, the two-story building on the left of Main Street in the second block.

(Sketch from West Shore by Kay Woodman)

FIGURE 27—The town of Adams on lower Wildhorse Creek in 1885. The Vaughan ranch lay on the middle horizon about three miles beyond town. After their marriage in 1878 Hank lived with Louisa Ditty in the mountains nearby.

(Photo Courtesy Howdeyshell Studio)

FIGURE 28—Centerville, now Athena, as it appeared in the late 1880s when more saloons lined its streets than any other businesses. The crowd is gathered in front of F'roome's Hotel where Hank was an occasional lodger.

Originally the Treaty of 1855 had designated that the reservation would began at the mouth of Wildhorse Creek in Pendleton and proceeded to its terminus on Wildhorse Mountain near where Hank had lived with Louisa, thence southwest past Lee's Encampment (Emigrant Springs) to a point near the head of Birch Creek and then generally down Little McKay and main McKay Creeks (near Pilot Rock) to its confluence with the Umatilla River and up it to the point of origin.

The first reduction of the reservation had occurred in June of 1882. Six hundred and forty acres of reservation land were sold to increase the city limits of Pendleton. After this initial infringement, pressure became relentless to further decrease the size of the Indians lands. The United States Congress began debating an Allotment Act which would reduce the reservation by about one-fourth of its area and parcel the remaining area to resident Indians: 160 acres to a family head and forty or eighty acres to children according to age.

As this legislation was pending, the settlers began jockeying for position to buy the Indian land. The Indians also were making arrangements to be in residence at the appointed time so that they would qualify for allotments on the remaining reservation lands. It was not only the local farmers and Indians who watched the progress of this bill as it made its way through the legislative process. Opportunist like Hank Vaughan, with his interest in Martha Robie, kept himself well informed. As later events would prove, he had positioned himself well before the Allotment Act became law. Some Indian families would relocate from as far away as Idaho Territory in time to be included in these allotments. Hank would see to it that Martha Robie and her children were among those who relocated in order to claim their share.

This move from Idaho Territory did not happen until mid-1883 or at least Hank's association with Martha was not common knowledge in Umatilla County much before then. One obstacle to him establishing an identity with Martha Robie at this time was the pending divorce between Louisa and himself.

Louisa had filed for divorce on October 9, 1882. She claimed she had not seen Hank since they parted on Indian Creek in Union County during the fall of 1881. Summons for Hank to appear for the proceedings ran six consecutive weeks in the Weston *Daily Leader*. The order, signed by A.S. Bennett, circuit judge of the Centerville Precinct, was also displayed in the post office of Star City, Idaho Territory. That was where Louisa thought Hank was residing.

Louisa's attorney was Steven V. Knox. Other officials involved in the divorce process were District Attorney T.C. Hyde, Umatilla County Sheriff Wm. Martin, and Referee Fred Page-Tustin. Witnesses appearing for Louisa were her brother-in-law, David Howdeyshell, and J.C. Davis who recalled for the court that Hank had been willing to give him a bill of sale for Louisa. Hank did not appear in his own behalf. The divorce was granted on June 22, 1883.[1]

In testimony during the trial, Louisa accused Hank of dalliance with another woman (Nancy Tucker). Since she did not mention Martha Robie, it is certain Hank's relation with Martha was not known to her. As soon as Louisa was legally out of his life in the area, Hank lost no time in relocating Martha and her children to the Umatilla Reservation.

Sometime during the summer of 1883, Martha and three of her children moved there from Idaho Territory. Her only son, Hugh, was about fifteen at the time.

Daughters, Mary and Minnie, were twelve and eight. The two older daughters, Clara and Lizzie, were both married and did not come to the reservation until later.[2] Martha's children had all attended parochial school in Boise City and were well educated. The two older girls were accomplished pianists. Their prized piano was one of the possessions freighted to Oregon.[3]

At first the Vaughan/Robie's lived near lower Wildhorse Creek on what was later the Bill Ferguson ranch. The area they chose for their farm was in nearby Spring Hollow. It was here they laid claim to a share of the Umatilla Indian Reservation. Although Martha's mother, Isabel Craig, was Nez Perce, a tribe closely kin to the Cayuse, this did not necessarily give Martha the right to take up land here. She did, however, and this was to cause considerable dilemma for future Indian agents.

During the summer and fall of 1883, along with his horse trading ventures, Vaughan plunged into his new role as farmer. Construction of a home, fencing, and preparing the ground for planting were among the major undertakings. That considerable fall planting was accomplished in 1883 is verified by a jotting in the *East Oregonian* of April 12, 1884, which said. "Hank Vaughan has 640 acres of the finest looking wheat in the country." That number of acres is about what Martha's entitlement would be if she and her children were legitimate residents on the Umatilla Reservation.

How much of the ranch work Hank did is open to question but there can be little doubt he directed the effort. He entered this venture at the same time as Thomas P. Page, Sr., of Walla Walla, who become his ranching neighbor. Page was married to a part Indian woman whose grandfather was of the Walla Walla tribe, and he, like Vaughan, could see the value of establishing residency on the reservation before allotments were settled.

Vaughan was not new to the Umatilla Indian Reservation. He was a familiar figure there, having lived among these Indians and run horses with them since 1878. This association had given him access to conveniently located holding grounds for horses. In turn Hank was a good agent for selling Cayuse Indian horses as he was familiar with buyers throughout the country. He frequently employed Indians who were excellent drovers and well adapted to the horseback travel required in that work.

Although Hank got along with the Indians and accepted them as equal partners, this was not the usual white and Indian relationship. As Hank was to find out, and certainly must have expected, his own family had some trouble with his association with Martha. After Hank and Martha were settled on their reservation ranch they visited their respective families in the Boise Valley. Upon arriving in their spring wagon at his sister Amanda Butler's place, Hank asked his little niece, Henrietta, to run out and greet his wife, "Gus," as he affectionately called Martha.

Hank pulled a diamond ring from his vest pocket, telling Etta, "This is yours if you go out to the wagon and say 'Hi, Aunty Gus!'" Etta grabbed the ring and ran to the window. When she pulled back the curtain, her mouth fell open. Turning away she handed the ring back to her uncle saying, "I could never be related to any Indian." Later Hank was said to have pawned the ring at a saloon in Boise City for a handsome sum.[4]

A number of years later, Henrietta was to recall another incident regarding her relationship to Aunt Martha Gus. At the dedication ceremony for the first permanent bridge built across the Boise River, a number of dignitaries were gathered. Henrietta had recently married the president of one of Boise City's principal freighting companies and she was among those greeting the distinguished visitors who included chieftains from various Indian tribes.

At the main reception in city hall, Etta, in the presence of her new mother-in-law, was introduced to Chief Minthorn of the Umatilla Reservation. While attempting to make conversation with the chief, Etta said her uncle, Hank Vaughan, lived on the reservation and did Chief Minthorn know her Aunt Martha Gus? He looked her in the eye and said in a loud voice, "I know Gus, Gus my aunt, too." Upon comprehending this, Etta's mother-in-law nearly swooned in front of the notables of Idaho.[5]

It was perhaps when Hank and Martha visited in the fall of 1883 that Vaughan and his cronies, including his brother-in-law and Henrietta's father, Butler, got called into court. The District Court Proceeding printed in the *Idaho Statesman* of November 23, 1883, reported that Vaughan was indicted on the first of five counts and given until the following day to plead.

Several of these indictments stemmed from criminal activity occurring four years previous on April 15, 1879, for which Vaughan had never been brought to trial. Ada County court reports contain the indictments but no information describing prior legal actions such as warrants or complaints has been found. The indictments from the Grand Jury on November 21, 1883, stated Case No. 3, The People vs. H.C. Vaughn-Assault with a deadly weapon; Case No. 4, same as above; Case No. 5, The People vs. H.C. Vaughn and William Moody-Grand larceny; Case No. 6, The People vs. H.C. Vaughn-Assault and battery; Case No. 7, The People vs. H.C. Vaughn-Grand Larceny. Hank was well prepared for his defense against the charges when they were brought against him this time. Case No. 3 was quickly set aside with the explanation "impossible date as to the offense charged." On the 22nd of November, Vaughan pleaded guilty to assault in Case No. 4 but not guilty to all other charges. Judgment was deferred until November 24.

Bill Moody was charged with Hank in Case No. 5, but he did not appear on his own behalf or make a plea in the charge of a joint crime with Hank. It can be assumed he was not apprehended for the offense nor was he in custody of the court at the time of this follow-up trial.

Following Vaughan's plea of guilty to one count, the District Attorney then shifted his attention to William Butler. He made a motion to the court to place on the calendar an earlier grand jury indictment against Butler for assault with intent to commit murder. This indictment resulted from charges brought against Butler on April 10, 1873, fully ten years earlier. It was soon after this date he had appeared in Elko and married Amanda.

Four years previously, Vaughan had appeared as a defense witness in an assault charge against his brother-in-law. All that can be found concerning the outcome of the trial was that the case was discontinued. Perhaps it was discontinued after plea bargaining between Butler and the court.

Butler had evaded prosecution for many years, but as a result of the current court action, he was found guilty and according to the *Tri-Weekly Statesman*,

December 4, 1883, he was sentenced to five years in the Idaho Territorial Prison at hard labor.

Vaughan escaped a jail sentence, received only a light fine and was discharged on the assault charge. The courts may have felt justice was accomplished but Hank evidently was not satisfied. He was almost immediately hustled back into court on another charge of assault and battery. Less than two weeks after his last appearance in court, the *Statesman* of December 6, 1883, reported a new case of The People vs. H.C. Vaughn. "The defendant fined $20 and costs, on indictment for assault and battery, and *nolle prosequi* entered in two cases. Defendant discharged." The Dalles *Mountaineer*, December 15, 1883, may have printed the nearest explanation of this complication:

> A rumor reached Pendleton on Saturday that Hank Vaughn had trouble with a lawyer in Boise City, resulting in the former shooting his antagonist. It is said that the trouble grew out of several cases in court in which Hank Vaughn was interested.

A reconstruction of what led to this flurry of court cases might be that Vaughan and his Boise Valley cronies were having some fun as they celebrated Hank's visit to Boise City. As a result they were arrested on a minor assault charge. In an effort to rid Ada County of this lawless element, the authorities searched their criminal files for more serious charges. As long as they had this bunch in custody there was no justification in turning them loose without making them pay for past misdeeds.

The District Attorney who brought charges against Vaughan was T.D. Calahan. Judge H.E. Prickett heard the cases in district court session. Other officers taking part were U.S. Marshall Fred T. Dubois and Ada County Sheriff I.L. Tiner. Hank's lawyers were Wuston and Grey.[6]

Vaughan extricated himself from these court cases in Boise City through a process of plea bargaining as he was becoming expert in using the law to his advantage. It is noteworthy that reporting about Vaughan in recent months remained very guarded. Words were carefully chosen and quotes about him were not offensive. Editors besides Wager of Pendleton and Parker of Walla Walla had been admonished by Hank and all were unquestionably gun shy.

With this problem behind him, he returned to Eastern Oregon and proceeded to make a name for himself in Centerville. Ever since living on upper Wildhorse five years before, he considered Centerville his home town. Although a post office had been maintained here since 1878, it was still little more than a collection of saloons and a trading center. Pioneer George Lynde remembers:

> . . . Centerville . . . was a rough town with more saloons lining its main streets than any other business houses. Being halfway between Walla Walla and Pendleton, the town caught all the tough riff-raff that roamed the country at the time.[7]

One of these toughs was a rowdy by the name of Wilse Coyle. By use of force and bribery, Coyle had intimidated the folks in eastern Umatilla County for a half dozen years. The *East Oregonian* of May 1, 1880, said:

> Willis Coyle is again a free man. He was arrested nearly a year ago, charged with assaulting Barney Prine, [founder of Prineville] marshal of the city of Weston, and

has been under bonds since. He was most ably prosecuted and defended and the jury acquitted. Willis and all his friends, and they seem legions, left the court room happy.

Coyle was not above influencing local politics and the *East Oregonian*, May 6, 1884, scolded the newly established Centerville press for not recognizing this:

The Centerville *Examiner* gives its views on various candidates quite fairly, but is silent about the candidates for sheriff. We would rise to inquire if it has any knowledge of who Wilse Coyle and a man named White, two noted desperados, and their crowd, were voting for and hurrahing for sheriff at the election in Centerville two years ago. And can it tell who furnished the keg of whiskey that was cached away in a convenient place on that occasion? And who was it that said he had been promised $25 to vote for Morton, and wondered why it had not been sent? And lastly, why have [not] more of that crowd of cut-throats ever been brought to justice for their misdemeanors?

The law was slow to stop Coyle, but Vaughan would soon put him on his good behavior. Vaughan happened across Wilse Coyle in a Centerville saloon that spring of 1884 and Coyle who had been bragging, did not recognize Hank. When Coyle overheard someone mention the name Vaughan, he proceeded to remark rather grandiloquently on what he would do to Vaughan if they ever had a difference. According to old timers:

Hank made no move for his artillery, but he stood there and talked to Coyle about the error of his ways in the plain manner that the plainsman had. Coyle experienced a change of heart.[8]

Another incident involving Hank and Coyle took place in Weston about six months later. It was one of the first of many incidents which Hank was fond of setting up in order to play a trick on an adversary. Editor Emsely Ridenour of the Weston *Leader* gave this account of the affair on January 4, 1885:

A most disgraceful row occurred last Tuesday between Ben Anderson and J.C. Hart, two "thimble rig" gamesters, and Wils Coyle. The trio, with a party named Bush, were engaged in a game of poker in the Orion saloon. Quite a sum of money was in the "pot" when Coyle raked in the stakes in the true style of a bay man. At that moment two pistols were leveled on him and Coyle was made to "disgorge." It is said that the strangers not only made Wils give up all the money that was up as stakes, but all he had besides, and then forced him to dance and otherwise amuse his audience, after which one of the two emptied a chamber of his pistol at the ceiling, and Coyle broke for dear life. Bare headed and excited, Wils ran up Main street and, rushing behind the counter of Mr. Proebstel's hardware store, appropriated to himself a 48-calibre Colts and a box of cartridges, and started out after revenge. Meanwhile, through the assistance of Hank Vaughn, Anderson and Hart got away. Coyle swore out a complaint against the two of robbery, and some officers were out scouring the country.

The pair were later apprehended in Walla Walla and brought back for trial, but Coyle skipped out of appearing against them. Anderson and Hart could have gone to prison for armed robbery had Coyle testified. Everyone figured that Hank, who was some how affiliated with Anderson and Hart, had persuaded them to return part of the loot in exchange for Coyle agreeing to absent himself from the trial. This was another example of Hank's ability to settle cases out of court.

Coyle avoided Umatilla County from then on, but within six months he was in trouble in his new location. The *Eastern Oregonian* of June 30, 1885, reported the law caught Wils following a later shooting altercation in Warrington, Washington. He was jailed for two months, fined $418, and required to post $1000 bond at the end of the sentence or lay out the whole cost at $2 a day. The *East Oregonian* editorialized, "Wils always did have a hankering after trouble."

Hank may have rid Centerville of its main trouble maker when he influenced Coyle to leave, but he quickly filled the void. His troublesome behavior often followed a period of drinking in one of the local saloons. Hank's ex-brother-in-law Howdeyshell claimed to have seen him drunk many times in Centerville.[9]

Being under the influence of alcohol didn't appear to spoil his aim. Lute Lane of Centerville recalled:

> . . . one time Hank stood in a store and shot through the open door of a grocery across the street, down through the aisle and put six bullets into a sack of flour which was resting against the back wall of the grocery, much to the discomfiture of the merchants and patrons of the store.[10]

When he was not intoxicated, Noah N. Brown claimed Vaughan was gentlemanly and courteous. He recalled frequent meetings with him when Hank was in his best spirits as well as in his most sullen moods:

> In 1884, when I was clerking for Tillie & Kirby in the Villard hotel in Pendleton, Hank came in and registered for a room. It was quite visible that he was not in his best mood, and as Tom Bradley, a mixologist known as the best in his calling, was tending bar, the firm consulted with Tom regarding the course to pursue in case Hank "got bad." Hank did not tarry long but went across the street to Cass and Bill Matlocks' gambling hall, and was soon mixed up in a "stud poker" game.
>
> The Matlocks had a nephew by the name of Johnson, a dapper young lighthaired fellow, hailing from the Willamette valley. He was dealing the game. Johnson did not know Vaughn, and as Vaughn was an expert dealer with cards he soon detected Johnson was giving him the worst of it by favoring his friends. He gave Johnson a few significant expressions that any one would have caught. Johnson, however, persisted, when suddenly Hank jumped from his chair and, reaching across the table grabbed Johnson by his pompadour hair, and pulled him out of his seat around the end of the circular table and sent him hurling across the floor. About the same time Hank landed in Johnson's chair.
>
> Tossing the deck of cards promiscuously over his head and reaching in the side drawer he took out a new deck, and, without saying a word, continued the deal. Johnson made his exit to the front part of the building and to the barroom. He informed his Uncle Cass what had taken place. Cass used an ear trumpet and was quite deaf, but it did not take long, however, to learn the true situation. Cass, in his characteristic way and fine feminine voice, advised Johnson to go up to the

house and remain with the women until he sent for him. Johnson took the hunch, and acted accordingly.[11]

There were other times when Hank himself was not above trying some sleight-of-hand dealing. Deputy Jim Johnson described one incident:

> Playing poker in Wallula one night, he spread a large silk handkerchief on his lap. Into this he dropped an ace when he considered himself unobserved. Later in the game he slipped the ace into his hand and prepared to take the pot. Bill Johnson [brother of Jim] was playing. Bill whipped out a gun, poked it into the wishbone of Hank and ordered him to put the ace back in his lap. Naturally, this broke up the game. Hank quietly left the cardroom and went out into the night to a saloon down the street.[12]

Hank had not been noted for his ability to win at cards, but an item in the *East Oregonian* of September 4, 1884, indicated that his gambling luck was improving:

> Joe Crabb of Walla Walla has had bad luck lately. His "George S." lost him money at Helena, and it is reported that his faro banks lost heavily lately, Hank Vaughn winning $1500 at one sitting and a Chinaman another large sum.

Joe Crabb had been on the local scene for many years. His establishment at Marshall's Station was granted the first liquor license in the country in 1862.[13] Crabb had always been a gambling man. Perhaps his most noted gamble was on a horse race featuring Cayuse Chief Howlish Wampoo's famous pinto.

> . . . Several ranchers near the reservation had secretly caught Chief Wampoo's pony and staged their own private race with Crabb's best race horse. The pinto was fast, but during this preliminary race, Joe's horse won handily. Knowing that the thoroughbred of Joe's could beat the pinto, the Pendleton bettors put up everything against the Indian bets. What the whites did not know was that they had really raced a half brother of Wampoo's best pinto. This nearly identical horse had been conspicuously planted for Joe's benefit. Even though that momentous race took place in 1871, the event was known as "the day Pendleton went bankrupt," for the blooded horse made a noble race, but he was no match for the pinto.[14]

Hank relished this kind of antic and it became a favorite story to be retold to him by his friend, Chief Wampoo. While setting up on the reservation, Vaughan made other close friendships. One such relationship was with S.P. "Doc" Whitley. Doc was described by Blankenship as follows:

> Doc is an all-but-forgotten character who came to Umatilla County from Arizona. Rumors of his reputation in the Southwest seeped into his new community, and the tenor of these reports was hardly reassuring. It seems that he had born so conspicuous a hand in the Earp-Clanton feud in Tombstone that when the famous gun battle at the horse corral was over, Doc found it advisable to absent himself from Arizona until the odor of his misdeeds evaporated.[15]

Doc Whitley had become a rather well-to-do rancher in the Milton area by the early 1880s.[16] He owned a saloon and hotel there and ran a ranch as a sideline. The growth and prosperity further south attracted his eye for business and in the spring of 1885 he removed his interests to Adams where he became a saloon keeper. The October 13, 1885, issue of the *East Oregonian* stated that Doc was doing $50 to $60 a day worth of trade.

It is likely that Vaughan had known Whitley for some time but with Doc now only a few miles from the Vaughan ranch their friendship grew. These two had much in common, not the least of which was an interest in horses, booze and recklessness. The results of one of their wild blasts in Pendleton was reported in the *East Oregonian* of June 9, 1885, under the caption "A Nose Broken:"

> Last Friday afternoon, while turning the corner of Main and Court street rather suddenly, a buggy drawn by one horse and occupied by Hank Vaughn and Doc Whitley, was overturned, throwing the animal flat on his back and the occupants out. The vehicle fell on Vaughn, who was driving, breaking his nose in two places. His wounds were dressed by Egan and Vincent. Doc Whitley escaped uninjured. Hank was out again, right side up, on the following day, ready for another turnover.

These crashes were not unexpected when Vaughan had been drinking and held the reins of the team in the wagon traces. He had the reputation of being a fearless though accomplished driver. According to Drake, an old timer around Pendleton, he "could drive a six-horse team where most men would be afraid to lead a horse."[17]

Blakenship told of another spectacular buggy crash:

> One day Vaughn, pretty well illuminated, drove up before Whitley's saloon behind a halfbroken team of lively young horses hitched to a light buggy. Doc came out to admire the festive animals and in the ensuing conversation jocosely twitted Hank.
>
> "It seems to me that you're scared of your team, Hank. Why don't you hire a man to break them for you?"
>
> Hank answered by inviting Whitley to take a ride. Doc jumped into the buggy, seized the whip, and poured the lash to the horses. Dare-devil Hank, instead of trying to control the team, threw the lines to the ground and gave an Indian yell. The runaway was one of the most successful that Adams ever saw. Down the street the team dashed pell-mell, Doc whipping the horses and Hank yelling. The team was going much too fast to make a turn, and the frantic horses, the smashed buggy, and the men all ended in a heap beside the road. Doc and Hank were so severely injured that for a few days hopes were entertained for their demise, but the reckless devils were too wiry, Hank survived to plague the community for years.[18]

Not all of Vaughan's upsets were as spectacular. One time in the late 1880s, Hank was alone when he wrecked his buggy. According to John Kelly:

> Much under the influence of hard liquor, Vaughn started home from Pendleton one day, driving a pinto hitched to a buggy. Somehow, the buggy upset throwing Hank to the ground. The pinto browsed on the roadside. A couple of Vaughn's friends came along and found him asleep, surrounded by gold pieces. Hank, had a winning streak and the money had been in a buckskin poke when George Horseman, then of Umatilla, and now of Portland, rode up, Vaughn's friends had recovered $6,000 in gold from the dusty road.[19]

That Vaughan would be carrying such large amounts of money was not unusual. People wondered where the money came from as the supply seemed bottomless. Pioneer editor Clark Wood said:

> . . . He carried plenty of money, in gold as a rule and was a liberal spender. I have seen him walk into Pat Kine's saloon, invite all present to have a drink, and tell the bartender to keep the change from a twenty he tossed on the bar.[20]

One of the benefits of having an established home was that now Hank had a place to entertain his parents. He was pleased to have them come for a visit and see the progress that had been made by the end of his first full year of reservation ranching. The *East Oregonian*, September 26, 1884, reported:

> Mr. A.H. Vaughn, of Ada County, Idaho, was in town last evening, and made this office a pleasant call. Mr. and Mrs. Vaughn have been visiting their daughter [Fannie] in Willowa [Wallowa] valley, and their son Hank Vaughn, near Centerville. And Mr. Vaughn is now on his way to visit his parents in Lane County. Having seen a few numbers of the *East Oregonian*, while at Hank's, he of course came around to subscribe for it himself.

As Hank got into his role as a permanent resident, he took an active part in community affairs. People soon learned they could count on him for unusual diversions. The Centerville correspondent to the Walla Walla *Union* of June 27, 1885, reported that Vaughan would be providing Fourth of July entertainment. He related, "Pendleton will celebrate the Fourth. There will be a grand procession, races at the fair grounds, and a fight between Hank Vaughn's cinnamon bear and a wild bull." No other reference has turned up about Hank's cinnamon bear, but in one way or another in his own style, he found ways to liven the scene during this period. It is interesting to note from the tone of newspaper reports, the local people seemed to be developing a tolerance to him, considering him an amusement rather than a threat. To all appearances, Hank Vaughan, the notorious horse thief, was directing his energies to carving out a ranch on the Umatilla Indian Reservation.

REFERENCES

Chapter 12

1. Umatilla County Circuit Court Case, No. 191-30, *op. cit.*
2. Census, Umatilla Reservation, 1887, Office of Indian Affairs, National Archives. This document showed the children's names and dates of birth as Clara (Moody), 1860; Lizzie (Perrin), 1864; Hugh, 1868; Mary, 1871; and Minnie, 1875.
3. Personal interview, Areta Barrett, Athena, Oregon, May 10, 1973. This fine upright piano was acquired by Chas. A. Barrett and was used by Areta Barrett when she taught piano lessons.
4. Personal interview, Mrs. Sophia Riede, *op. cit.*
5. *Ibid.*

6. Ada County Circuit Court, The People vs. H.C. Vaughan, Criminal Case File 3, 284-290, Ada County Court House, Boise, Idaho.
7. Pioneer Ladies Club. *Reminiscences of Oregon Pioneers*. Pendleton: East Oregonian Publishing Co., 1937, 252.
8. The *Spokesman Review*, January 29, 1911.
9. Umatilla County Circuit Court Case, No. 191-30, *op. cit.*
10. The Dalles *Chronicle*, September 30, October 6, 1926.
11. The *Spokesman Review*, August 31, 1913.
12. Kelly, John, *op. cit.*, 20.
13. Searcy, Mildred. *Way Back When.* Pendleton: East Oregonian Publishing Co. 1972, 252.
14. Pioneer Ladies Club, *op. cit.*, 110-1.
15. Blankenship, *op. cit.*, 226.
16. Gilbert, *op. cit.*, Portland, 65.
17. Drake, *op. cit.*
18. Blankenship, *op. cit.*, 227.
19. Kelly, John, *op. cit.*, 14.
20. *East Oregonian*, March 27, 1948.

XIII.

WORKING THE RESERVATION FARM
(1884-1885)

Hank's managerial ability had not been so evident when he was directing his efforts in illegal channels, but now that he was concentrating on constructive pursuits, this talent became apparent. Hank, himself, may even have been surprised at the success of his farming venture, but he wasn't above boasting of his accomplishments. The writer from the Walla Walla *Journal* whose article was reprinted in the *East Oregonian* of June 27, 1884, undoubtedly received much of his information from Hank. His description of the farm follows:

HANK VAUGHN'S WONDERFUL FARM

> One of the finest farms in the United States is said to be that of Hank Vaughn, on the Umatilla Reservation. Features are 900 acres of wheat, 480 acres of barley, 15 of Russian oats, 30 of miscellaneous vegetables, 160 acres of pasture, 600 acres broken for fall sowing, an orchard planted and in thriving condition, 600 or 700 chickens, countless ducks, a large number of hogs and hundreds of horses and cattle; a good residence and fine barns and outbuildings; an abundance of the best machinery; the land all fenced; several hundred thousand feet of lumber hauled from the mountains; 150 cords of wood. This year's crop is magnificent; the wheat is as high as an ordinary man's head, and very thick. Mr. Vaughn calculates to clear $22,000 from this year's products. On the 18th of May 1883, the land was unbroken prairie, with no sign of civilization; it now blooms like the rose. Hank Vaughn is said by the *Journal's* informant, to be one of the most capable and hardworking farmers in the Northwest. Certainly the results of his past years operation on what was before virgin soil are well-nigh astounding.

The local press could not find enough good things to say about the economic developments brought about both by the new farms like that of Hank's on the reservation lands and the improvements in transportation with the new railroad link between Pendleton and Walla Walla. A reporter's description of his trip on this branch line reveals his awareness of the part Vaughan played in this development. The location of the Vaughan ranch relative to Pendleton and environs was described in a feature article in the *East Oregonian*, May 1, 1885:

> The trains run twice a week, leaving here Tuesdays and Fridays at 1 o'clock, returning the same afternoon at 4:15 o'clock. On the roof of the "caboose" you perceive as you leave Pendleton the top of the high hills ahead, in the direction of Centerville. . . . Up the "Wild Horse," with the winds ahead and the smoke from the struggling engine in your face, but the prettiest and simplest pastoral views repays you a thousand times for suffering the ills of a little smoke. The square checkerboard farms to the left, and the uninhabited reservation to the right, suggest an idea of the "sublime and the ridiculous." Away to the east can be seen the beautiful wheat fields of the Vaughan and Page farms, green and flashing in the sunlight. This road is through the "God's country" of Umatilla County.

Such a ranching operation as Hank was now into could not have gotten started without capital or credit and Hank, who understood how to use other people's money, quickly went into debt. Those with whom he dealt were to find his attitude toward repayment most irritating. When he was indebted to another, he felt little concern to pay up. In fact, Vaughan felt little obligation toward contracted debts and this attitude seemed to become a fixation as he went to great lengths to outsmart his creditors.

In 1884, he accumulated considerable local indebtedness in the form of 90-day notes. These notes were in Martha's name with Hank signing as her agent. In all legal matters he was careful to be only an agent for Mrs. A.H. Robie. Between March and November 1884, there were seven loans of from $100 to $850 mostly for purchase of farm materials such as $162 for a freight wagon and $853.34 for lumber and logs. One loan for $120 was made in Walla Walla from Frank Rayburn and was later transferred to Virginia Everts.[1]

Having a permanent residence, Hank learned, also made it easier for creditors to catch up with him and some of his earlier creditors now descended on him. He and Harry Vaughan had signed two notes to Frank Bros. in Spokane Falls in 1880; one for $25 on April 1, another for $42 on April 16, both at 1 percent interest per month. Together with lawyer fees, these small bills now amounted to $175. This was at a time when $5 would buy a week's board at Bill Gray's California House. The Spokane firm decided to go after its money and on November 14, 1884, Sheriff William Martin presented Hank with a District Court summons and a Notice of Attachment to his reservation holdings. Attorney for the plaintiff, Cox and Minor, had done their homework well and this was one of the debts Hank Vaughan paid off.

Other creditors had their own style of collecting from Hank. This story comes from one of Fred Lockley's columns:

> Hank owed a man named O'Brien $20. O'Brien struck him for his money a time or two. Hank said, "Go ahead. Why don't you collect it? Start something whenever you are in the notion. You will collect something you don't need and you aren't expecting." O'Brien knew Hank could pull his gun awfully quick. He met Hank one day and before Hank could reach for his gun he grabbed Hank around his arms, threw him on his back, reached under him, got Hank's gun and threw it out into the middle of the street. Then he sat on Hank. "How about it, Hank? Do you owe me $20 or do I get it?" he said.
>
> A big crowd had gathered around them. Hank looked up and grinned. "Do you know, I have been studying about that matter and I have a sort of hazy

recollection of owing you some money—I think you are right about it being $20. You might let me up. I have an idea I have your twenty with me right now."

When Hank had gotten up he brushed the dust off of his clothes and said. "Come on into the saloon, boys." He pulled out a handful of twenties, slid one along the bar to O'Brien and another across to the barkeeper. "Never mind the change," he said to the barkeeper. "Drink it up," he said to the boys at the bar, and out he walked.[2]

Few of Hank's creditors possessed the courage of O'Brien. Some creditors made attempts through legal channels to collect on Hank's charges, but didn't thoroughly follow through, deciding to absorbed the cost rather than push Hank. One example of the latter occurred on March 1, 1887, as Hank did some shopping in Baker City. He purchased on account from the firm of Charles St. Louis, Jeweler and Watchmaker, the following items:

1. One gold horseshoe scarf pin	$ 5.00
2. One gold hunting case Elgin watch	50.00
3. One diamond ring	50.00
4. One rolled plate gold chain, ladies	20.00
5. One rolled plate gold neckchain, ladies	14.00
6. One rolled plate band ring	2.50

It did not take the jewelry firm long to realize their mistake in opening an account for H.C. Vaughan. By March 25, St. Louis filed suit to recover payment for these items but the Baker County Sheriff could not find Hank nor could he attach any property in Baker County belonging to Hank.[3]

For some reason, the jewelers did not attempt to collect the bill in Umatilla County and so forfeited their $141.50. Vaughan never did have a high regard for Baker County or many of its people ever since his Auburn trial back in 1865.

Two days after charging the jewelry in Baker City, Hank was passing through Island City in Union County. He and A.R. Matoon cosigned a note for $300 to purchase four horses from F.S. Ladd. The horses must not have met Hank's expectations as a year later he still had not paid for them. Mr. Ladd died in the meantime and perhaps Hank felt his debt would be overlooked in the settling of the estate. However, the executor of the estate successfully filed suit to collect the debt.[4]

The *East Oregonian* of April 27, 1888, noted:

> Two horses belonging to Hank Vaughn were sold at sheriff's sale this afternoon under an execution of the Ladd estate. They brought $104. Two more will be sold on the 8th of next month under a like execution.

This was not the first time some of Hank's horses had been attached in order to collect an account. A district court record shows that, in 1886, Centerville merchants, C.W. Hollis and Charles Cleve, were attempting to recover on a promissory note for $3,054.45 issued to Mrs. A.H. Robie and C. Meek. Since Hank Vaughan was their agent, fifty-six of his horses had been seized as security for the loan.[5]

In attaching the horses, very detailed descriptions as to color, age, sex, and brands were recorded by the sheriff. Nearly all the horses carried different brands. Those horses carrying the "P" of Tom Page, Sr., and the "J" and "CT" of the Thompson brothers were probably purchased locally. The ones branded "N" and "C" probably came from the herds of Fred Nodine, Union, and the Circle C ranch in Idaho Territory.

Among the band was one horse with a "V" branded on both left and right shoulders. This could have been Hank's special mark. Since he often operated on the reservation and Indians commonly mount from the "off" side, Hank may have chosen this rather unusual identification.

Occasionally it only took a bit of imagination to manipulate Hank into paying up. Friends who knew how to approach him were sometimes successful in getting their dues. A long-time resident of Pendleton, Billy Mays said:

> Nearly everyone was afraid of Hank, and he took advantage of it to bluff collectors out. I used to be constable, and they would give me a bill to collect from Hank. Just as he took a pride in refusing to pay his debts, he also took pride in helping anybody who was up against it and needed a loan.
>
> When I had a bill to collect from Hank I would meet him and say, "Hank, I am strictly up against it. I know you have a heart as big as a steer. Loan me $20."
>
> "Sure I will, is that all you need?" he would say. He never struck a man to return a loan, so my system worked fine.[6]

Vaughan delighted in making life difficult for his creditors as it gave him an opportunity to needle the law. At the same time, this kept his lawyers busy with miscellaneous matters until he needed them for more serious business.

Most of the debts connected with his farming were eventually paid but only after court attachments against horses, cattle or wheat owned by Hank and Martha. How many smaller debts Vaughan never paid back because going through the courts was too expensive for the creditor to collect can only be surmised.

The fact that he was doing much of his business dealings on credit which he was reluctant to pay was not well known. He was acclaimed only for his obvious achievements at the farm. As befitted the increased social status that followed this accomplishment, he acquired the garb of a proper gentleman. For social occasions and trips to town he was usually attired in a Prince Albert-style coat which he wore over a linen shirt and black woolen pants. A favorite plaid vest completed his costume (fig. 29.)

Hank had always been know as a good story teller. On April 21, 1885, a roving reporter, the *East Oregonian* Tramp, visited the Vaughan home and was entertained by one of Hank's anecdotes:

> . . . we met Mr. Vaughn and wife, accompanied by a gentleman who was from Sacramento, California, by the name of Anthony Greene, who contemplates going in the brick-making business at Adams. Of course, we had to stop for a chat and "Hank" told us a story as follows: "Two prominent citizens of Centerville came over to the ranch to call on us a day or so ago, and of course I passed some of my best Scotch whiskey. The result was I had to pass it again, until one of the prominent citizens had to go out and lay down on the cellar door to cool off. He was pleasantly

(Courtesy Laura Belle Rogers)

FIGURE 29—Hank Vaughan, at about age 35 (ca. 1885), is portrayed in his customary city attire. The Prince Albert coat, vest and linen shirt gave him the deceptive air of a circuit riding preacher.

> situated and slumbering, when without warning the supports gave way and he was precipitated about ten feet below.". . . . The prominent citizen felt very much humiliated that Scotch whiskey would allow him to break into a man's cellar without knowing it.

Another description of Hank's reputation as a host was found in stories written in 1887 by George Hunter. Hunter didn't use any names since "some of the parties are alive, and I have not asked their consent," but the broad details fit what is know about Hank Vaughan. Hunter had been camped within earshot of the shooting episode involving Sheriff Maddock and he knew Hank had spent time in prison over that affair. Hunter felt Hank had become a good citizen despite his earlier problems:

> He . . . still lives in this country, and is noted for his hospitality and genteel behavior among gentlemen, as he also is for the pluck and daring which he has shown on several occasions since his release [from prison] in different personal encounters with men equally ready with "popguns."[7]

Most visitors to the Vaughan ranch were treated with generosity. However, two men who attempted to take advantage of Hank's hospitality found they had stopped at the wrong place. Billy Mays told the following story about Hank during this period of affluence and gentlemanly behavior:

> One day a couple of campers drove up to Hank's ranch on the reservation near Athena. They asked Hank if they could camp there over night. He took them in, fed their horses and said, "My woman is visiting friends in Walla Walla. But between us we can get up a good supper." They stayed all night with Hank. In the morning one of the men said, "What do we owe you?" "Not a cent," Hank answered. "I'm always glad to entertain gentlemen. All I ask is that you shut the gates when you drive out. I have to go to Athena." Hank had ridden a mile or so when he found he had forgotten something he had promised to take to Athena with him. He rode back. As he passed his granary he happened to look in. He had sent for four sacks of seed oats. Two of the sacks of oats were gone.
>
> He followed his guests, saw the two sacks of oats in their wagon. He stopped them and said, "Didn't I treat you like gentlemen? If you had asked me for a couple of sacks of barley you would have been welcome, but like a couple of low down skunks you pay me for my kindness by stealing my seed oats."
>
> One of the men said, "We have been feeling mean about it ever since we took them. We will drive back with the oats and return them."
>
> "Oh, no you won't," Hank said. "Those poor, thin, worn out horses of yours didn't steal my oats. It wouldn't be fair to make them return back. Tie your team. It's only a couple of miles back. Each of you can pack a sack on your back. You don't want to rile me, though, so you had better hurry." He rode back of those two fellows while they tramped back. If either of them lagged, Hank swung his revolver toward him and it was as good as a spur. The fellow would hustle right along. Hank talked as pleasant as you please and entertained them all the way back.[8]

The following story was told of a stranger who became a regular and welcome visitor to the Vaughan ranch:

> . . . a farm implement salesman from Portland arrived in Athena and went to F'roome's Hotel for the room he was accustomed to get on his annual trip there. It was harvest season and it had rained driving all the harvest hands to cover and taking all the hotel rooms as well as hay mows of the livery and fee yards. At the desk Mr. F'roome informed the salesman that the only room he had left was the sample room and he would have to share it with another man who was now in the room. The salesman accepted the room and the other man was Hank Vaughn. They hit it off fine together and became good friends. While Hank was cleaning his guns he told the salesman that whenever he came that way again to be sure and stop at his farm and he would be treated to a fine chicken dinner as his guest. The salesman dined with him many times after that. What influenced him to do so could have been the guns, the chickens or just friendship for this extraordinary man.[9]

Martha Robie/Vaughan had settled comfortably into her home on the reservation. It was with her help the couple acquired their reputation for hospitality. J.L. Sharon remembered a time he was at the Vaughan ranch. The purpose of his trip was to adjust an insurance claim resulting from a fire which had burned a hay barn, some crops and equipment. Sharon stopped briefly at the Ferguson place near Adams, then went on to the Vaughan farm. He said, "it was almost noon when we arrived and Mrs. Vaughn had prepared one of the nicest dinners I ever expect to participate in. Six hungry men sure did justice to that dinner."[10]

Harvesting that first year was big business. The *East Oregonian*, July 28, 1885, said Hank had fifty men hired in the fields for harvesting. "Vaughn threshes 2,700 bushels a day, and expects a total of 60,000 bushels." But the price of wheat at 50 cents a bushel was not good news for growers. The note in the August 25, 1885, *East Oregonian*, was more about the low price of wheat than the benevolence of Vaughan:

> Among the Umatilla County farmers who have contributed to the "missionary car" of Oregon produce sent East are Hank Vaughn, J.R. Murphy, D. Coffman, Jas. Jones, Wm. Penland, Geo. Wallinhoff, J. Despain, and J.R. Porter.

Hank did, however, make some money as, in the fall of 1885, he invested some of his profits in real estate in Adams. Later when a judge converted part of this building into a courtroom apparently without his approval, Hank found an opportunity to shut down the law. An article in the *East Oregonian*, September 4, related how Vaughan turned the tables on the law and further embellished his reputation as a news maker:

ADJOURNED SINE DIE
How Hank Vaughn Upset a Justice Shop

> There was a stabbing affray sometime ago in Adams, and the way the prisoner got clear of an examination is thus told by a Walla Walla *Journal* correspondent:
>
> Just as I got to the door, in marched Hank Vaughn, and, in less time than it takes to write it, he adjourned the court—drove every mother's son out of the house and closed the doors, and had it not been for the serious countenance of his honor as he silently and solemnly stalked out, the scene would have been supremely ridiculous. No one seemed to comprehend it till they got outside—then the boys

began to yell. One thing was certain, however, the court had adjourned and the prisoner gone hence without delay. This at first seemed a high-handed piece of business, but the inquiry revealed the fact that his honor, without leave from Mr. Vaughn, who owns the building, had taken possession of it and converted it into a courthouse. This little intrusion Mr. Vaughn did not relish, and having just arrived from Walla Walla, acting as an envelope of about three thumbs of blue ruin, he was just in the proper mood to declare himself emperor.

His honor would have been Judge Baker and the prisoner probably some reservation friend of Vaughan's. Whether the culprit was a friend or not, the idea of embarrassing the court would have been excuse enough for Vaughan's behavior. As usual it was the presence of alcohol in his system that touched off his disorderly conduct.

Lute Lane who once lived in Centerville tells this story of how the local populace grew to expect and accept this liquor-related conduct of Hank's:

Hank was want to ride into Athena about Saturday noon, patronize the various bars until he attained his western frame of mind and then he would ride up and down the streets shooting out the few lights or go in stores, two guns on his hips, and take without pay whatever he wanted. The merchants never worried over this, for Monday morning Hank was sure to come to town with a repentant headache, and ask the various storekeepers what he had "charged" Saturday. He would then pay what they asked and go out without a word.[11]

Another resident of Centerville, R.S. Erb, related a similar episode that happened there in the mid 1880s:

. . . Erb watched the men line up at the bar and order drinks. After several rounds had been indulged in, the men decided to set their glasses on the bar, retire to the far side of the room and shoot at the glasses. The one who missed was to pay for the next round. Hugh Langdon was the barkeep and mildly protested against this noisy outburst, for fear the sheriff would think some one was in trouble and arrest the whole bunch for disturbing the peace. But the fun continued and the barkeep was kept continually ducking behind the bar to escape the fate of his glasses. After the demonstration was over, dozens of glasses were shattered, all the bottles back of the bar were broken, and the big mirror was a wreck. Feeling that they had a real good time, the men mounted their horses and rode out of town. The next day, when Vaughn had partly sobered up, he returned to Athena, told Langdon to fix up everything damaged in the way it should be and send him the bill. This was done and Hank cheerfully paid the several hundred dollars of damages, feeling he had an experience well worth the money.[12]

In other towns where Vaughan's reputation preceded him, saloon keepers were more protective of their stock. Lee Drake related:

Hank's favorite hang-out was the Bureau Saloon in the Transfer [Villard] House (fig. 30) in Pendleton near the Union Pacific depot. He would ride up in front and shoot out the transom over the front door. When this would happen, Ed Horton, who owned the saloon, would tell his bartender: "Take Hank out a drink so he

(Sketch from West Shore by Kay Woodman)

FIGURE 30—The Villard House which contained the Bureau Saloon was Hank's Pendleton headquarters for ten years. The manager, Dave Horn, and bartender, Pat Kine, were good friends of his. This hotel was one of the most popular overnight houses for travelers in eastern Oregon.

won't ride in and shoot all the glasses and bottles off the back bar." And Hank would get prompt service.[13]

In September 1885, Vaughan received the news that his mother had died. He had always had a great affection for her and was deeply appreciative of her efforts in getting him pardoned from his life sentence in the Oregon penitentiary. Elizabeth Fields Vaughan was buried in the cemetery in Star, Idaho Territory. Carved on her tombstone was: "Remember me to thy last days, husband and children, I must leave you . . . all alone . . ."

Before a year had passed, Hank's father, who had not enjoyed his lonely life, proposed to a widowed acquaintance, Isabella Arnold. According to the family, Aleck made all the preparations necessary for the wedding and sent for Mrs. Arnold. When the train carrying the bride-to-be pulled into the station, the ceremony commenced. As soon as Isabella stepped off the train, Aleck took her to the waiting preacher and they were married right there on the station platform.[14]

REFERENCES

Chapter 13

1. Umatilla County Circuit Court, Case No. 270-31. Frank Rayburn vs. H.C. Vaughan.
2. Lockley, *op. cit.*, 47.
3. Baker County Circuit Court, Civil Case No. 96-149.
4. Union County Circuit Court, Civil Case, F.S. Ladd vs. Henry C. Vaughan and A.R. Matoon.
5. Umatilla County Circuit Court, Civil Case No. 44-53, Book 11, Hollis and Cleve vs. A.H. Robie.
6. Lockley, *op. cit.*, 47.
7. Hunter, George. *Reminiscences of an Old Timer*. San Francisco: H.S. Crocker and Co. 1887.
8. The Oregon *Journal*, August 11, 1913.
9. Drake, *op. cit.*, 9.
10. *East Oregonian*, April 10, 1948.
11. The Dalles *Chronicle*, September 23, 1926.
12. Bailey, Robert G. *River of No Return.* Lewiston: R.G. Bailey Printing Company, 1947 (rev. ed.), 155.
13. Drake, *op. cit.*, 8.
14. Personal interview, Mrs. Sophia Riede, *op. cit.*

XIV.

RUSTLERS AND VIGILANTES
(1883-1884)

It was inevitable that with increased settlement, the days of the rustlers were numbered. But for a brief period, Hank and his kind teamed up with the homesteaders to take one last pound of flesh out of the big cattle ranchers. The Robin Hood element of robbing the rich to give to the poor was some how associated with this activity. While some factions contended stealing was stealing, others felt the cattle kings could well afford some scattered losses. If the little guy benefitted in the process that made it okay.

By the mid 1880s, the bunchgrass range that once provided abundant winter forage for the livestock of the cattle ranchers was under cultivation and fenced. The homesteaders or "nesters" had the best water holes and choicest bottom lands.

Not only were the cattle barons finding it more difficult to get cheap pasturage for their stock, they were experiencing considerable loss from rustling activity. Rustlers continued to drive branded cattle off the range, alter brands and sell the animals, but in company with some unprincipled homesteaders, the rustlers latest trick was to brand free-ranging slick-eared calves with the settler's mark. The animals were then sold to buyers in the normal fashion and the rustlers and their local confederates pocketed what should have been the big cattleman's profit.

It was becoming increasingly difficult for the large cattleman to get convictions in law suits against the homesteader. The homesteader had closer links to the developing settlements and seemingly more sympathy from the courts. Many of the large cattle companies were backed by capital from California and Nevada. For this reason the local press did not show much sympathy for the economic woes of the big cattle operators. The *West Shore* of January 1885 grumbled:

> The cattlemen are nearly all non-residents; the cattle sold out of county and the money used elsewhere, all the benefit the county derives is the presence of the few men needed to care for the stock.

Along with the pressures of population, the cattlemen suffered from a new agricultural innovation. Barbed wire appeared everywhere. This wire was only something newfangled to talk about back in 1875.[1] However, by 1880, hundreds of miles had been strung out in the Columbia basin lowlands and its benefits were not all good. The wire was dangerous to livestock, particularly horses. Accordingly, the *East Oregonian* of April 17, 1880, reported:

> J.G. McCoy seems to be among the unfortunate kinds; burnt out two years ago and this Spring he informs us that he has had 15 head of good horses killed or ruined by their turning into the wire fence, so extensively used between here and the Columbia.

The wire was not just being used on pastures in the lowlands. The Dalles *Times Mountaineer* January 5, 1884, quoted the Union County *Record* on a report of fencing which was occurring in the mountain valley sections:

> Messrs. Charles McConnell and Daniel Chaplin are about to commence the fencing of 6,000 acres of their land in the valley [Grande Ronde] with wire fence. A small pile driver weighing 325 pounds, for setting the posts, has been received. The whole length of fencing, including exclosures and cross lines, will be twenty miles.

Horse thieves too were finding there were few place where they could operate without being confronted by people or fences. One strategy successfully used by Vaughan and his riders to avoid the restraints of the barbed wires was to follow the main unfenced travel routes but to move their illegal herds by night. Stolen horses were cached in secluded spots, like the Horse Ranch on the Minam River, until enough were accumulated to make up a small band. Then on a prearranged date, teams of thieves would begin relaying the horse herd from one hideout to the next at night. These points were located at distances of from twenty to forty miles apart, depending on the terrain.

The first team of "night riders" would relay the band from their hideout to the next and return to their home place and continue normal activities, being absent less than twenty-four hours. The horses were held at the hideout during the day and then the next team of night riders moved them on down the line until they were far enough out of the country of origin not to be recognized.

In more populated areas, one hideout arrangement was a fake hay barn. Inside the hay in the haymow was a fully enclosed compartment large enough to hold a small band of horses. In less populated areas the horses might be day-herded in more remote basins or box canyons.

Night riders were clever in their operations. They took advantage of their intimate knowledge of equine behavior and would use an older bell mare who knew the route with each new bunch. This was especially useful when the route lay through timber or when wide rivers had to be crossed. While moving horses in and about fence lanes and corrals or when removing horses from home pastures, night riders often carried horse-hoof sandals. These devices could easily be slipped over their boots before dismounting, thus no telltale man tracks were made.

Sharon described the follow-up operations of a night riding venture like those for which Vaughan was suspected to control:

> When the stock were successfully spirited far enough away from their home range the head or "brains" of the gang would appear on the scene, have the stolen stock driven to the nearest shipping point and either dispose of the lot outright to waiting

> buyers or car and ship farther east, the "head" and one or two men accompanying the shipment. As soon as possible after the disposal of a shipment all "hands" concerned were to be seen back in their accustomed haunts, each with a few dollars extra in his pockets, while the ring-leader took life easy, waiting the assembling of another livestock cache. Then stealthily disappearing as though on a visit or business trip and again returning in a few days with the proceeds of his visit.[2]

Vaughan had several routes in operation beginning on the reservation. The first stop to the east was in the mountain prairie at Starkey. The next point was on the North Powder River below Haines. Here the relay was taken over by Hank's in-laws, the McCarty brothers, who had been on their Swamp Ranch since 1882 (fig. 31). From there the night trail led to the big pasture on the oxbow formed where Pine Creek entered the Snake River. Here more McCartys and other relatives lived. Across into Idaho Territory and up river from Weiser the route was met by the Fuller boys, noted horse thieves.[3] From here it was an easy run into Boise Valley through the Star and Dry Creek area and Vaughan's father's ranch.

Hank's many contacts in the Boise Valley not only arranged for the sale of stolen stock, but they assembled animals appropriated in Idaho Territory or Nevada and relayed them back to Oregon for disposal. Those who worked as night riders

FIGURE 31—The McCarty's Swamp Ranch was along the banks of the North Powder River. Many of their criminal activities were staged from here in the late 1880s and early 1890s.

and kept hideouts along the trail were careful not to jeopardize their positions and for the most part did not pick up stray stock too close to home.

There is evidence that another line of night riders crossed from the Umatilla Indian Reservation through the Wallowa country into a holding ground on the Nez Perce Reservation. This route then followed along the Lolo Trail into Montana Territory. There were still so few people living along this route that it was hardly necessary to resort to night riding, however.

Hank's links with this route were easily established. He had spent considerable time developing the haven for stolen horses on the Minam River and through his Indian riders knew the trails from there over the Wallowa valley to cross the Snake River into Idaho Territory. Many of his relatives were establishing homesteads in this most northeasterly corner of Oregon. There were Vaughans among the first pioneers along the Imnaha River, and some of the McCartys were setting up in the Chesnimnus area, giving Hank close contacts all along the route.

It was during this period when Vaughan was actively moving horses from eastern Oregon to the Lapwai reserve that he became infamous in Lewiston, Idaho Territory:

Hank Vaughn, Lewiston's Bad Man

> Whenever Hank Vaughn came to town it was raised abroad and all the small boys took their fill of peeking around the corners in awe and with bated breath watching to see what new comedy was to be enacted.
>
> His most noted exploit in Lewiston was pulled off in the Green Front cigar store building. . . . It was erected by M. Dongac in 1879, and at the time of the Vaughn episode was used as a saloon. . . . Hank was in the saloon engaged in a card game. His opponent did something to anger Vaughn, and was invited to settle the matter with six-shooters. This was acquiesced in and the opponents rose to their feet, their left hands clasped and a gun held in the right hand. A bystander was requested to count three with the understanding that on the third count firing was to begin. This amicable arrangement was adhered to and, when the smoke of battle had cleared away, each man was found to have absorbed six bullets from the revolver of his adversary. None of them proved of lasting injury, though the opponent of Hank always afterward walked with a stiff leg.[4]

No records have been found as to who Hank was duelling with in this Lewiston encounter. If, indeed, each man "absorbed six bullets," the wounds must have been bloody, but superficial.

Vaughan's link to the Lapwai area was through his connection with Martha and the Craig family. Martha's father, William Craig, who came here in 1840, was recognized as the first white settler in Idaho. He died in 1869, but by right of his marriage to Isabel, daughter of Chief James of the Nez Perces, his relatives remained on land that was ceded to them in the Treaty of 1855.

Hugh Robie's first wife, Julia Rice, was also from the Lapwai Reservation.[5] It is through either her family or the Craig family that an article that once belonged to Hank is now in the Fort The Dalles Museum. According to The Dalles *Daily Chronicle*, July 22, 1926, Judd S. Fish presented a pair of saddle-bags or Spanish cantinas to the historical society (fig. 32). The cantinas had been sent to Fish by

Wasco pioneer Ferndal "Fenn" Batty who located them in Grangeville and knew them to be the property of Hank Vaughan.[6]

Vaughan would also continue to use the route through Dayton to Spokane Falls to move his stolen herds. He would vary the routes according to his calculation as to the risks involved.

Regardless of innovations, Hank's lawless kind were to reach the end of their free moving days. Even in remote places like the Wallowa country resistance was growing to rustling activities. In Umatilla County, the stockmen were at the limit of their tolerance for the brazen rustler who stole stock and made a clean getaway or if caught somehow managed to slip out of the hands of the law. Drawing from the ranks of the old guard stockgrowers, they formed their own vigilante committees. If justice would not be served in the courts, then it could be served at the site of a hanging tree.

When a suspected rustler was running free due to a smooth talking lawyer or a corrupt jury, the vigilante committee singled him out and soon he was the main attraction at a "necktie party." Hangings were not that common, but when they occurred they set an example easily understood by others involved in the same shady dealings. Milder warnings took the form of signs posted conspicuously on the violator's property.

If these warnings were heeded by the drifting professional or part-time rustler there was a temporary halt in local rustling activities. J.M. Bentley, an early day

FIGURE 32—These cantinas of Vaughan's are at the The Fort Dalles Museum. Cantinas like these hung from each side of the saddle horn and were a handy place for a cowboy to keep such things as food and ammunition.

Umatilla lawman who had dealings with Vaughan, put it, "Though I don't approve, it had the effect of purifying the air for about three months."

These vigilante practices were becoming increasingly unpopular with the people, the local officials and the law in general, but there was not much that could be done when the evidence was scarce and the fear of intimidation was strong. Especially indignant were the big city reporters who, protected by distance, clothed their attack in sarcasm. The following is a comment from the Portland *Oregonian* as it was reprinted in the *East Oregonian*, June 13, 1884:

A Thief on General Principles.

> *Sunday Oregonian:* Somebody in Pendleton telegraphed to this city, about a week ago, a dispatch which said that "the body of an unknown horse thief was found hanging to a tree in Vansycle canyon." Now, what I wish to ask is, if the man were unknown, as the telegram states, how did anybody know that he was a horse thief? I once lived in one of the southern counties of this state, where, at one term of the Circuit Court, five different cases of attempt to take life were suffered to go unpunished. At the same term of court two men were convicted of horse stealing and two boys of killing a calf belonging to another man. All four of these parties were found guilty of grand larceny and sent to the penitentiary for terms varying from one year to five. The old adage "touch a man's horse and you touch his heart," was manifest in those cases and it seems to hold good in the ethics of the Vansycle canyon case. The *onus probonl* (sic) is thrown upon the defence rather than the prosecution, and the supposition is that every man is a horse thief until he can, by competent witnesses, establish the fact that he is only a poor and honest murderer.

Although Vaughan was outwardly busy raising wheat on the Umatilla Reservation, the local vigilantes had not forgotten he was suspected of being the boss horse thief in the Pacific Northwest. On two different occasions, the vigilantes left a very impressive symbol and a warning for Hank. At least two years in succession they captured one of his gang and strung him up at the edge of the reservation on the lane leading to the Vaughan ranch. The first instance was reported in the *East Oregonian*, of May 30, 1884:

A Cattle Thief Lynched

> Walla Walla *Union*: Mr. Epler of this city, returned from Umatilla County last evening and reported the finding of a man hung on three rails a short distance below Centerville. The rails were tied together in a tripod and the fellow was suspended in the middle. The man is unknown, and no due as to who did the job can be obtained. Parties well acquainted in the neighborhood say that the man was one of a band of cattle and horse thieves who have been infesting the neighborhood for some time past. Ranchers in the Cold Spring and Centerville neighborhood are much worked up by the depredations of the thieves, and express themselves as bound to break up the nefarious business. Should they succeed in breaking up all the organized bands in this and Umatilla counties, they will find use for about 1,000

rails. A number of men possessed of considerable property are strongly suspected as being in league with the cattle thieves.

One reason vigilante action was disliked by law abiding citizens was that often so-called vigilantes used that cover to hide violent retaliations connected with their personal vendettas against neighbors, former associates or rivals. It could be for reasons such as these that Hank Vaughan, Sam Vincent, William Carlow, and a Mr. Shepherd, were listed among "numerous others," as organizers of the "Vigilance" or "601 Committee" that operated out of Ainsworth. Many citizens appeared to back the activities of this organization since for much of Ainsworth's existence there was no law enforcement in the immediate area. Ainsworth was situated in Whitman County and the county seat at Colfax was two days away. The nearest civil law was in Walla Walla which was about forty-five miles distant. As one Ainsworth citizen declared:

> When the 601 got in working order they made things count and were feared. When a party received an envelope with a piece of rope about one or two inches long and a slip of paper with six or twelve hours' notice to leave, you can bet it was heeded.[7]

In the fall of 1885, after considerable trouble with horse thieves along the foothills between Pilot Rock and Walla Walla, the *East Oregonian*, of November 6, 1885, related how several citizens handled a group of alleged thieves who had been brought to trial but acquitted. Following the trial the members who had not already left the territory were escorted to the train by a mob of about three hundred citizens headed by prominent stockmen.

One of the suspected thieves, Oliver H. Stanley, defied the order to leave and returned to his home at Pilot Rock. The next evening about thirty neighbors helped him change his mind and started escorting him to the train station in Pendleton. About halfway there, the Pilot Rock troupe was met and confronted by some fifty men from Pendleton. Stanley, figuring this was it, "put spurs to his horse" and tried to escape. The next day, the coroner found his body along the road with seven bullet holes in it.

Not quite a month later, the *East Oregonian*, of December 1, 1885, reported on more vigilante violence:

THE VIGILANTES AGAIN
George H. Keatch, a Supposed Horse Thief, Found Hanging Beside the Walla Walla Road near Adams

> About three o'clock Sunday afternoon Will C. Stimson arrived in town in charge of George Keatch, a supposed horse thief, on his way to Adams, where the prisoner would be given an examination before the justice of the peace of that precinct, for the theft of a horse, the property of John Adams. Quite a crowd collected around the officer and his prisoner as soon as he reached town. Keatch appeared perfectly at his ease, although handcuffed and tied to the pommel of the saddle. He had been overtaken and arrested in the Desolation country, on the other side of Camas prairie. As he surveyed the crowd who were intently gazing at him,

he remarked: "I must be a bad man, don't you think so?" About an hour after arriving here, Stimson determined to push on with his prisoner to Adams. They started about four o'clock and reached a point about four miles this side of Adams, where they were called to a halt by a crowd of about twenty men on horseback, who demanded the prisoner and took him in charge. The greater portion of them were masked, but acted quietly and deliberately. Keatch was taken from his horse and the animal was turned over to Stimson, who was ordered to leave without further inquiry into the matter. He did so and without further delay returned to town and reported the circumstances to the sheriff.

Early yesterday morning news reached here that a man had been found hanging beside the Walla Walla Road, about four miles this side of Adams. Coroner McKay was notified and summoning a jury, he repaired to the scene at once. As reported, the man was found hanging to a pole supported by two uprights securely set into the ground. The cross piece was sharpened and placed in auger holes bored in the top of the uprights. It appears from the evidence at hand that the crime was premeditated and the executioners had for some hours awaited the coming of the prisoner.

The following is the verdict of the coroner's jury:

STATE OF OREGON
COUNTY OF UMATILLA

In the matter of the inquest upon the body of George H. Keatch, deceased, now held by the Coroner of said County, November 30th, 1885, on the Umatilla reservation, four miles south of Adams, Or., we, the Coroner's jury, impaneled to investigate the cause of the death of the said George H. Keatch, find from the evidence of but one witness, Will C. Stimson, that the deceased came to his death by hanging, at the hands of masked men, the names of whom are to the jury unknown, on the 29th day of November, 1885, at about 5 o'clock, p.m., of said day.

Keatch was about twenty-eight years of age, unmarried and a halfbreed. Some claim he was a Mexican. Anyhow, his reputation, wherever he lived, was bad and his acts suspicious. The theft of John Adams' horse was the main cause that led to the unceremonious ending of his life on the vigilantes' gallows. The persons who superintended the hanging understood their business, as every arrangement, even to the hangman's knot, was perfect. When cut down the neck of Keatch was found unbroken, the fall of three feet not ample enough to produce death at once. The unfortunate man simply was choked to death at the end of the rope, with his feet about a foot from the ground. His hands were left hand-cuffed as Stimson last saw him alive, and his feet were tied in order to lessen his death struggles.

On the same page with the grisly story of the death of the unfortunate Keatch was a short note from the Adams *Times* that "Hank Vaughn has gone to the Yakima country for a few weeks to try the vicissitudes of camp life." It may have been that Hank was bored of ranch work and needed a change of scenery but he probably preferred to make himself scarce until the vigilantes cooled down. December was hardly the time to go camping in the Yakima country.

REFERENCES

Chapter 14

1. Osgood, Ernest Staples. *The Day of the Cattleman.* Chicago and London: University of Chicago Press, 1929, 190.

2. Sharon, *op. cit.* 136.

3. Beal, *op. cit.* 24-28.

4. Bailey, *op. cit.*, 155-6.

5. Personal interview, Royal Robie, Mohave Valley, Arizona, January 26, 1987.

6. The Dalles *Weekly Chronicle*, September 20, 1926. Ferndal Batty's obituary noted he had come to The Dalles in 1887 where he first managed the Columbia Hotel and later the Umatilla House.

7. Meyer, Bette E. "Ainsworth: A Railroad Town." Manuscript. No Date. Copy in the Northwest Collection, Spokane Public Library, Spokane, Washington.

XV.

MARKING HIS TERRITORY
(1886-1887)

Hank did not give ground for long to the vigilantes. In the next few years his actions suggest a man who is out to intimidate, not be intimidated. He went about his affairs in a way that was certain to attract attention. Not one to shy from publicity, he was one of the most reported characters of his day. He made no attempt to hide at least certain aspects of his operations. Through 1886, Hank's presence was conspicuous in local politics, in real estate ventures, in horse trading, and in a variety of ways calculated to keep the legal system busy and the press provided with copy. Like a dog marking corner posts, Vaughan went about putting his mark on his territory.

Hank's political affiliation is not known, but he took an interest in the local campaigns when the results of the elections would have an effect on his activities. In January of 1886, there was a hot local contest between J.P. Wager and Major Cornoyer. A few years earlier, Wager had been roughed up by Vaughan over the uncomplimentary obituary printed prematurely in the Pendleton newspaper. Wager's opposition for the state senatorial race that year was Republican Narcisse A. Cornoyer, ex-Indian agent of the Umatilla Reservation. Vaughan's support would logically have gone to Cornoyer who understood the regulation of reservation business. Like Vaughan, he was married to an Indian woman. If Cornoyer were elected he might be expected to have some influence in protecting Hank's interest in reservation land.

Wager, running on the Democratic ticket, was supported by C.S. Jackson, editor of the *East Oregonian.* According to Jackson, supporters of Cornoyer were ". . . Tustin, Leasure, Sommerville, Kaufman, McCall, Hank Vaughan, 'Doc' Whitley, Howlish Wampo *et id omne genus.*" Howlish Wampo had been dead for several years, but his name was synonymous with a certain clique of men who along with Cornoyer were accused by Jackson of everything from stealing horses to operating a whiskey ring. Cornoyer's loss to Wager was to the benefit of the county if Jackson's observations were the least bit accurate.

Later that month, Hank, prompted by some unexplained surge of generosity, gave a local political figure a gift. The January 25, 1886, *East Oregonian* reported: "Hank Vaughan presented James Marston with a very handsome seal skin vest yesterday." Marston, a prominent businessman of Pendleton, ran for the office of State Treasurer that fall.

Vaughan was not willing to leave his future in the hands of politicians. If he lost his bid to stay on the reservation, he was readying an alternative site. In the spring of 1886, according to the March 8, *East Oregonian*, he and Martha were improving their property in Centerville. Their lots were on the upper end of town west of the school block and it was said they were preparing to erect a brick residence. The supplier would be their friend, Anthony Greene, who had come from California the previous year to set up a brick building business. Hank would be fortunate that the house was completed or at least habitable by August as it provided him a comfortable haven in which to recuperate after a painful injury.

Later that spring, according to *The Times*, April 23, which was then publishing in Adams, Hank even talked of starting a newspaper. The paper commented, "He would make a good (fighting) editor."

During this period Hank continued wrecking buggies. How one buggy met its demise was told by Richard Cox:

> A friend of mine named Hollis, from Virginia, was one of the early-day merchants of what was then known as Centerville, but is now know as Athena, in Umatilla County, Oregon. His partner's name was Charlie Cleve. One day Hank Vaughn drove into town with a brand new buggy, to which was hitched a spirited team. Seeing Cleve on the sidewalk in front of the store, Hank cramped his buggy and invited him to take a ride. As they drove up Main Street, Hank said, "Do you think you can hang on, Charlie, if I let 'em out a little?"
>
> Cleve said, "Sure. I can hang on."
>
> Hank unbuckled the reins, threw them over the horses' backs, gave each of the horses a slash with the buggy whip, and the frantic horses started down the street on a dead run. Someone tried to head them off, and they swerved and struck a rail fence. The body of the buggy was detached. It flew over the fence and lit in the field right side up with Cleve still sitting in the seat, hanging on for dear life.
>
> Hank turned a double somersault, and when he had quit rolling, he got up, saw Cleve sitting in the seat, and said, "Well, you sure can hang on, can't you."[1]

The Times, April 23, reported that Hank then bought from Charley Bolin a new buggy for $250 and that the old one "now stands waiting as a charity boon for some good Indian."

Besides buying buggies, Hank was investing in some fancy horses. He was observed to be chief bidder at several horse sales that spring, taking home the top animals to upgrade his herd on the reservation ranch. The Adams *Times* reported:

> Hank bought of Samuel Vess, of the Willamette Valley, a fine three-quarter-blood Arabian stallion, the like of which was perhaps never seen in this county. He was snow white, dotted over thickly with dark blue spots not much larger than a trade-dollar; he was 16 hands high and as "beautiful as a dream." No better description of him could be given, according to the editor, than that he was just what a boy's imagination would conjure up after reading Mrs. Heman's lines so familiar to all boys, beginning thus: "Thou art sold, my Arab steed, thou'rt sold." The price Hank paid was reportedly $600.

A month later, Hank was still buying horses. The Adams *Times*, May 21, 1886, reported there was a large attendance at the sale yesterday. In tallying up Hank's purchases, the article said:

> The stock sold reasonably well. Hank Vaughan was one of the principal purchasers and got away with the choice of the band. Liberal in everything, Hank was a liberal bidder, and to him is due the generosity of the prices paid. For a fine span of two-year-olds he paid $320. Another one of the same age, he paid the handsome sum of $175. There were 60 head sold at the average price of $82 per head. This not considered high as this band was undoubtedly the finest ever sold in this part of the country.

Shortly after branding time that spring, Hank was in the town of Adams for a little entertainment. What followed became one of the more complicated practical jokes he is remembered perpetrating. He had a few drinks and was playing poker, relaxing in the saloon of his friend, Doc Whitley. Not long before, Hank and some of his Indian hands had turned their cattle up McKay Creek for summer pasture. In doing so, they may have crossed some rangeland belonging to Dick Stewart. As a result of this and earlier range mixups, Vaughan and Stewart had never developed a cordial relationship.

At the Adams saloon that evening in May 1886, Hank took it upon himself to settle accounts with Stewart who like Vaughan was not a stranger to the sort of ruckus that followed. Stewart had been involved in a similar brawl two years earlier which was reported in the *East Oregonian*, June 13, 1884:

> Last Sunday the people of this burg witnessed one of the most disgusting scenes that has ever taken place in Pilot Rock. Four or five of the Upper Stewart Creek men fairly captured the town with their drunken brawls and insulting language. They finally wound up with a knock down between Dick Stewart and Al. Acton, the former getting his right hand badly bruised and knuckle thrown out of place, the latter a black eye and a scratched face. Monday a complaint was sworn out and all interested were fined $5 and costs. Scott and Co., who run the saloon here, were also arrested for selling liquor to minors, and were fined $50 and costs. We are beginning to get civilized now.

Perhaps civilization had reached Pilot Rock then, but two years later, according to the *East Oregonian* of May 11, 1886, Stewart found conditions still pretty rough and uncivilized when he visited Adams. Three items relating to the Vaughan/Stewart case appeared in local papers. The first one, a bit lurid and distorted due to its travel along the grapevine, said:

> According to report, Stewart was asleep in Whitley's saloon, when Vaughan approached him with a hatchet, and pounded and cut him until he was battered almost to death.

The second item by the Adams "Corncracker" reports the assault in more believable details. The local reporter said, Stewart, of Birch Creek near Pilot Rock, had been drinking and gambling and had won $70 to $75 when he felt too woozy to continue the game and retired to the back room for a nap. As he slept someone disarmed him and chopped up his boots and hat and robbed him. Sometime later out front he got into a fight with Hank Vaughan and was badly beaten about the head and face. The "Corncracker" ended by saying that he was not insinuating that any parties mentioned actually robbed Stewart and that in reporting he was only giving the facts as he could gather them.

The third account appeared in the columns of *The Times* of Adams, on May 5, 1886:

> Last Friday evening there was a rough and tumble fight in town between Hank Vaughan and Dick Stewart, of Pilot Rock, resulting in black-eyes, defeat to a Pilot Rock man and considerable talk. The latter feature of the affair will result more harmfully to the participants and others than either black-eyes or defeat.

A fourth version of this altercation was told by Billy Mays. It conflicts considerably from earlier reports, but it gives the reason the case came to trial. Mays' first hand account follows:

> . . . One morning, I met Colonel Stewart's boy walking into town early in the morning. He had been playing cards with Hank at Adams and Hank caught him helping himself to a card from the discard. Hank beat him up till he was a sight to behold. Colonel Stewart vowed vengeance. He swore out a warrant against Hank and had him bound over to the grand jury.[2]

Actually both Hank and Doc Whitley were named in the suit and were both charged and released on bond.[3] Being bound over to the grand jury didn't curtail their activities, however. They continued about their business and two months later they found themselves in Pendleton short of funds. On July 13, 1886, they co-signed a note to cover their purchases. The note was made out to E. Hahn for $120 at 10 percent interest, payable in 30 days. Hahn waited patiently one month past the 30 day period. Then on September 17, as time drew near for the circuit court to hear the Stewart/Vaughan case, Hahn filed suit to recover his money.

On the following day, Matt Taylor, acting in behalf of Sheriff Bentley, attached Whitley's horse and single-rigged buggy and harness for the amount of the debt.[4] Doc posted money to get the release of his outfit, then he and Hank hired lawyer Fred Page-Tustin to file for a dismissal saying the complaint misrepresented their agreement to pay. The matter was settled before it came to court, but with legal fees and related complications it became an expensive loan.

By the time the Stewart case came to trial, Vaughan was in no shape to appear in court. He been seriously injured as a result of misjudging the disposition of a new person in town. On the 8th of August, while in a jovial mood in a saloon in Centerville, Hank decided to create a bit of excitement by carrying out one of his favorite jokes.

This joke involved selecting someone from the bar room and obliging him to entertain the patrons by dancing to the tune of Vaughan's six shooter.[5] Hank would lean back against the bar and practically shoot the heels off his protege. The crowd and Hank thoroughly enjoyed this fun. If it was a particularly good performance, Hank could usually be counted on to buy a round of drinks.

The stranger, Bill Falwell, was the actor Hank chose to perform this time. He had come into town the day before and just happened to be in the saloon when Vaughan decided it was time for another dance act. Some said Falwell was a high-spirited southern gentleman and perhaps that was why he was singled out by Vaughan to provide the afternoon's entertainment. Falwell courteously declined the first request but after a well placed volley from Hank's gun, he was stepping unceremoniously high, wide, and handsome.

Such an insult was not taken lightly by this Dixielander. Falwell went out and traded his fine horse, "Pack-saddle," to R.S. Erb for the fancy handled 7-inch .50 caliber revolver Erb was wearing. Erb was quite pleased with his trade. Armed with the gun he got from Erb, Falwell looked for Hank Vaughan and found him in one of the main street stores. Erb was a witness to how the Southerner evened his score with Vaughan:

> . . . . The next day Erb was in the store of Dick Doneca when the door was violently thrust open and Folwell burst into the room, acclaiming in a loud tone of voice that he was after Vaughn and intended to kill him. Vaughn was in the corner of the store at the time, talking to the proprietor. He was standing close to a spool case. Catching sight of his intended victim, Folwell began to shoot. One bullet found its mark, hitting Vaughn in the right arm and breaking it. Vaughn dodged behind the spool case, and every one of the next five shots went through this case. When the sixth shot sounded, Vaughn, though unarmed and with a broken arm, rushed his assailant, struck up the gun arm, smashed Folwell a few good lusty blows, and was treating him in approved roughhouse style when the sheriff arrived and separated the combatants.[6]

This retaliatory attack took place in the store of Dick Donica, Hank's childhood friend from the Waldo hills. Donica's name first surfaced in 1865 when Hank tried to locate him to testify concerning the black mare which Hank was alleged to have stolen at Durkee's Express Ranch before the Burnt River shootout. Donica had operated a main street business in Centerville since the mid 1880s.

Fortunately for Hank, Falwell's aim was a bit off that day for apparently Hank had picked on someone like himself who was not adverse to shooting other people. If conditions had been right, this might have been the end of Vaughan's career. According to Parsons, Falwell had ". . . been a member of the Younger Brother's notorious gang of desperados. . . ."[7] This may have been why Falwell was able to find his mark at least once with a pistol unfamiliar to him.

The spool case that took the brunt of the attack became the possession of Mrs. Areta Barrett (fig. 33). Three shots can be detected through it. The gun described as used by Falwell only shoots five bullets, thus the accounts of the affray have been somewhat distorted. Vaughan, however, was seriously injured because the wound affected his ability to protect himself from challenges to his quick draw ability.

The Union *Scout* of August 14, 1886, carried this abbreviated story, "Hank Vaughn was shot by W.H. Falliwell (sic), at Centerville, Umatilla County, last Monday. He is lying in a dangerous condition."

The Walla Walla *Union* of the same date gave more details:

HANK VAUGHN SHOT
Full Particulars in the Centerville Shooting Scrape —Hank Vaughn Not to Blame

(Special to the *Union* Pendleton, Aug. 10)—Wm. Falliwell [sic] shot Hank Vaughn in Donica's store, Centerville, at 6:15 last evening. Vaughn was making purchases at the time. The ball a 50 calibre, entered about two inches to the right of the right nipple, coming out back of the right arm, making only a flesh wound. No cause other than whiskey and a desire for notoriety can be given for the act. Vaughn was unarmed at the time, but secured a gun as soon as the firing ceased and pursued and captured his assailant. Falliwell fired five shots at Vaughn, the first of which took effect, the other four being lodged in a spool case behind which Vaughn took shelter. Vaughn is suffering considerably today from his wound, but it not considered in danger. Falliwell was taken immediately to Pendleton where he has preliminary examination tomorrow.

In spite of the fact that some people may have approved of Falwell's attempt to rid them of Hank's tormenting, the state quickly charged Wm. Falwell with assault with a deadly weapon with the intent to commit murder. Less than a month after he shot Vaughan, The *East Oregonian*, of September 10, 1886, recorded that Falwell was found guilty and sentenced to four years in the state prison.

The newspapers were not aware of the seriousness of the wound Hank had sustained to his right arm—his shooting arm. But there were those who learned of

FIGURE 33—The spool case that Hank ducked behind shows three bullet holes from Falwell's five-shot .50 caliber revolver. One shot broke the glass frontal piece of the second tray and the arrows point to where two other bullets hit the case.

the injury who would attach considerable significance to it. Hank set about to protect himself against anyone who might seek to take advantage of his disability. William Parsons recollected how Hank developed the dexterity necessary to defend his reputation:

> A few weeks afterward the writer had some business of a legal character with Mr. Vaughn and called at his house in Athena [then Centerville]. He was met at the door by a stepdaughter, who advised the visitor to be careful about entering Hank's room as he was practicing target firing. On entering the room Vaughn was found propped up by pillows with a pistol in his left hand and several boxes of cartridges upon his bed, engaged in target practice, the target being an ace of clubs pinned to the wall near the foot of his bed. He explained to his visitor that as his right arm had been crippled in his last encounter he had decided to learn to shoot with his left hand, and was now practicing with that end in view.[8]

Mrs. Charles Barrett who was the community's good Samaritan visited Hank while he was still in pretty bad shape. He told her, "Well, Mrs. Barrett, they damn near got me this time."[9]

> . . . . Mrs. Barrett, who always helped anyone in trouble or sickness, called on him. He remarked that he guessed while he was in bed he'd have a little peace as those he owed would probably leave him alone.[10]

Hank was mistaken about being left alone for on September 15, 1886, Sheriff John Bentley came to serve a bench warrant for his appearance in court in the matter of the Stewart case. Bentley was new to this office having just been elected in June of that year. He found Vaughan in no condition to travel and returned to the court with an affidavit from Hank's personal physician, Dr. E.R. Barker, to the effect that Vaughan was incapacitated. It was the doctor's opinion that the shot had severed or injured certain muscles and that an operation was necessary. Vaughan also submitted his own statement:

> . . . on the 9th day of August 1886 I was shot with a pistol by one Falwell the ball entered my right breast and passing through come out the inner side of my right arm near the elbow . . . I have consulted with Doctor N.G. Blalock of Walla Walla . . . [E.P.] Eagan and [Fred W.] Vincent of Pendleton . . . E.R. Barker of Centerville.[11]

The court would not accept the affidavit of either Vaughan or his Centerville doctor so the following day two other doctors were asked to evaluated the situation. Dr. Vincent submitted this statement:

> . . . in my opinion the condition of the said H.C. Vaughn is wearing on him physically and he cannot exist much longer unless he gets some relief other than his present constant use of morphine by hypodermic injection and this is almost as fatal to his life as the exhaustion from pain. That unless said operation is successfully performed in a very short time it is my opinion that said Defendant H.C. Vaughn cannot live.[12]

Dr. Barker's statement was essentially the same. However he seemed to understand what was bothering the court as he added: "This affidavit is not made for the purpose of delay." The judge finally accepted the fact that Hank's physical condition had not improved enough for him to attend the current court session and the Stewart case was deferred until the next sitting of the circuit court.

Vaughan wasted no time getting medical attention for his injured arm. On September 21, the *East Oregonian* reported that Hank Vaughan had departed for Portland to obtain surgical assistance for the repair of the damage to his right arm; he was accompanied by Dr. Barker of Centerville. The article continued that Vaughan would be operated on by a team of three surgeons and that the operation promised to be successful.

It was essential for Vaughan to receive the best surgical attention available. He had to have complete recovery of the use of that arm or it would one day cost him his life. There were many men carrying scars of one kind or another inflicted by Vaughan. Such men would follow his recovery very closely. Any number of them would be willing to be first in line on the chance that Hank's draw was not as quick as it was when they first met. Vaughan's wound was very serious for a man who lived by the gun and he was well aware of it.

By October 7, he was feeling fit enough to make a public appearance. He came to Pendleton making threatening remarks about what he planned to do in regard to the Dick Stewart affair. This outburst caused him trouble with his bondsmen—the second set to bail him out in the course of this case. Court records show Whitley and Vaughan were first released to bondsmen S.L. Moore and T. Milarkey on May 11, 1886, in lieu of being jailed for the Dick Stewart assault.

Five months later, the bondsmen were William F. Matlock, occupation-speculator, and George Darvau, liquor dealer. His current bondsmen were not happy hearing Hank's threats and by October 8, Darvau turned Hank over to Sheriff Bentley and asked to be released from his bond obligation. The following story, with a slightly different cast of characters, was related by Daniel M. "Mat" Taylor who played a part in that transaction:

> One time when George Darvau and Gus LaFontain had gone his bond for $500 they got uneasy for fear that Hank would skip out. They asked John Bentley, the sheriff, to go out and arrest him. Bentley replied, "No, you go and get him and bring him to me. Then I'll release you from your bond." That same day Darvau said to me, "Mat, what'll you take to go and get Hank Vaughn?" "I'll do it for $20." I replied. When I got my money I went over to where Hank was standing and told him that they wanted him over at the Court House in connection with his bond. "Come on, let's have a drink before we go," he said. John Bentley told him that his bondsmen were nervous and that he must get new ones or surrender and go to jail. "I'll be back in a few minutes," he said. In a little bit he was back with Tom Milarkey and Bill Matlock as bondsmen.[13]

Shortly after this Vaughan was in Walla Walla possibly to have Dr. Blalock check his arm but he also sold a horse. The *East Oregonian*, of October 22, 1886, quoting from the Walla Walla *Journal*, said: "Hank Vaughn brought over from the reservation his spotted stallion, 'Glorious Fourth,' and sold him, Tuesday, to Jerome Gammon of Pendleton for $300." This spotted stallion may have been the

Arabian stallion bought from Vess for $600 last spring. If so, Hank must have been in dire need of cash to have taken such a loss on his sale.

Selling the horse at a loss was not the only misfortune for Vaughan on this trip. His wallet was taken by a man whom Hank had considered a friend. The report was carried in the *Weekly Union* of October 23, 1886:

> On Thursday morning, Hank Vaughn was robbed of his pocket book by a man named McIntyre. It appears that McIntyre was an old friend of Vaughn's and that he arrived in the city from Portland in the morning. Upon representing to Vaughn that he was broke the latter paid for his board. Later on Vaughn retired to his room, complaining that his shattered arm was paining him badly. McIntyre followed Vaughn to the room and after the latter fell asleep, McIntyre took Vaughn's pocket book, containing between five and six hundred dollars, from under the pillow and skipped out. He shortly afterwards met Vaughn's boy [Hugh Robie] and cautioned him not to disturb his father; that he had placed Vaughn's money in a place of safety. Since that time McIntyre has not been seen. Vaughn offers $200 reward for his capture and has sent telegrams to all points to apprehend the thief. Mr. Vaughn is reticent in the matter and the meager details were obtained from his friends.
>
> Late in the night McIntyre was arrested in Ed William's while attempting to change a $100 bill. The thief had up to that time spent $150 of the bootie.

Vaughan and Doc Whitley managed to stall the due process of the law in the Stewart case until the spring of 1887. Then, according to the *East Oregonian*, May 6, Vaughan's lawyer, Fred Page-Tustin, pleaded with District Attorney Morton Clifford for a dismissal of the pending case. Clifford hung tough and said he would definitely continue to prosecute. Shortly thereafter Hank met the district attorney on the street and "viciously attacked" Clifford. Bystanders were able to pull him off before serious harm was done. The article ended on the note that, "Vaughn seems to own Pendleton."

Since he was not able to convince Clifford to drop the charge, Vaughan proceeded to carry out an elaborate strategy to get rid of the complainant. One version is told by Billy Mays whose memory may have switched the roles played by the Stewart father and son:

> . . . . Hank came to Colonel Stewart and, pulling out a handful of $20 gold pieces, he said, "How much will it take for you to be absent from the trial?"
>
> Colonel Stewart said his reputation was at stake and he couldn't afford to be absent for less than $500. Hank and Colonel Stewart went to Gip Will's saloon and Hank put five stacks of double eagles, five in each stack, in a drawer in the safe. He said to the barkeeper, "The morning after my trial, if Colonel Stewart does not appear against me, those five stacks of coin are his." The trial was held. There was no complaining witness, so Hank was discharged for want of evidence. That night Gip Will's saloon burned down. Colonel Stewart did more lamenting about that fire than all the rest put together. He told everybody he had deposited $500 in gold in the safe. It was a couple of days before the safe got cool enough to open. Colonel Steward and a big crowd were on hand to see the safe opened. When it was open, Colonel Stewart reached in and got his five stacks of twenties. They were what is

> called "dummy stacks," made out of dross to imitate a stack of $20 gold pieces. They were worth about 15 cents a stack as paper weights. Talk about mourning and wailing and gnashing one's teeth. Colonel Stewart could have given Shylock cards and spades and beat him when it came to lamentation.[14]

Sheriff Bentley's version of the Vaughan/Stewart case has a slightly different set of characters and more money changing hands. It also describes the farce in great detail from beginning to end:

> . . . . I always wore a gun on the outside of my leg, not really to use, but just so folks would know I was sheriff. One day a man came in and complained to the judge that Hank Vaughn and "Doc" Whitley had robbed him. I went to Hank's place, four miles from Adams, to arrest him. Did I arrest him? Sure, I did. He had made his brag that he would never be arrested. When Hank saw me drive up to his place he came out with a rifle across his arm and his six-shooter in its holster. He said, "Sheriff, have you come out to get me?" I said, "Well, Hank, that's what I was sort of figuring on doing." He said, "Have you got a warrant for me?" I said, "Yes, do you want to see it?" He shifted his gun so it lines up in my direction, and said, "Do you aim to arrest me and take me in with you?" I said, "Hank there's no call for you and me to be getting unfriendly about this little matter, but I sort of figure you ought to come in to Pendleton and fix it up." He said, "You go back to Adams and arrest 'Doc' Whitley, and wait there for me. Along about an hour from now I'll drift into Adams. You can sort of deputize me to help you bring in 'Doc' Whitley; that will be the best way to fix this thing up without making hard feelings between us." I said, "That suits me, Hank, I guess you'll make a good deputy." He came into Adams and I turned 'Doc' Whitley over to him. He said, "You drive on ahead, Sheriff. I don't like to be seen in your company. I'll be in soon." I told him to bring in $1000 in gold for each of them and I would turn them both loose till the trial. He went out to some of the gamblers and saloon keepers and got $2000 in gold and brought it to me and I locked it in my safe.
>
> Then Hank hunted up the complaining witness—the chap that was going to appear against him at the trial. He took him into a saloon, counted out $2000 in bills, and, handing it to the saloon keeper, said "Keep this in your safe till after the trial. If Dick here disappears till after the trial, hand it to him. If he appears against me, return it to me." 'Dick,' the chap Hank and 'Doc' Whitley had robbed, said, "Give me a couple of the 20-dollar gold pieces you got off me and I'll beat it and stay out of sight till the case is dismissed. That's making $2000 pretty easy."
>
> When the case came up, the witness could not be found, so the case was dismissed and I returned the bail money to Hank. A few days later the missing witness turned up and went to the saloon to get the $2000 in the safe. The saloon keeper turned it over to him. When he tried to spend the money he was the maddest man you ever saw. It was counterfeit money.[15]

For Dick Stewart, the final insult came almost two years after his boots were chopped up. The February 7, 1888, *East Oregonian* reported that he had been fined $150 for failure to appear at the trial of H.C. Vaughan and S.P. Whitley. Only one of the defendants, Vaughan, appeared as Whitley was reported to have been in Missouri at court time. The case against Vaughan was dismissed. Charles F. Hyde who succeeded Clifford as District Attorney decided to continue the case against Whitley. The case came before the circuit court three years later on June 9, 1891, but Judge James A. Fee had it dismissed for lack of sufficient evidence. The records were signed by Clerk W.M. Pierce, who later became governor of Oregon.[16]

Hank's good friend and co-prankster, Doc Whitley disappeared from the scene shortly after this. It was learned that he died in Congress, Arizona, as a result of gun shot wounds. The circumstances surrounding his death were never clear but according to his family, who thought he was suffering from an incurable disease, the wounds were self inflicted.[17]

As Hank's role in the Stewart case came to an end, he was shortly again in the limelight, appearing as an important though minor character in an intriguing case of blackmail in Pendleton. The details of this case were sensationally exposed in the *East Oregonian* between February 7 and 17, 1888. It seems Dr. A.W. Burg while treating the sexually transmitted disease of a rather notorious lady about town had been given the name of the local businessman from whom she had contracted it. This man was the bank manager who had earlier attempted to collect a loan from Dr. Burg. The doctor thought he could use his inside information to change the banker's mind about the need to foreclose on the loan.

As Dr. Burg negotiated with the banker, rumors got started which made it appear he was attempting to extort money from the banker. More parties got involved and the situation became so overwhelming, Dr. Burg decided to leave town. He hired Hank Vaughan to take him into hiding in the Puget Sound area.

Hank willingly did his part to escort the doctor into obscurity until he found Burg hadn't brought enough money to pay for the trip. At that point, Vaughan turned about and returned Burg to the authorities, collecting the reward that had been offered for the doctor's arrest. Dr. Burg was tried, convicted and sentenced to prison for blackmail.

After his recovery from the Falwell shooting, Vaughan began carrying two guns. Before his injury, he had only carried one gun as an ordinary practice and that gun was rather common in appearance. As he became more affluent and had more occasion for the need of a gun he invested in one of a special cut—this was a silver mounted six shooter valued at $300. Several times when he was in Pendleton, he would pawn the gun with Joe Basler who ran the hotel side of the Villard House. He would ask for $100 worth of gold in twenties and Basler always loaned it to him.[18]

There were times when Hank found himself in trouble when even two guns couldn't help. This anecdote was told by Lee Drake:

> On one occasion when Hank emerged from the Bureau Saloon about half illuminated, he ran into a crowd standing on the sidewalk outside who were merely talking among themselves. Hank, feeling his oats, told them to start dancing and backed up his order with both guns blazing into the wood sidewalk at their feet. There was one big six foot, 200 pounder in the crowd by the name of Geo. Clark who took exception to this demand. Clark was a member of the railroad bridge gang and the home run clouter of the Pendleton professional baseball team and did not know the meaning of the word fear. Clark walked right up to Hank, grabbed his gun and with one mighty swing knocked Hank Vaughn down. Then handing the gun to one of the bystanders, he casually walked away.

> Hank's friends, aghast at this unheard of occurrence immediately helped Hank to his feet and asked him why he did not shoot the man. To this Hank replied, "There's a real man. There's not enough of that kind around these parts. It'd be a shame to kill him and let the chicken livers stay. . . ."[19]

Hank was usually a good judge of who he could intimidate and who he couldn't. When he felt a real man had the better of him, he was wise enough to back down.

REFERENCES

Chapter 15

1. Lockley, *op. cit.* 284.
2. The Oregon *Journal*, January 12, 1928.
3. Umatilla County Circuit Court, The State of Oregon vs. Hank Vaughn and S.P. Whitley, Criminal Case No. 26-416.
4. Umatilla County Circuit Court, Case No. 26-416, *op. cit.*
5. Personal interview, Ted Stickler, August 12, 1967, Starkey Cow Camp, Union County. Ted Stickler's father witnessed a similar performance with Hank as master of ceremony in a saloon at Pilot Rock in about 1885.
6. Bailey, *op. cit.*, 157.
7. Parsons and Shiach, *op. cit.*, 258.
8. *Ibid.*
9. Personal interview, Areta Barrett, Athena, Oregon, May 10, 1973.
10. Pioneer Ladies Club, *op. cit.*, 251.
11. Umatilla County Circuit Court, Criminal Case No. 26-416, *op. cit.*
12. *Ibid.*
13. Taylor, *op. cit.*
14. Lockley, *op. cit.*, 284-5.
15. Oregon *Journal*, August 13, 1923.
16. Umatilla County Circuit Court, Criminal Case No. 26-416, *op. cit.*
17. Mrs. Thelma Martin, Personal Correspondence, Bremerton, Washington, February 9, 1973.
18. *East Oregonian*, April 10, 1948.
19. Drake, *op. cit.*

XVI.

TWO VENTURES TERMINATE
(1887-1888)

The enforced inactivity brought on by the need to let his shooting arm heal gave Hank time to plan his strategy to continue his presence on the reservation. Ever since Hank and Martha became established on the reservation, there had been attempts to evict them:

> The Indian agent notified them to get off the reservation. Hank sent him word that he couldn't put them off. Before the agent's posse got started Hank had left for Washington, D.C. He came back with a permit from the Indian department, and so made his boast good. He was a man of great ability as well as courage.[1]

That Hank actually made that trip to Washington, D.C., is questionable, but he and Martha did continue to occupy this choice piece of land on the reservation, and the controversy of why continued to plague the Indian agent. An article in the *East Oregonian*, October 13, 1885, entitled "The Agent's Dilemma," outlined the current status of trespassers.

The whites were keenly interested in getting the reservation Indians to agree to a bill which Congress had recently passed. This bill was introduced by Senator James H. Slater, who twenty years ago had defended Hank at his trial in Auburn. The Slater Bill would reduce the reservation by about one fourth. The remaining land in the reservation would be parcelled out to individual Indians living on the reservation. The Indians were holding out on ratifying the Slater Bill. One of their reasons for refusing to sign was that they considered some of those who lived on the reservation not qualified to receive allotments.

Agent F.J. Sommerville reported the Indians' complaints to the Commissioner of Indian Affairs, Department of Interior. He explained their resentment against the presence of half breeds and whites married to Indian women. He particularly described Thomas Page and Hank Vaughan and their considerable land developments. The instructions he received back from Washington seemed to authorize the removal of "certain half-breeds and whites" with the exception of those who could clearly establish their membership in the tribe.

Opponents to this purge deferred to the 30-year-old Treaty of 1855 which made no distinction between mixed or full bloods. Agent Sommerville was uncertain of his position in regards to Vaughan and Page, but some stockmen with questionable rights were removed from the reservation. It can be assumed Hank was receiving expert legal advice allowing him to prolong his title to the allotments.

Hank had not waited for the legality of his position to be determined. Since 1883 he and Martha had proceeded resolutely to developing their reservation land. That strategy worked then but events were changing. Hank, always a keen observer of the mood of the times, interpreted correctly that he would likely be forced off the reservation. Certainly they would never qualify to hold the two thousand plus acres he and Martha were described as having in the summer of 1884. A correspondent from Adams wrote to the Weston *Leader*, on August 6, focusing on the change in attitude toward those whites who had developed reservation land:

> To the Editor of the *Leader:*
>
> The E.O. is exercising itself over the reservation question in its usual "original" style of fairness. A year or two ago it was lavish in its praise of the enterprising parties it is now so ready to abuse, men who were so peculiarly situated that they were enabled to enter that fertile waste and make it "bloom like the rose:" men who came, not as paupers but some of them—aye, many of them—with wealth which they have lavished unsparingly. Vaughn has spent nearly $20,000 opening his farm which is a model for any country; Page nearly as much; McLeferre and Woodward have built residences and made farms at the cost of many thousands of dollars. Not they alone have been benefitted by this outlay of time, toil and money; everybody in this part of the country has been either directly or indirectly benefitted. But the benefit that has accrued to this side of Wild Horse is not a tithe to the great and lasting benefit the Indians themselves have received by the instructive example of these white men. Many of them have been induced to open farms on quite an extensive scale. This course will, if adhered to and encouraged, prove the greatest civilizing process yet discovered, especially when such men as now occupy this reserve can be induced to occupy the reservations.

About this time, Vaughan filed for and shortly purchased a preemption claim east of Pilot Rock on the south fork of McKay Creek not far from his horse corral at the mouth of the North Fork. This would provide him an alternative to the holding ground he was utilizing on the reservation. For a number of years, he and Pat Kine, a bartender at the Villard House who was his partner in this venture, would run cattle in this area, using the Blue Mountains toward Starkey for summer range. The deeded land was 160 acres. Apart from some fencing and corrals, it contained little in the way of improvements.

Before there was a clear decision to evict Vaughan from the reservation, an opportunity arose which enabled Hank and Martha to divest themselves of the ranch and the impressive improvements they had made. In October of 1886, they sold their ranch on the reservation in a complicated deal that was to receive the attention of the Commissioner of Indian Affairs in Washington, D.C., before it was settled.[2] The new owners were Augustus Russie and Tom Page, Jr., son of Vaughan's former neighbor who was considered along with Vaughan of having no right to reservation land.

The sale included a dwelling house with four rooms, two granaries, a smoke house, a lodging house, a buggy shed and storage room and also fencing to enclose one thousand acres of cultivated land then held and cultivated by said Mrs. A.H. Robie and H.C. Vaughan, her agent, and all the right and title and interest of said Mrs. A.H. Robie and H.C. Vaughan in all the lands enclosed in said fence.

Hank must have felt there was still some profit to be derived from farming this tract as, on December 22, 1886, he leased back a portion of the land to use during the year 1887. Very shortly it became apparent there were problems regarding the outcome and intention of this lease. Page claimed in a statement signed March 7, 1887:

> I intended to lease only the 600 acres of unplowed land—400 acres of this farm was already in crop by Russie and myself and it was not my intention or meaning to lease only my half of the 600 acres of unplowed land. The agreement calls for all of said farm—this was not my intention.

The ambiguity of the statement written and signed by Page only served to confuse the issue but, perhaps, showed the talents that would later make him a good lawyer. Page also admitted in this statement that he and Russie had purchased the property of Vaughan and Robie for a reason. Their object in buying the land was "to get rid of Vaughan and make him leave the reservation. The Indians did not want Vaughan on this Reservation as he is a bad man." One wonders why, if Page felt that way in October, he later leased land back to Vaughan giving him a reason to remain on the reservation.

In the spring, Vaughan plowed a portion of the six hundred acres and planted grain on it. The unplowed section produced a bumper crop from the grain heads that had shattered and dropped seed following the preceding year's harvest. Russie wanted a division of the "volunteer" crop of wheat and barley. Russie and Vaughan agreed that Russie should have about eighty acres of the barley and about thirty acres of the wheat growing on the southern portion of the land. However, Russie claimed Hank went in and cut all the grain even from those portions allotted to Russie. He believed the barley to be worth $1,600. When Agent Coffey heard Russie's complaint, he confiscated the barley until the rightful owner could be determined. The barley was left stacked and curing in the field.

Agent Coffey, in his report to Commissioner J.D.C. Atkins, on July 13, 1887, understood that Page had sold, not leased, his portion of land back to Mrs. Robie and that the land division in this new agreement was what was not satisfactory to Russie. Mrs. Robie then agreed to a new division of the plowed lands and both parties seemed satisfied. Again, according to Coffey, Russie came back to the agent with the complaint that Mrs. Robie had harvested barley that belonged to him. From what Agent Coffey could determine this barley was not even grown on land embraced in the original agreement.

Coffey was impressed with the fact that Martha in an effort to establish "good feelings and harmony" had offered Russie one hundred sacks of the grain—no matter how much it may yield after being threshed. He was disgusted that lawyers had been hired by both parties "although there was not the slightest occasion for the expense." He requested that the Commissioner send his decision in the case at once as the grain might be damaged "as it stands now—if left too long—the expenses attendant on this measure will have to be paid for—out of the grain—or the loser—as may be agreed upon."

U.S. Commissioner Fred Page-Tustin had discussed this matter with Agent Coffey. Page-Tustin was also a member of the firm hired by Hank and Martha to represent them in the dispute. A representative of that firm showed up at the July 12 hearing with a chattel mortgage on two hundred acres of spring wheat located on the Vaughan ranch. This, according to Russie, defeated him. Russie further stated he could not receive a fair hearing because he had not been on good terms with Mr. Coffey for some time past. This was said to be a result of Russie requesting the service of the ex-Indian Commissioner Pearson to mediate the grain issue instead of Coffey since Pearson had been in on the original deal between Page-Russie-Robie-Vaughan.

Both parties eventually agreed to submit their facts to an arbitration as suggested by the Office of Indian Affairs on September 28, 1887. The arbiters decided on October 13, 1887, that Mrs. Robie should hold the barley but she should pay for the cost of arbitration. Supposedly the matter ended there, but Russie certainly had reason to question the objectivity of one of the arbiters, R.W. Donica, one of Hank's old friends.

Hank continued to raise grain on leased reservation land, but since 1886, he and Martha lived in their home in Centerville. From this location, he caroused with his friend Doc Whitley, became embroiled in the Dick Stewart case, and was shot by Falwell. By the spring of 1888, apparently completely recovered from his injuries, Hank was back to his normal behavior. The *East Oregonian*, of March 2, 1888, reported:

> Tuesday evening Hank Vaughn was indulging in some of his accustomed amusement at Centerville. He and another man came to blows and finally drew guns on each other, but no one was hurt.

While Hank's more legitimate operations received the most publicity during this period he was still the mastermind behind much of the horse thefts in this region.

An appalling event involving horse thieves was about to become public. In the winter of 1886-87, a small group of horse thieves taking advantage of the remoteness of the Wallowa Valley in northeastern Oregon were involved in a deadly attack on a group of unarmed Chinese miners. This unfortunate episode was to have international repercussions.

It is thought the decision to kill the Chinese was made on the spot and without any advanced planning. The names of the accused murderers, with the exception of one minor but important participant, were never associates of Hank. Mass murder was not anything Hank had been involved in nor was he ever known to shoot other than in self defence . . . or in jest.

This band of horse thieves almost got away without being connected to the crime because of the isolated nature of the area where they carried out their cowardly deed. Only for the past ten years had this area been considered available for white settlement. Until that time, this secluded area was off limits to white settlement as it was the homeland of a small group of Nez Perce Indians.

These Indians led an idyllic existence in this Land-of-Winding-Water. Their winters were spent in the warm canyon country along the Imnaha and Snake Rivers. In the spring they moved their camps up higher into the Chesnimnus area where they gathered roots and fished for steelhead. As summer progressed, they migrated onto the relatively flat valley land drained by the Wallowa River. Occasionally they ventured out east to hunt buffalo in Blackfoot country or south to raid horses from the Snake Indians.

In the fall they caught and preserved the sockeye salmon or redfish that were so numerous the streams appeared to run red. The Indian horses and cattle stayed sleek feeding on belly-high bunchgrass. By late fall the Wallowa band returned to the wooded Chesnimnus to hunt deer and elk and, as cold weather set in, descended again to the shelter of the deep canyons of the Snake River tributaries.

This routine was not affected by white encroachment until the Tulley boys and a few other stockmen brought several hundred cattle over from Forest Cove to winter them on the breaks of the Imnaha in 1872.[3] From then on settlers began trickling into the main valley. When the Indian agents at Lapwai tried to persuade the Indians to move onto the Nez Perce Reservation in accordance with the treaty of 1855, they retorted that they had not signed their home over to the whites and never would.[4]

Choosing to ignore the wishes of the Indians and the pleading of Joseph, their chief, the settlers continued coming. Pressure from those who coveted the Indian land finally forced Joseph and his people toward the Lapwai Reservation across the Snake in Idaho Territory. The tragedy of this move, which developed into a war, made a legend of Joseph as he and his band outmaneuvered the army on a 1,600 mile flight toward a refuge in Canada.

The whites, after a brief moment of fear that the Indians might be back, set about in earnest to homestead the Wallowa Valley. This was one of the three major valleys in the corner of northeastern Oregon which in 1862 were lumped into one political subdivision called Baker County. Two years later in 1864, the two more northerly valleys were split off from Baker County to become Union County. It would be twenty-three years before there was a further division of the two adjoining valleys and Wallowa County came into its own political right.

Development was slow not because there wasn't great natural potential but because access into the valley was so difficult. The valley was cleaved on the east by Hell's Canyon of the Snake River, the deepest canyon in the North American continent. The south and west of the valley was barricaded by the 10,000-foot peaks of the Wallowa Mountains and the northern side of the valley was protected by the canyon of the Grande Ronde River.

Stockmen looking for rich grazing land for their animals were not the only types attracted to this region. Its isolated nature appealed to those who preferred to live on the fringe of society, according to T.T. Geer, one-time governor of Oregon:

> . . . The fact is, at the beginning of its settlement it was thought that only those went to Wallowa who cared little for the advantages of civilization and were willing to bid farewell to their friends, if they had any, and embrace the life of a hermit.[5]

Although law and order had more or less arrived in Umatilla and parts of Union County, it was slower to come in the Wallowa country which was notorious for horse thieves. Those like Hank Vaughan who needed to shift their stolen products to market undetected were frequent travelers along the difficult but secluded trails through the Wallowa area.

The first trail Hank's group used was from the Horse Ranch on the Minam River to Blue's Den where the prairie met the timber north of Wallowa Valley. From there, the trails dropped down along the Imnaha River then up over Lone Pine Saddle to the crossing of the Snake River near Dug Bar. This was the same route taken by Chief Joseph when he led his band of Nez Perce out of their homeland during the spring of 1877. From the river, it was only a day's ride to reach the Lapwai Reservation.

A short-term holding ground for stolen horses was located high in Dug Basin, several miles up the creek from the river crossing. From this vantage point, a watch could be kept over activity on the river. A band of horse thieves, operating from here during the winter of 1886-1887, observed some Chinese miners working gold out of the potholes and eddies along the Snake. A flurry of excitement amongst the Chinese alerted the outlaws to the possibility that a new deposit of gold had been found. They decided to kill the Chinese and take their gold.

Later testimony said the scheme of the thieves was not only to take this gold but to rid the area of the Chinese who might observe and report suspicious activities on the river. The thieves carried out their plans quickly. While four men acted as lookouts at strategic spots along the river, three men hid in the rock outcroppings above the miners' camp and gunned down thirty-one unarmed Chinese without mercy. The assailants crept down the hill to finish off their slaughter pushing bodies into the Snake River and ransacking the camp for gold.[6]

After the conspirators regrouped at their hideout in Dug Basin, they hurriedly collected their horses and moved to their next rendezvous. Apparently no one else heard or saw any of this atrocity. Not until spring when the bodies of the Chinese began appearing downstream near Lewiston, Idaho Territory, was there any indication of the tragedy. Although an investigation was begun immediately no clues were found to point to the killers.

It was not until later that summer following the apprehension of a band of horses thieves that some solid leads developed in the case. The seemingly unrelated event was first mentioned in an article in the Union *Scout*, of August 6, 1887, which reported:

> Fred Nodine returned from Wallowa last Tuesday. He says that about three hundred of his horses are missing. As he had a pretty good idea what became of them, further developments may be expected.

The further developments were that Sheriff R.H. Coshow, Wallowa County's first sheriff,[7] caught four men in the act of changing brands on Nodine's horses and arrested them. Having no jail facilities, he locked the prisoners up in Joseph as best he could. One by one the prisoners were released on bail until the leader of the gang and one young boy were all that remained. Those who were released secreted a pistol in the outhouse and passed the word to their leader. At the appointed hour, the older prisoner asked Deputy Sheriff Humphreys to escort him to the toilet. The next thing the deputy knew he was looking a loaded .44 in the eye and he was obliged to let the prisoner go. The escapee made his way to a saddle horse staked out by his friends and disappeared. The one remaining prisoner, a school boy, then secretly implicated the rest of the gang in the Chinese massacre. He was released with the promise he would testify if the gang could be brought to trial.[8]

The above information comes from the memoirs of an early day resident. When it is fitted into court records of that period, it is possible to reconstruct what happened. John T. Canfield and others were arrested by Sheriff Coshow while changing the brands on stolen horses. Canfield was charged with "altering and defacing a brand upon an animal which was the property of another." He was then released on bail.

When the Wallowa County Circuit Court met for the first time on August 22, 1887, the Grand Jury returned a true bill in the Canfield case. At the time of the hearing, "Neither Canfield nor his bondsman appeared and the bond was declared forfeited."[9] While Canfield was free on bail, he helped plan and carry out the escape of Bruce Evans and Omar LaRue. They left the school boy, Frank Vaughan, in jail feeling certain he would not talk about the Chinese killings for fear of retribution from the gang which was now running free.

But Frank Vaughan decided to confide in the authorities and described the gang's brutal treatment of the Chinese miners. He was released pending investigation of his charges. As a result of his cooperation plus the tenacious and skillful work of J.K. Vincent, who was hired by a Chinese company to investigate the massacre, indictments were issued for the murders.

The murder indictments were issued March 1888 against six men: Hiram Maynard, Carl Hezikiah Hughs, Robert McMillan, J.T. Canfield, Bruce Evans, and C. Omar LaRue. The men suspected of doing the actual slaying were Evans, LaRue and Canfield. Although a heavily armed Canfield was observed in the area that summer, neither he nor Evans nor LaRue were apprehended and brought to trial.

The *Scout* of July 20, 1888, under the heading "Imnaha Jottings" said:

> J.T. Canfield was seen a few days ago on the Imnaha. He was armed with two six shooters and a Winchester rifle. He was one of the Chinese murderers. He is one of the horse thieves that Nodine caught and had bound over to the Grand Jury and who afterward went and shot some of the Nodine horses. It is believed that those Chinese murders will come clear although they do not deny doing the deed.

The three accomplices in the murder of the Chinese, Maynard, Hughs, and McMillan, were put on trial August 28, 1888. They pled not guilty to the murder charges. On September 1, they were found not guilty and released. Frank Vaughan appeared before the Grand Jury at this time and because of his testimony he was also released and his bond ties discharged from all and any further liability in the case.

Frank Vaughan who turned state's evidence was one of the younger members of the gang. His job that terrible morning was to remain in Dug Basin camp, prepare the meal, and head off any unexpected visitors. Frank was son of Enoch Vaughan who settled on a ranch on the Imnaha River along with his sister and brother-in-law, Mr. and Mrs. Joseph Smith.[10] The Smiths had moved here in 1883 shortly after their son, Joe Jr., committed suicide in Walla Walla.

Living with the Smiths was Harry Vaughan who for a short time was also a suspect in the Chinese murders. Nothing was ever established to implicated him in the crime.[11] Harry had been running horses with Hank Vaughan in the Spokane Falls area where, as described in his biography, he led a "frontier life" for three years before settling on unsurveyed lands near Wallowa valley in 1883.[12]

How much Hank was directly involved with this horse stealing operation through Wallowa County is not known. But there is little doubt he had much to do with the way it was organized and shared in the profits if any were made. At the time of the massacre of the Chinese miners, Hank was recovering from the wounds inflicted by Falwell and about to appear in court to answer Dick Stewart's charge of assault. He also was deeply involved in the struggle to maintain his favored position on the reservation. It was unlikely he could have spared the time to be moving stock across the back routes through the Wallowa country.

Hank's name was never attached to this crime or directly connected with this particular bunch of horse thieves. There is no question but that he was well informed of how and when the group operated through this area. He may have been one of the first to receive word that some Chinese had been shot along the Snake River. He could have heard these rumors from his relatives, the McCarty's, when he contacted them in March of 1887.

The indication he visited them on the Powder River near Baker City at that time only became evident because attempts were made to have him pay for the purchases he had charged during the visit. The evidence of this trip surfaced in obscure ways—the case filed against Hank by the jeweler, St. Louis in Baker City, and the news item that some of Hank's horses were being sold to cover a debt to the Ladd estate. Much more can be said about this early 1887 visit to Baker County, but for the sake of brevity the whole story will be told later.

In Hank's visits and business dealing with the McCarty's over the past few years he had kept informed as to the whereabouts of his two sons and their mother. He must have decided that now that he had a proper home and reputation he should press for a visit from his boys.

In July 1888, Alexander, or "Jake" as he was known, came to spend the summer. Jake who was thirteen quite impressed Hank whose fatherly impulses became so strong he decided to try and gain custody of both boys. Hank figured to accomplish this through initiating divorce proceedings against their mother, Lois.

One can imagine the apprehension his lawyers felt as Hank unfolded his scheme. But such cases provide the bread and butter for legal counsels so Fred Page-Tustin did not hesitate long. Hank's next step was to find a lawyer to appear for Lois. He first approached Lawyer William Parsons in Pendleton. Parsons later described the meeting:

> He noticed that I did not wear a finger ring, and said he would like to present me with one. I told him that I did not desire one, that I seldom wore one and that I preferred he should not give me one. He insisted, said that he had given several other persons rings and watch chain charms. His persistence finally overcame my

> reluctance as he seemed to think it was unkind to him to refuse. To avoid that appearance I allowed him to buy and give me a ring, the price being seven dollars.[13]

Several weeks later, Hank asked Parsons to appear for Lois and make a statement for her in the divorce case which was soon to be started. On August 22, 1888, Hank signed a complaint against Lois, charging her with deserting him without cause. He asked for a divorce and custody of their two boys. The summons for Lois to appear was filed on August 28.

Parsons appeared for Lois on September 13 and waived the service of summons. On the following day he made a statement for Lois that she denied that her desertion was without any or just cause or provocation and alleged that Hank's conduct fully justified such desertion. She further stated Hank was not a proper person to have care of the minor children and that she should be allowed to continue their care and custody.

Page-Tustin and Parsons, acting for their clients, then signed an agreement that Lois should have the boys in the event of the divorce being granted. Charles H. Carter was appointed to referee the case. Hank repeated that Lois had deserted him while they lived in Boise City in 1878. This was new information as before it was only known that they lived together in Elko, Nevada. He felt he had "treated her well, very nicely," he thought, while they lived together.

Giving testimony to Carter next was Joseph R. "Pap" Hunsaker who claimed that he was a general laborer and had known Lois to reside in Douglas and Josephine Counties, Oregon, since 1879. He knew that she had taken good care of the two boys and sent ". . . them to school, right along." He also affirmed that Lois had no intention at all to again cohabit with Hank.

Carter then retired to consider the facts. His findings led him to report back to the circuit court that the bonds of matrimony should be dissolved, that Lois Vaughan should have custody of the two boys, and that H.C. Vaughan should be taxed for the costs and disbursements of this suit.

This was not the outcome Hank had expected at all. The divorce was not granted immediately because Parsons ran into difficulty when he attempted to collect his fees from Hank. He claimed his fee was $50 and that to this time he had only been paid $5. Hank filed back that he had not only paid $5 but given a $9 ring to Parsons and that in his opinion that was sufficient compensation for all the services Parsons had rendered.

Parsons refused to budge from his claim that Vaughan must pay the remaining attorney fees. Hank must have given in, as on October 8, Circuit Judge James A. Fee granted the divorce. Later Parsons was to return part of his fee to Hank. From that time forward Hank displayed the greatest admiration for the lawyer, showing that he appreciated those who could fearlessly meet him on his own ground.[14]

The divorce gave Lois continued custody of Jake and Albert or "Bert" as he was known, but from now on Hank did have contact with his boys. Bert later married the granddaughter of Hank's friend, Doc Whitley, after becoming acquainted with her during visits to Hank in Centerville.[15]

Information not brought out during the divorce trial was that Lois and Pap Hunsaker had been married for several years. They eventually moved to a ranch on the Snake River below the Oxbow in Baker County. Their family consisted of their boy, Little Joe; Pap's boy, William; and her boys, Bert and Jake (fig. 34).

Once Hank's marriage to his first wife, Lois, was legally ended, he and Martha went to Walla Walla and were married. George T. Thompson, who officiated, signed along with L.R. Hawley as witnesses to the event.[16]

Earlier in 1888 when Hank had several unsettling affairs on his mind—investigations going on in Wallowa County which involved his relatives and hampered the horse trading business, the coming divorce proceedings against his first wife and the matter of the horses purchased from Ladd—a news item seemed to indicate he was finding a way to relax and get away from his problems. The *East Oregonian*, of April 17, 1888, describes Hank in the unusual role of sportsman:

> Centerville *Home Press:* Hank Vaughn and party were over on the Umatilla fishing Sunday and met with quite good success in catching the speckled, numbering 253 mountain trout and half dozen salmon [steelhead]. Pretty good day for suckers, hey?

(Courtesy Laura Belle Rogers)

FIGURE 34—Joseph R. "Pap" Hunsaker (left) married Lois McCarty Vaughan after she and Hank separated. This picture taken in the late 1890's shows Pap and Lois' son, Joseph L. Hunsaker, next right, followed by William Hunsaker, Pap's son by a former marriage; Jacob "Jake" Alexander Vaughan and Albert Irving "Bert" Vaughan, children of Lois and Henry C. Vaughan.

It is difficult to picture Hank Vaughan fishing, therefore it is suspected that this item and others like it were coded messages to out-of-town associates. It is known that Vaughan and the McCarty clan had some kind of an elaborate "bush" telegraph system that kept the syndicate informed of clandestine affairs. One suggested method was to advertise for the return of strayed horses of particular descriptions or brands. This type of advertisement frequently appeared in early-day newspapers.

One more significant event was to take place this hectic year of 1888. Noah Brown tells how Hank came face to face with Charlie Long, the man with whom he shared a vivid memory:

> In 1888 when in the hotel business in Ellensburg I saw Hank Vaughn and Charlie Long together. . . . This was the first time they had met since their shooting scrape, from which both escaped full of lead. Long and a friend were sitting at a four-chair table in the dining room of my hotel, the Oriental, when Hank and a citizen of the town came in. They placed their hats on a rack and as Hank turned around to take a seat his eyes met those of Long. I was in a position to look Long squarely in the face, but could only see a part side view of Vaughn's. I surely thought there would be something doing and presume felt more frightened than either of them. After looking at each other for the better part of a minute Long greeted Vaughn and at the same time Hank advanced and extended his hand, which was met by Long's. The four sat at the same table and ate a good square meal. An uninterested observer would have thought them to be friends. . . . They were in town several days and, while they did not act as cronies, the past to an extent appeared to have been as only an episode of the past.[17]

The man who told this story later added more details naming the other men at the table. Vaughan's companion, a citizen of the town, was Dave Correll, a professional gambler and gunman; Long's friend was James "Popcorn Jimmy" Muldowdey, a faro dealer. Long was said to have been in town several days after which he returned to his ranch in the Conconully area of Washington Territory.

Vaughan was reported to have been in Ellensburg for only a few hours. During that time he saw Ben E. Snipes, banker and cattle king of The Dalles. This may have been the first and only direct contact between Vaughan and Snipes, but they were later indirectly involved in a matter which eventually ruined Snipes financially.

REFERENCES

Chapter 16

1. The Portland *Telegram*, July 30, 1926.
2. Office of Indian Affairs, Letters Received, 1887-1907, No. 13337-E, National Archives, Washington, D.C.
3. Western Historical Publishing Company. *An Illustrated History of Union and Wallowa Counties*. Spokane: W.H. Lever Company, 1902, 531.
4. Josephy, *op. cit.*, 445-510.

5. Geer, T.T. *Fifty Years in Oregon*, New York: Neal Publishing Co., 1912. 278.

6. Tucker, Gerald J. "Massacre for Gold." *Old West*, Fall 1967, 26-8, 48.

7. Hawley, H. William. Historian, Oregon State Sheriffs' Association. Lake Oswego, Oregon. Personal correspondence, February 4, 1973.

8. *Chief Joseph Herald*, January 8, 1959. *Wallowa County Chieftain*, February 16, 1995.

9. Wallowa County Circuit Court Docket A.

10. Western Historical Publishing Company, *op. cit.*, 568, 641.

11. Tucker, Gerald J. Correspondence, Imnaha, Oregon, April 14, 1974.

12. Western Historical Publishing Company, *op. cit.*, 641.

13. Umatilla County Circuit Court, Divorce Case No. 191-31, H.C. Vaughan vs. Lois Vaughan.

14. Parsons and Sciach, *op. cit.*, 256.

15. Thelma Martin, Correspondence, February 9, 1973, *op. cit.*

16. Walla Walla Valley Genealogical Society, compilers. *Early Marriages of Walla Walla County, 1862 through 1899, Washington Territory and State*. Walla Walla: Walla Walla Valley Genealogical Society, 1976.

17. Wenatchee *Daily World*, December 19, 1922.

XVII.

RESERVATION TROUBLES
(1889-1890)

The bullet wounds and broken bones which Hank's body had endured over the years were causing him constant pain. In the year 1889, Hank wrote to his sister, Amanda, in Boise City (fig. 35), telling her he was suffering and that he would soon be seeking some relief through medical help from doctors in the East.

At Home May 18th, 1889

Dear Sister,

As I have not heard from you for a long time I thought I would write. We are all well but me I am in a bad fix. I suffer all the time. I have got in 2700 acres of grain and the finest grain you ever saw and as soon as I harvest I will start East to Doctor. I wish I could see you all. Why don't you send Etta down and let her stay a month with me. I could fix her up nicely if you will let her come down. I will come up and pay you a visit. I just got a letter from father. They are all well. Alleck is a going to get married. So goodby. Tell Joe to write to his uncle Hank.

Is he a going to school? If not send him. Write soon and all the news.

With love to you all, your brother

H.C. Vaughan[1]

Hank says he has not heard from his sister "for a long time." It is quite certain that Hank has had news of Amanda's family, however. Her husband, William Butler, who had been involved in several court cases with Hank, died in 1888, possibly just after being released from prison. No information has been found concerning his death. Amanda then married Joseph Hahn.

One of the qualities which made Hank a favorite with his family was his personal interest in even the youngest of his relatives. This was evidenced in the letter to his sister as he invites his niece and nephew to come visit him. This willingness to socialize and share time with people also brought him a host of friends outside the family circle.

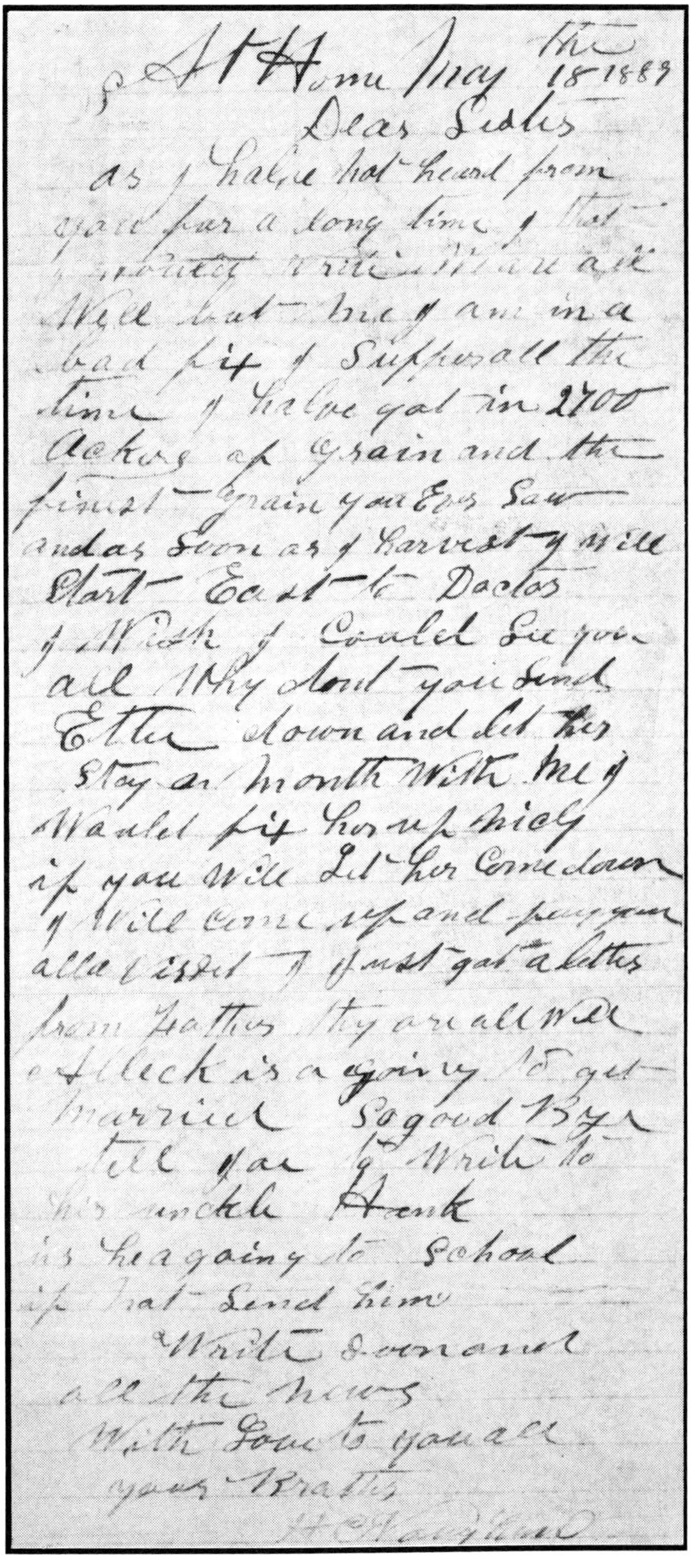

(Courtesy Courtney DelCurto)

FIGURE 35—Hank wrote this letter to his sister, Amanda Butler who was living near Star City, Idaho Territory, with her children, Henrietta and Joe. After Amanda's husband, William Butler, died in 1888 she married Joseph Hahn.

At Home May the 18 1889
Dear Sister
as I halve not heard from
you fur a long time I thot
I woulld write we are all
well but me I am in a
bad fix I suffer all the
time I halve got in 2700
ackers of grain and the
finest grain you Ever saw
and as soon as I harvest I will
start East to Doctor
I wish I could see you
all Why dont you send
Ettie down and let her
stay a month with me I
would fix her up nicly
if you will let her come down
I will come up and pay you
all a visit I just got a letter
from Father they are all well
Aleck is a going to get
married So good Bye
tell Joe to write to
his unckle Hank
is he a going to school
if not send him
Write soon and
all the news
With Love to you all
your Brother
H C Vaughan

Because of his interest in other people, it is certain that Hank had observed with amused curiosity the recent antics of his old friend and former neighbor, Tom Page, Sr. Comfortably married for over thirty years Tom had started chasing another woman. Mrs. Page took exception to his philandering and sued him for divorce.

The case received wide publicity because of the prominence of the parties involved. Francis Ellen Page was, according to an earlier report in the Portland *Oregonian* of February 12, 1882, ". . . among Walla Walla's most refined and estimable ladies." Mrs. Page was the daughter of Joseph Gale, one of the provisional governors of the Oregon Territory. Her mother was a descendant of the Walla Walla chieftain, Peo Peo Mox Mox. Thomas P. Page had long figured prominently in the history of eastern Oregon.

The *East Oregonian* broke the story of the breakup of their marriage on January 26, 1889. According to the newspaper, the Pages, formerly residents of Walla Walla, had developed a fine ranch adjacent to that of Henry Vaughan. Lately Tom had been seeing a lot of an old acquaintance of his. It was claimed that ". . . Page had formed the design of eloping to Arizona with . . . Grace Darling, who is described as being a very handsome and fascinating woman." Grace and Tom, it was alleged, were living in one house on the ranch while Mrs. Page and her children were living in another. When the humiliated Mrs. Page moved out, Tom sued for divorce claiming desertion. Mrs. Page in a countersuit claimed Page had been abusive and had threatened her and the children.

The *East Oregonian* observed that thousands of pages of testimony were being taken from witnesses in the case and that attorney fees had reached $5,000. Tom had sold eighty head of horses, the grain off the reservation, and liquidated real estate assets throughout the Inland Empire to help cover his lawyer's fees. The divorce was granted in June 1889.

What the paper didn't report was that Grace Darling was also a daughter of Joseph Gale and that she and Ellen Page were sisters of sorts. It was not relevant to the divorce as there was no mention of Hank being involved in the case, but Grace Darling had figured prominently earlier in Hank's life. Not many people knew that she was one of the bondpersons who posted bail to keep him out of jail back in 1864 when he had his first serious encounter with the law. This was in the heyday of mining activity in Canyon City. Why Grace was there at that time is not known, but the fact that she was and that she was in a position to post bail for a youngster in trouble shows that even at that early date, Grace knew her way around.

After the divorce Tom and Grace moved off the ranch into Centerville. Their behavior which preceded the divorce surely caused lots of tongues to wag. Such impropriety was becoming less acceptable to the citizens of this community who were beginning to take their civic responsibilities seriously. For example, the Centerville *Home Press*, of March 22, 1889, reported a violation of the new city ordinance against shooting a gun in the city. It also reported that the city council had passed an ordinance providing for a city jail and levied a two mill tax to pay for the construction of the jail.

At the same time, the local residents were going through the procedure of incorporating their village. After more than eleven years of settlement, Centerville was to be incorporated as a town but it first had to select a new name to avoid confusion with Centerville in Washington County. A name was suggested by school headmaster, D.W. Jarvis, in honor of a Grecian goddess. Since the city council and most of the eight hundred citizens liked this characterization, Centerville became Athena.[2]

Little more was reported about Vaughan during the remainder of 1889 which turned out to be one of the driest years on record. Stockmen were short of summer range and fires raged throughout the forested lands until the fall rains fell.

It is possible that after harvest Hank did go East to doctor. He and Martha began spending part of their winters visiting some of the more famous hot springs around the country, trying to get some relief from the aches and pains Hank's abused body was suffering. But by the next spring, Hank was reported back in town celebrating the grand opening of a new bar. The *East Oregonian*, of March 17, 1890, reported the following:

> The opening of a new saloon in Athena was the occasion of considerable gaiety in which many participated. The reservation element was out in full force and took a prominent part in the celebration. Several fights and an occasional pistol shot were among the specialties introduced.
>
> The old city marshal had relinquished his office and the new marshal had not yet been installed, so neither felt inclined to take an active part in the program. At last, however, it became absolutely necessary to escort Big Hank the most obstreperous of the revellers to the city jail.

That night Hank was introduced to the amenities provided by the new Athena city jail. A month later he would wish there were also hospital facilities in Athena. The March 21, 1890, *East Oregonian* said:

> H.C. Vaughan, arrived in Pendleton last evening, and immediately hunted up a physician to dress a wounded hand which he received while branding an unruly bull. The member is badly mutilated.

From this story, it appeared that Hank still took an active part in the annual spring roundup activities and unfortunately had been injured in an accident while working with his cattle.

Hank had accumulated a sizeable cattle herd and, like his neighbors, he often allowed them to stray off his property onto the reservation. There were periodic attempts by the Indian Agent to have these trespass cattle rounded up and removed from the reservation. The *East Oregonian* of June 11, 1889, reported on this activity:

> The band of cattle fired from the reservation and rounded up on the Tutuwillow has been separated and driven to the four points of the compass. Okanogan, Snake river, Grande Ronde, John Day, Starkey Prairie and other ranges have each served as a refuge for a portion of the stock. Now the reservation is but a grazing place for Indian ponies.

The Indian Agent may have believed this, but the fact remained the reservation continued to be a holding ground for stock of questionable ownership. Complaints were frequently registered against this trespass. A letter from a bona fide Indian,

Lucretia Simpson, to the Commissioner of Indian Affairs dated April 21, 1890, said in part, "I have also told him (Agent Coffey) that Jerry St. Dennis, Thomas Page, Hank Vaughan and a man named Pierce were running large bands of cattle on the reservation having no rights."[3]

While there was criticism of Hank's cattle being on the Umatilla Reservation, there would be no question that Martha had the right to keep cattle on the Nez Perce Reservation. According to the *Idaho Free Press*, June 3, 1890, she had excess to sell:

> Grant Benedict and Tom Aram started Monday with 150 head of beef steers for the Spokane market. Mrs. Robie and Grant have 120 head in the bunch and Arams the other 30.

This proved to be a bad health year for Hank. It wasn't long before he had another accident on the reservation. This time it involved horses and was much more serious than the torn up hand he suffered in the branding accident. The *East Oregonian* of May 9, 1890, reported, "Hank Vaughan was brought into town in the Agency wagon late this afternoon." It said his right leg was broken in two places.

More details were given in the May 11, 1890, *Sunday Oregonian* under "Notes From Pendleton:"

> From Mr. H.L. Boomer, editor of the Pendleton *Tribune*, who is now in the city, the following items have been obtained:
>
> Hank Vaughn was very severely injured by a horse Friday, while attending a "roundup" on Umatilla reservation. One leg was broken—a complete fracture—one rib fracture, and internal injuries probably sustained. He is in the Hotel Pendleton and is suffering intense agony. Physicians are doubtful of his recovery.
>
> The Indians were engaged in catching a number of horses that were confined in a corral. Vaughn was standing in the corral, watching the Indians. While not noticing a large horse ran over him, knocking him down and kicking him.

On the 14th the *East Oregonian* said Hank was slowly recovering but that his suffering was severe. Though laid up, Vaughan continued to run parts of his operation through the help of a partner. The *East Oregonian* of May 26, 1890, said, "Van Shull, who is looking out for Hank Vaughan's band of 325 cattle at his ranch on McKay Creek, at the foot of Wood Hollow, was down today."

The Pendleton paper continued to report on Hank's recovery. As the following reports show, his recuperation from having broken his leg in two places was probably without incident. Since it would be several years before plaster of paris casts were used to immobilize broken bones, the doctors would have strapped Hank's leg in splints. Wrapping his chest would be all the care given his broken rib. Six weeks would be the minimum time before the doctors would let him be up and leave for home.

> (June 7) Hank Vaughan is slowly improving. He will probably be able to leave his room in three weeks. Hank is a tough one and hard to put down, but this last experience has been the worst yet.

As the next item shows, Hank was as usual preparing himself for the time he would be allowed out of bed.

> (June 16) Hank Vaughan will be able to navigate on crutches in a few days. He has had a pair manufactured ready for use.

Just six weeks and a few days after his leg was broken, Hank was able to go home.

> (June 21) Mr. and Mrs. Hank C. Vaughan left this morning for Athena. Hank is now able to get about on crutches.

It was unusual for Vaughan to recuperate in the Hotel Pendleton after his accident. His preference in hotels for the past ten years had been the Villard House. An announcement in the *East Oregonian*, April 1, that Rose and Parsons had taken over the Villard House perhaps explained this switch. Parsons was the lawyer who represented Lois McCarty Vaughan in the divorce case two years earlier. In those proceedings Parsons had infuriated Vaughan by his legal maneuvering to extract fees due him. Vaughan must not have found conditions to his liking in the hotel after Parsons acquired it for he began staying in either the Hotel Pendleton or in the Transfer House near the depot on the south end of Main Street.

An incident that happened later may have been related to this recent accident of Hank's on the Umatilla Reservation:

> Hank rode into this small saloon town one sunny afternoon and everything was boresomely quiet. He looked up and down the street to see what might be done to break the monotony and uphold his reputation. Nothing was in sight but the usual loafers leaning against the corner saloon, and two Umatilla Indians riding slouched on their ponies like bags of meal. Hank took heart, and riding quickly beside one of the Indians leaped from his horse to the flanks of the pony of the Indian. He then wrapped his arms around the Siwash, prodded his heels into the ribs of the horse and gave a war whoop. When the horse started to buck, Hank wrenched the Indian off and fell on top of him in the street. He then jumped up, a revolver in each hand, shot in the air and yelled. The poor Indian nearly scared to death, ran one way and his horse the other.[4]

Though the story is undoubtedly true, there is a question as to the motives reported for Hank's attack on this Indian. Rather than creating the disturbance to break the monotony and maintain his reputation, it is more likely that Hank had a score to settle with that particular Indian and he used this act to retaliate for some misdeed he felt the Indian had done to him. Perhaps it was this Indian who had been on the horse which ran over Hank in the corral. Vaughan had too much invested on the reservation to indiscriminately pick on Indians and harass them in this manner just to uphold a reputation.

That Hank was respected for his honest dealings with the Umatilla Indians was indicated in this article from the Adams *Times* of April 2, describing Hank officiating at a reservation horse racing event:

Furthermore, for the benefit of the sporting public, allow me to state that the 999th Annual Meeting of the Umatilla Reservation Speed Association will commence on May 1st, at the old fair grounds. Everybody is invited to come and take part with us. The managers of this association have made special arrangements to furnish every accommodation necessary for those desiring to train on the ground—all that will be needful for them to do will be to bring their stake ropes and hobbles. Entries for all races shall positively be made at least fifteen minutes before they are to come off. Positively no deviations from this rule. Aged horses will be required to carry 180 pounds; 3 years and under, 150 pounds. No saddles are to be used in any race. Distance of races from four to ten miles. The directors will reserve the right to declare all races off—in case said directors should happen to put up their blankets on the wrong horse. This is a slight departure from their old rules, but it is a trick we have learned from our white brothers at Pendleton, who conduct the races at the E.O.A.A. track, and will be strictly adhered to at our coming races. The services of Hank Vaughan have been obtained to officiate as pool seller on the occasion. He is not the best talker in the world, but is better than a raw hand. The management will spare no time or expense to make this meeting one of the grandest ever held west of the Rocky Mountains.

Vaughan's name was conspicuous in its absence from eastern Oregon newspaper accounts in the summer and fall of 1890. His activities would have been restricted somewhat by the fact he needed to let his broken leg mend. Either he avoided Pendleton or the editors were ignoring him, for his name did not appear in the local press during that period. However, the Seattle *Post Intelligence*, August 30, 1890, recorded one event that occurred during this period. It revealed that Hank was still involved in farming and still attempting to take the law into his own hands. But it would appear he had met his match when he came up against his old adversary, John Hailey, Jr. The article follows:

NOTORIOUS HANK VAUGHN COWED
WALLA WALLA, Aug. 29

The notorious Hank Vaughn, of Umatilla county, Oregon, came near meeting his death Wednesday evening from a Walla Walla man, who has just returned from Athena. Your correspondent gleaned the following facts: Mr. Vaughn had mortgaged a quantity of grain which he was hauling to his place on the reservation. The mortgagee objected, but received no satisfaction, Hank proceeding with his work. Deputy Sheriff John Hailey, of Pendleton, and Constable James Stamper, of Athena, were summoned and demanded, as officers of the law, that Mr. Vaughn return the grain, which was refused. Vaughn was met by them on the street in Athena Wednesday, and when Constable Stamper read the order of the court to him he whipped out a revolver, quick as a flash, and covered the officer. Deputy Sheriff Hailey was too quick for Hank, and in the instant, when the latter pulled his pistol the deputy also levelled a cocked revolver at Hank's head, ordering him to drop his gun and surrender or he would be a dead man. This was complied with, after which it is said that Hank walked to one of his horses and leaning his head against the animal wept like a child. When asked the cause of his grief, he said: "It's all right, but I do hate to give up." Had he not, immediately obeyed the officer's order there is no doubt he would have received his death wound, as his record as a dangerous man is well known, and no chances would have been taken.

John Hailey Sr., the father of the deputy sheriff who got the drop on Hank in the above episode, had been threatened by Hank many years earlier for not being quick enough in releasing money due Martha from the Robie estate of which Hailey was executor. Now it seemed John Hailey Jr. was in charge of keeping Hank under control. If the report of the August episode is correct, Hank was indeed slowing down. He had been out drawn by Hailey. Considering the several injuries he had sustained that year, there is little wonder that he was slower on the draw. It was fortunate for Hank that the person outdrawing him was a law officer and not a rival gunman. Although the story must have exaggerated when it described Hank weeping like a child at having to give up, one now is alerted that Hank's ability as a gun slinger is on the decline.

However, there was no sign that Vaughan had put up his guns. Under the influence of strong drink, he continue to create excitement in the neighboring town of Weston. George Bird, an early day visitor there, remembered:

> I was with my father, in my brother-in-law's saloon in Weston, Oregon, when Hank cleaned out the place. I was pitched unceremoniously behind the bar, from where I could not see much but from where I heard a-plenty.[5]

Hank did not confine himself to eastern Oregon in 1890. That fall he had been to Portland, perhaps for medical attention for his broken leg. While there he had a run in with one of the local toughs and the repercussions of this fight followed him back to Pendleton. The *East Oregonian*, gave a series of reports about the antics of a man named McDonald who claimed Hank had shot his brother:

> (November 14) It is said that a tall broad-shouldered Irishman, with a cartridge belt and six-shooter made the rounds in Pendleton last night in search of Hank Vaughan, swearing he would shoot him on sight. He remarked that he was a brother of "White-haired Ross," which, however, left his identity in doubt.
>
> (November 15) The big Irishman, who had been hunting for Hank Vaughan in Pendleton with a revolver and a look of wild-eyed determination, ran across Tom Johnson last evening, and was taken in tow by that officer. He went peaceably to quod.

McDonald was not a very stable character as within a week he was in trouble with the law for selling drinks to Indians. He escaped back to Portland but was returned to Pendleton to face charges. The *East Oregonian*, November 27, reported:

> A man named McDonald, the same tall, rawboned son of the Emerald Isles who was seeking the blood of Hank Vaughan in Pendleton a few days since, claiming to be a brother of "White-haired Ross" who he said Vaughan had shot, was brought up from Portland this morning by a deputy United States marshal. He was taken below by Deputy U.S. Marshal Watrus for selling liquor to Indians, and was sentenced to one day in the Umatilla County jail by Judge Deady. Hence a return trip with the prisoner was necessary.

There was grumbling in the press about wasting tax payer's money escorting prisoners hither and yon. As to whether Vaughan shot White-haired Ross while in Portland, neither court records nor newspaper reports have been found to verify the charge. If McDonald came to Pendleton looking for a fight with Vaughan to avenge his brother's shooting, Hank may very well have sought protection from the law and sworn out a warrant for his arrest.

During this period, Hank appears in the role of rancher, taking part in harvests, roundups and horse races. His painful accidents have been reported in detail. His run ins with the law have stemmed from over exuberant celebrations. Despite the fact that the newspapers report his activities as the expected behavior of a typical roughneck of the wild western scene, not everyone forgot that Hank Vaughan was still very much a renegade.

About this time several milestones in municipal development were reached in Pendleton. In 1883, the Western Union Telegraph Office was opened. The town was receiving piped water by 1887. Oil and kerosene lights were starting to be replaced by electric lights in 1887, and in 1889 a phone system began serving patrons in Pendleton.[6]

These were all visible signs the area was emerging from frontier days but the problem of horse thieves continued to be a major concern of the local ranchers especially in the area around the reservation. On October 1, 1890, the *East Oregonian* after expressing irritation at the number and frequency of such occurrences, attempted to explain the success of the thieves:

> It is believed that the horse thieves are perfectly organized, that they have a chief who plans and conducts operations, and that the band is composed of several reservation toughs who have disappeared, and some men from Wallowa valley.

The reporter was describing the very type of operation Hank was thought to mastermind. No names were mentioned in the article, but it was likely he was a prime suspect. The allusion to men in Wallowa Valley makes one wonder if there was suspicion that Tom McCarty who had established a ranch in that area during the early 1890s might be a part of Hank's band.

Tom's ranch was in the hills above Chesnimnus Creek about thirty miles northeast of Enterprise. It is reported he ranched and ran a few horses but, for the most part, he used this as a hideout between bank holdups and as a cache for stolen horses and cattle. Tom also maintained a winter headquarters and hideout on the Oregon side of the Snake River in what remains some of the most remote and rugged territory in the west.

About fifty miles south up river from the latter place through what is known today as Hell's Canyon of the Snake River were the holdings of other McCartys and their relatives. Since the early 1880s, their winter range had included what became the mining boom town of Copperfield at the mouth of Pine Creek. They laid claim to all of the pasture on the Oxbow of the Snake. Few people were aware of the close ties that connected Hank with these families who were discretely gaining a reputation for robbing banks and trains. It might have been surmised by those in the know that Hank was involved with Tom McCarty trading horses, but evidence would soon come to light that Hank was also planning a bank robbery.

REFERENCES

Chapter 17

1. DelCurto, Mrs. Courtney, Sunnyside, Washington. Personal correspondence, January 15, 1973. This letter belongs to Mrs. DelCurto. Mrs. Sophia Riede, granddaughter of Amanda to whom the letter was addressed, established the relationships. Etta (Henrietta) and Joe were the children of Amanda and William Butler. Alleck refers to Hank's brother, Francis Marion, now twenty-four years old.
2. McArthur, Lewis A. *Oregon Geographic Names*. Portland: Binfords & Mort, Publishers, 1952, 23. According to the *East Oregonian*, August 24, 1878. the settlement was once known as Richards' Station. It also went by the name of Yellow Dog or Squawtown according to Searcy, *op. cit.*, 102.
3. Contreras, Ina, Chula Vista, California. Personal correspondence. July 26, 1973. *Also* Office of Indian Affairs, Letters Received, 1887-1907, No. 13337-E. National Archives, Washington, D.C.
4. The Dalles *Chronicle*, September 30, October 6, 1926.
5. *Spokesman Review*, May 7, 1911.
6. Mcnab, Gordon. *A Century of News and People in the East Oregonian 1875-1975*. Pendleton: East Oregonian Publishing Co., 1975.

XVIII.

BIG-TIME OPERATIONS

(1891-1892)

The abuse Hank had inflicted on his body over the years was catching up with him. In the past five years, he had suffered a crushed hand, a broken leg and a gunshot wound to his chest and elbow. Besides broken bones, he was still carrying at least one lead bullet—the one from Charlie Long's revolver which was lodged near his spine. When the cold Eastern Oregon winter weather started his body aching, he had in previous years spent time in the Willamette Valley where the weather was more moderate. While there he was known to cause a bit of excitement in the Portland gambling saloons.

That he considered travelling in search of medical help was known from the letter he wrote his sister saying that after harvest in 1889 he was going "East" to doctor. No record was found that he took the trip in 1889, but the papers do tell of an extended trip he and Martha started early in 1891. They went south to California and then clear across the United States.

One purpose of the trip appeared to be to try some health spas. Soaking in their mineral waters might give him some relief from pain. Knowing how Hank operated, he had probably talked to enough people to have a very good idea of distances and locations of hot springs. Most of their trip would be by passenger train as this was in the heyday of rail travel. The *East Oregonian*, January 5, 1891, carried this brief note on the Vaughan's sojourn:

> Mr. and Mrs. H.C. Vaughan leave Friday for California, and will go east from San Francisco, visiting New York, Chicago, and other cities. They will stop for a time at the Paso del Robles springs in California and the Arkansas hot springs, where Hank wishes to try a health restorative. They will return in April next.

Shortly before leaving on this extended trip, Martha was able to conclude a business deal that had been dragging on for over twelve years. She had been in correspondence with the Indian Services as recently as May 13, 1889, attempting to receive reimbursement for horses lost through Indian hostility during the Paiute-Bannock Indian war of 1878.[1]

When her first husband, the late A.H. Robie, sold the Diamond Ranch in southeastern Oregon to Peter French in 1877, the Robie cattle, but not the horses, were sold in the deal. During the summer of 1878 when Robie returned to collect his horses, the Bannock Indians swept across the ranch taking his horses in an affray that eventually cost Robie his life. The *Morning Oregonian* of July 19, 1878, had reported that Glen and French lost five hundred head of horses to the Indians. Presumably some of these horses belonged to Robie.

A special agent of the Indian Service was recently in Pendleton settling claims resulting from this activity. The *East Oregonian*, of December 28, 1890, printed a list of those who qualified for payments and Martha Vaughan "ne Robie" was one of them. The settlement which Martha accepted may have helped finance that winter's trip.

The reason Hank would return from their trip by April was that it appeared the long awaited auction of reservation land would take place that month. Several years earlier, the Umatilla tribe had ratified the congressional act drawn up by James H. Slater to allot lands to individual Indians.

This allotment left a calculated surplus of land which was to be put up for auction to the highest bidder. It took six years of negotiations, land surveys and resurveys, before the auction could be scheduled. In anticipation of the auction, many prospective buyers preempted reservation land. As usual Hank was in a position to take advantage of the situation when it finally occurred. On February 11, 1889, the *East Oregonian* noted that "plowing on the reservation has started." An estimated one hundred squatters had moved onto the reservation.

A later recount of this situation which could have resulted in an act of martial law explained:

> This sort of thing, if permitted, would have caused great confusion when the land was auctioned, so the squatters were ordered out. A detachment of 42 men of the Second Cavalry, under Capt. S.W. Swigert, stationed at Walla Walla, was sent and "will move white settlers off the reservation unless they go peaceably," the E.O. said.
>
> It was April 1, 1891, before the public sale of the land actually started. The auction was held at the agency and a special train was run there from Pendleton each day through April. The first section put up for sale was 12 miles south of Pendleton: Section 1. Township 1 South, Range 32 East. There was no immediate bid on the first quarter—the limit was 160 acres—but the second [sic] went to P. Olson for $189, the second went to Charles Cunningham for $1,006 and the third to H.C. Vaughan for $936.[2]

A humorous incident is related about Hank's participation in this auction of reservation land. Ed Horton, his good friend and keeper of the Bureau Saloon in Pendleton, wanted to buy a certain piece of land that was among some lots being sold, but he had only limited funds for that purpose. He put it up to Hank to create some kind of distraction once the price got to that amount:

> When the price went beyond Horton's limit and his rival out bid him, he signalled to Hank and the fusillade was on. Frightened men scurried through the door and back to town. Others could not get out and sought shelter beneath the tables and behind the furniture. Hank was careful with his fire, but they were unaware of his discrimination. Horton's rival stood not upon the order of his going but speeded

back to town. The auctioneer then accepted Horton's bid. Later, Horton is said to have rolled over and over on his bedroom floor in an ecstasy of mirth.[3]

Lee Drake related the climax of this affair, saying: ". . . when Hank started shooting they all rushed to cover and as the stranger darted under the porch of one of the buildings the auctioneer cried 'sold' to the last bidder."[4]

Hank was busy that spring and summer setting up the ranch property. In acquiring cattle to stock his new acreage he became involved with the southeastern Oregon stock outfit of Miller and Lux. The story was told by Umatilla County Deputy Jim Johnson:

> Johnnie Austin and Guthrie [sic] stole 400 head of cattle belonging to the Miller and Lux outfit in Harney County and drove them to the yards at Pendleton. I saw the cattle and saw they had the "Wrench" brand of Miller and Lux and I knew that the cattle company offered a reward of $1000 for anyone stealing their cattle. Austin and Guthrie had gone up town. I took charge of the stock when Hank Vaughn came riding around the corner. He told me he had a bill of sale for the 400 head. I replied that was okay, and kept walking up to him. When I reached him I shoved my gun at him, yanked the revolver from the holster at his saddle and at the point of his own gun marched him to jail.
>
> We sent 106 cattle thieves to jail, but we couldn't get Hank on that charge.[5]

Deputy Johnson was undoubtedly a brave and honest lawman but it would have taken considerable courage and agility for a man on foot to remove a gun from Vaughan, especially if Hank was mounted at the time. A slightly different version of the arrest has also been told:

> It is related that in the eighties Johnson noticed some cattle in Pendleton with the Lux and Miller brand. Knowing that these men, owners of the biggest ranch holdings in the world, did not shop through Pendleton, Johnson suspected the cattle of being stolen and was told that they were the property of "Hank" Vaughn. He soon located the rustlers.
>
> While the desperado's back was turned, Johnson took his gun and knife from Vaughn's saddle bags and when Vaughn looked around, Johnson had him covered. Although the cattle were found to have been stolen, Vaughn got free as usual.[6]

The case did come to trial but Hank wasn't named in it. According to the proceedings of the district court reported in the *East Oregonian*, of November 6, 1891, John Austin and J.S. Guthridge had seven indictments against them. They were arrested and jailed in early September on a complaint of J.H. Keables, acting as an agent for Miller and Lux. Initially Austin and Guthridge pleaded not guilty and were counselled by Capt. N.B. Humphrey, Calvin Hyde, of Baker City, and E.B. McCormack. Before the trial they pleaded guilty to larceny and the other six charges were dropped. Guthridge being an accomplice received a light sentence but Austin received three years in the penitentiary.

The reward Johnson and Keables were after was no longer in force but Keables did receive a Miller and Lux check for $100 for information leading to the arrest and conviction of the thieves. The *East Oregonian*, of November 20, 1891, said

Keables immediately paid $90 of the money on an obligation. This was probably to Johnson for handling the arrest.

Although Deputy Johnson recalled he arrested Hank, there was no evidence brought out at the trial to link him to the theft and he apparently did not testify at the Austin trial.

Hank had appeared in another case before that same session of the circuit court in November 1891. Back in 1889, Harry Grastly and Charles Miller were caught on the reservation with horses stolen from Jesse Drumheller. Grastly escaped but Miller was tried and sentenced to the penitentiary in Salem. After two years had elapsed Grastly made the mistake of returning to Umatilla County where he was again arrested and charged with his part in the theft. He was indicted by the circuit court on November 3, 1891, on two counts.

Although Grastly could have hoped the evidence against him was old and forgotten, new and damaging evidence was introduced during this trial which had not come out in Miller's trial two years previously. It was at this point Hank got involved. The *East Oregonian*, of November 13, 1891, said:

> . . . Part of this new evidence was from Hank Vaughn, who testified that he met the accused parties and was told by Miller that they had the Drumheller horses "cached" up on the Walla Walla River and would drive them away. Grastly was seen on the reservation by two Indians who appeared as witnesses.

Miller was brought up from Salem by Deputy Sheriff Hailey. Although he testified Grastly had nothing to do with the theft, after several ballots, the jury concluded Grastly was also guilty. He was sentenced to two and one half years in the penitentiary. When it was one horse thief's word against another, the jury believed Hank Vaughan.

The business of the circuit court was not the only newsworthy note about Hank that winter. There was quite a stir of excitement when D.F. Smyer displayed a huge gold nugget he picked up while working his Susanville, Oregon, placer mine. Smyer deposited it for credit at Alexander and Hexter's as trading currency for supplies of which he bought several hundred dollar's worth. The *East Oregonian*, of November 6, 1891, described it as follows:

> It averages about four inches in length, two and a half inches in width and one quarter of an inch in thickness, and is about as pretty a piece of gold as a man ever feasted his eyes upon.

A follow up on November 13 announced that Hank was now the new owner of the nugget:

> The big nugget brought in by D.F. Smyer from Susanville has been purchased by H.C. Vaughn for a "specimen" and he is now displaying it to his friends. Hank paid $356.61 for his pretty piece of gold. He is undecided whether to wear it as a watch charm or a scarf pin.

Just before Christmas in 1891, Vaughan was feeling in a particularly law abiding mood. The *East Oregonian*, of December 25, said that three men were creating a disturbance in the Blue Front Saloon Monday afternoon and were arrested by Marshal Morgan with ". . . Hank Vaughan assisting."

The Vaughans stayed in eastern Oregon over Christmas, but they were so favorably impressed with the success of their trip south the previous year that they soon repeated the pleasurable undertaking. They may have left in January to leave the cold winter weather behind and visit warmer areas in California. The *East Oregonian*, of March 20, 1892, reported on their return:

> Mr. and Mrs. H.C. Vaughan have returned from an extended visit to California. Hank's health was greatly improved by a stay at Paso del Robles, and he feels like a new man.

This was at least the second winter Hank had gone south. Since it was not his nature to lie around in hot springs quietly nursing old wounds, chances are he produced some excitement in California, but if he did these stories have never surfaced. Apparently his name and fame weren't evident when he traveled. Even in Eastern Oregon during the six months following the Vaughan's return from California, there was little news of Hank's activity. But that was the period of calm before the storm broke in Roslyn, a mining town in central Washington.

Customers going into the Ben E. Snipes & Company bank came face to face with armed robbers ransacking the establishment. The bandits were going quickly about their separate tasks. One directed the patrons to line up against the wall, another kept the bank attendants under control while the third emptied the contents of the safe. The thieves eased out of the bank with their loot and mounted their waiting ponies. A few shots were fired into the air in the best wild west tradition and the bandits made their getaway.

The sound of gunshot immediately roused the law and a posse was organized and dispatched abruptly in the direction of the fleeing gunmen. Out in the mountains, several miles north of town, a woman waited nervously with a group of fresh horses. But even the best made plans sometimes go awry. The woman's husband was with the outlaws and only through her loyalty to him was she taking part in this escapade. The robbers, over exuberant in their successful haul and get away, had missed the fork in the trail leading to the rendezvous. As they milled around the mountain searching for the route, several times they almost came face to face with the posse.

Just before dark they found their way to the meeting spot. On the backs of fresh horses, they were able to flee the scene and evade the posse. What appeared to the law as a well executed robbery and escape was not without more bungles, but for several months it was a clean getaway.

Although Pendleton was 175 miles southeast of Rosyln, from the beginning Hank Vaughan was a prime suspect in the case. The reason for this was that a couple of his associates and an unusually marked horse were observed in the vicinity of the crime both before and after the event. Robert Ballou summarized two sightings that pointed toward Hank:

> Ben Snipes, main owner of the bank, an early day cattleman had many friends in all walks of life. A few days after the robbery took place, a professional gambler went to him privately and told him he had seen a half-breed Indian, whom he knew to be a first lieutenant of Hank Vaughn, eastern Oregon outlaw, looking around in Roslyn a couple of days before the robbery occurred.
>
> Soon after the gambler had provided the information for a possibility, a stockman friend of Ben Snipes told him that a few days after the bank robbery he had met two mounted strangers, riding southward on an isolated foothill road, toward the Columbia River. One of the riders had an off color horse with outstanding markings. The observer said he recognized a brand on the animal as that of a well known eastern Oregon stockman, noted as a horse breeder. He also said he recognized the rider as a man from eastern Oregon that he had known since childhood, but in spite of this, the rider did not extend any greeting.[7]

The law's first reaction upon receiving these tips was to start undercover operations in the Pendleton area to collect solid evidence against Vaughan. Hank's reaction was to take to the hills on an old fashioned Indian hunt. The newspaper report of this sporting event had the suspicious appearance of containing a message hidden between the lines. It was similar in style to the item in April 1888 which said Hank and party ". . . met with quite good success in catching the speckled, numbering 253 mountain trout and half dozen salmon." Ten days after the Rosyln bank robbery the *East Oregonian*, of October 4, 1892, gave full details of Hank's supposed hunting trip:

> Charles Downey, H.C. Vaughan and John McBean, the interpreter, have planned an old time "Indian Hunt."
>
> They started this morning in company with five Indian braves for Black Mountain, lying between Meacham creek and Grand Ronde River, the most inaccessible part of the Blues, where there is reported to be big game in abundance. They will have seven saddle horses, eight pack animals for transportation of camping outfit and provisions, and plenty of guns and ammunition.
>
> It is the intent to be absent two days or two weeks. Mr. Downey has brought in a small arsenal from the ranch, a Winchester and two double barreled shotguns. The latter are of the Johnson and Bonehill pattern, No. 8 and No. 10, respectively. He expects to make a record in bear and deer shooting.

This announcement could have been a tipoff to an accomplice as to where to meet Hank. It certainly contained a thinly veiled warning that Hank was well armed and guarded.

The undercover operators must have turned up some information but, according to Ballou:

> Just what they found out never became a matter of public record, but in late November, about two months after the robbery, three men were arrested in the vicinity of Pendleton and Heppner, on warrants issued in Kittitas county charging them with complicity in the Roslyn robbery.[8]

The three men were Cal Hale, Tom Kinzey and George Zachary. These men were well known and liked in their home towns and had no previous criminal records. While they waited in the Ellensburg jail, the authorities tried to get more evidence against Hank. Ballou's account tells how Hank took care of the evidence:

> . . . After the men arrested were locked up at Ellensburg, Kittitas county authorities attempted to get possession of the saddle horse seen by the stockman. This was said to have been foiled by Hank Vaughan in person, after Hank had consulted with a wily old eastern Oregon pioneer lawyer. It was said that officers searched a big pasture on the ranch of the horse's owner a few hours after Hank had been there with a Winchester and disposed of the evidence. It was also said that Hank even took the precaution to skin the horse, so as to remove the tell tale brand. The story further related that when officers came to the ranch on a certain creek and told the owner what they were after he waved his arm toward the big pasture and said truthfully, "He was out there when I saw him last."[9]

The three Oregonians went on trial in February 1893, but through lack of what was considered sufficient evidence, Kinsey and Zachary were released. Only Hale was declared guilty. The unfortunate Hale served several months before more evidence came forth that earned him a pardon and his freedom.

Hale's conviction was not popular. Rumors circulated that there was much more to this case than had yet come to light. One such story was spread by Vaughan himself:

> Enroute to his home in Oregon, one of defendant Hale's witnesses stopped in Walla Walla and saw Hank Vaughn who told him that he knew who the men were that robbed the Roslyn bank and that Cal Hale had nothing to do with it. As they stood at the bar in a saloon there, Hank said "a part of the money taken from the Roslyn bank was drank up right over this bar." He further said that one of the robbers told him he had a notion to go to Ellensburg and confess the whole thing as he could not bear to see an innocent man go to the penitentiary.[10]

This tender-hearted robber did not step forward, but it was not long before a letter postmarked Salt Lake City, Utah Territory, was received by one of the attorneys with the Washington Bankers Association. The letter contained information that incriminated Hank's former inlaws, the McCarty brothers. The testimony which reopened the case was given by Sarah Jane Morgan, sister-in-law of one of the men who actually took part in the bank robbery.

Accounts of the events that followed have been included in several books, all with varying details.[11] Briefly, George McCarty and Ras Lewis (alias "Matt" Warner, born Erasmus Christiansen) were captured without much difficulty and brought to the Ellensburg jail where they awaited trial.

An attempt was made to arrest Bill and Tom McCarty at their Swamp Ranch on the Powder River in Baker County, but this action backfired when the sheriff fell into a trap which permitted both men to escape. They hastily left Oregon. Along their route to Colorado, Bill McCarty wrote a letter to the Baker paper to give his family the excuses they needed to explain his departure. The letter was reprinted in the *East Oregonian*, April 27, 1893, about a month before the case against George and Ras Lewis came to trial.

WRITES A LETTER
Bill McCarty explains Why He Skipped From Baker County

The Baker City *Democrat* received Wednesday evening a letter from W.A. McCarty, one of the alleged Roslyn bank robbers. The letter was not dated, but the envelope bears the Pocatello postmark, the date not being discernable. It reads:

Editors *Democrat:* As I left your part of the country very suddenly and mysteriously I deem it proper to let my friends in Baker county hear from me, provided you will be so kind as to give space to this letter in the columns of your valuable paper. I want all of my friends to know that neither my brother or I had anything to do with the Roslyn bank robbery or any other robbery. We have always made our money honestly and if any man wants to look up our pedigree he can easily do so in Colorado, Montana, Nevada or Utah, as we have lived in all of those places and can get references from either of the places mentioned.

My reasons for leaving Baker county as I did are as follows: I sold a certain horse to my brother Tom while in the Big Bend country [Ephrata, Washington 7U Ranch], and he says the animal was stolen from him and was used by one of the Roslyn bank robbers. He advised me to pull out until the thing was cleared up; I knew well enough that if I went to law it would take all I had to prove my innocence. I have had something to do with the law in Oregon and Washington and don't want any more of it, and rather than take the last cent from my wife and children and see them suffer, I determine to face the strong arm of the law and bid them do their worst. However, I assure you that I will vindicate myself in due time.

Tom and I have had a very pleasant trip thus far. We have met with plenty of friends everywhere we have been, who offer us every assistance within their power.

I hope to see you all in the near future. If I had any way of sending you a mess of speckled beauties that abound in the pure mountain streams of these parts I would be pleased to do so. I am badly disfigured but still in the ring. Promising to write you again at some future time, I remain, yours, as ever.

W.A. McCarty

Bill wrote to give his neighbors an explanation for his sudden departure. Since he was under suspicion of being a bank robber, he gave his version of the horse sold, stolen and used in the Roslyn robbery. This horse was undoubtedly the one Hank skinned. Bill also claimed to have had something to do with the law in both Oregon and Washington, but he didn't elaborate. Not until Matt Warner's book came out in 1938 was Bill's name connected with bank robberies in Summerville and Enterprise, Oregon. Bill had been on the verge of being an outlaw when he was younger. After marrying Lettie Maxwell he had tried to stay clean. Upon moving to Oregon he took up cattle ranching but he slipped back into his old ways and undertook some illegal sidelines with his brother, Tom.

This letter is full of hidden meaning. Bill's allusion to the "speckled beauties that abound in the pure mountain streams . . ." was too poetic to come from the pen of a fleeing robbery suspect so it must have been a coded message for someone in the gang.

His attempt to clear his family's name was ruined when he, his son, Fred, and his brother, Tom, attempted to rob the bank in Delta, Colorado. Both Bill and his boy, Fred, were shot and killed while leaving the scene of the crime. Tom escaped uninjured, disappearing into obscurity. He later returned to Wallowa County. In his later years, he had an urge to write the story of his life and his autobiography eventually found its way into print.[12]

Matt and George were jailed in Ellensburg. But as Matt claimed in his book, they received help from outside and were able to escape. They were soon recaptured and went through a short trial. Effective legal advice provided by Hank and money by Tom capitalized on the earlier conviction of Hale and threw much doubt on the charges.

After his release George McCarty with his loyal wife, Nellie, moved into the depths of the Snake River country around Homestead and dropped out of sight. Ras Lewis became Matt Warner and lived a life of respectability after the turn of the century.

Hank came out of the Roslyn affair without even having to appear in court, but some people continued to watch him for any suspicious activity that might link him to the Roslyn robbery. The following story was told of Hank's disregard for the seemingly inept detectives who handled the investigation:

> . . . The detective agency that brought about the first arrests in the case, clung to the theory that Hank Vaughn, famous eastern Oregon outlaw, was the master mind in the robbery. Hank was kept under surveillance for a long time after alleged members of his gang had been excused by the law. It was said that Hank was aware of this and once did a little clowning stunt for the benefit of what he termed tin star detectives.
>
> . . . Hank and some of his most intimate cronies were on a trip to Portland. They stopped at what was then the most popular hotel for upstate visitors. Soon after they arrived Hank noticed two men in the lobby, who had been pointed out to him at Pendleton as detectives who were trying to fasten the Roslyn bank robbery on him. He and his friends went to their rooms for a brief period. When they came downstairs again, they headed for the hotel barroom with Hank in the lead. The detectives had anticipated this and were already in the saloon. Hank's pockets were literally bulging with silver dollars. He went at once to the center of the drinking bar and commenced to throw handfuls of silver dollars at the bartender with disregard for the mirrors and glassware on the back bar. As he heaved the money about he said to the bartender, "There is big dollars from Roslyn for you, you white coated — of a —. Fill 'em for everybody and the stool pigeons."[13]

Vaughan was never directly connected to any other bank robberies, but he was accused of being the mastermind of several. Some of Hank's antics which brought him under suspicion in the early 1890s were described in a story in The Dalles *Chronicle:*

> Shortly after the robbery of a Canadian bank of a large amount of money, Hank staged an unusually bad spree in Pendleton. He rode up and down Main Street all afternoon, firing his revolvers and giving war whoops. The police did not shoot him but had been trying to get hold of him and send him out of town so that the streets would be safer for law abiding citizens. When they approached, however, Hank would spur his horse and yell . . . "Look at him boys. This is the horse that packed the swag from the Canadian bank."[14]

Once Hank was accused face to face of robbing one of the local stores. According to Areta Barrett, daughter of Charles A. Barrett, her father's mercantile store was robbed one night in 1890. Barrett, later a state senator, knew Hank very well and suspected him of being involved. The next time Barrett saw Hank after the safe cracking, he went directly to him and asked boldly if he had robbed his store. Hank said. "Hell, no, Mr. Barrett," and that was good enough for Barrett.[15]

It is doubtful if Hank profited financially from the Rosyln robbery. For one thing, the $40,000 payroll for the Roslyn mine which was what the robbers were after was not in the bank safe. It been taken to the company office earlier that day. If he did acquire some of the loot, he shortly found a use for some of it by helping Mollie Robie who had lost her home on McKay Creek. The *East Oregonian* of November 8, 1892, said "H.C. Vaughn is building a $1,200 cottage to replace the house at the Robie place on the reservation recently destroyed by fire."

In May of 1893, Vaughan sold his homestead on the south fork of McKay Creek to E.L. Smith for $1,000.[16] This may have been the source of the money he later threw around in the Portland saloon.

Although the general mood of the country was terribly depressed during the spring of 1893 because of diphtheria which had taken a tragic toll of lives and the general financial depression of Grover Cleveland's term which had wiped out many fortunes, Hank appeared to be a survivor. There was no warning that his days were numbered.

REFERENCES

Chapter 18

1. Office of Indian Affairs, Letters Received, 1887-1907, No. 13337-E, May 13, 1889, National Archives.
2. Macnab, *op. cit.*, 78.
3. *East Oregonian*, March 27, 1948.
4. Drake, *op. cit.*, 8.
5. Kelly, John, *op. cit.*, 13.
6. The Dalles *Chronicle*, July 22, 1926.
7. Ballou, *op. cit*, 61-62.
8. *Ibid.*
9. *Ibid.*
10. Mires, Austin. "The Great Roslyn Bank Robbery," ed. by Terry Abraham, *The Record* 32:27-72 (1972) Pullman: Washington State University, 72.
11. Kelly, Charles. *The Outlaw Trail.* New York: Bonanza Books, 1959. Warner, Matt, and Murray E. King. *Last of the Bandit Riders*, Caldwell: Caxton Printers, Ltd., 1940. Sheller, Roscoe. *Bandit to Lawman.* Yakima: Franklin Press, 1966.

12. McCarty, Thomas. "A History of Tom McCarty," Manuscript, Utah State Historical Society, Salt Lake City, 98. This manuscript was printed in 1986 by Rocky Mountain Press, Hamilton, Montana.
13. Ballou, *op. cit.*, 57-58.
14. The Dalles *Chronicle*, September 30, October 6, 1926.
15. Personal interview, Areta Barrett, Athena, Oregon, May 10, 1973.
16. Umatilla County Court Probate, Henry C. Vaughan, Probate Book F, 113-116, filed August 27, 1895, Pendleton. Stephen L. Morse, administrator of Vaughan's estate had known Hank since 1878 when Morse was a deputy United States marshal.

XIX.

THE FATEFUL ENDING

(1893)

One of Vaughan's final acts was to defend the honor of his country against the overbearing boasts of a pompous Englishman. This seems a rather odd role for Hank to play as he was not known for his understanding of international affairs, but the type of rhetoric he used was common during this period. In this rather one sided argument with a scholar, Hank, through the straight talk and action of a frontiersman, was thought to have handily subdued his adversary. The background and dialogue were found in the May 8, 1893, *East Oregonian:*

Fights for His Country

> Last Saturday night H.C. Vaughan made the acquaintance at a hotel of a traveling man who had the florid complexion, sturdy form and self-satisfied air of a typical Britisher. It is related that the latter very soon began boasting of his country's glory and greatness. He remarked that "our navy, you know, is much superior to the Hamarican navy, and the superiority of our harmy, sir, over your harmy, is not to be doubted."
>
> Hank became nettled, and said something patriotic to the effect that no war vessel flying the United States flag would ever yield to a Britisher or a ship or any other nation. Rather than do so it would sink within the briny deep with the stars and stripes still unfurled.
>
> The Englishman was undaunted. He replied with a remark about the "superiority of the British tars."
>
> "You're an Englishman, aren't you?"
>
> "I was a lieutenant in Her Majesty's service, sir."
>
> "Well, I'm an American, and you weigh forty-five pounds more than I do, but I'm going to knock you down. Put up your props."
>
> They rushed at each other, Hank's fist struck the Englishman's head, the latter's body struck the floor, and in this little affair Uncle Sam's champion was the victor.

Hank came to Pendleton later that month to have some shoes changed on his horse.[1] Seth "Boss" Richardson was tying his team at a hitching rack when Hank stopped nearby and dismounted. Vaughan led his horse as he walked with Boss to a blacksmith shop on the corner of Main and Alta Streets where he said he was having the horse rough shod in preparation to ride in the hills after cattle.

While waiting for the horse to be shod, Hank stepped into the Quelle Restaurant where he had lunch and visited with the owner, Mrs. Gus La Fontaine. As he paid his bill, he commented on some rings Mrs. La Fontaine was wearing. Later Hank collected his horse at the smith's, but before he headed out of town he must have made the rounds of his favorite saloons.

Clark Wood was standing in front of Charley Reese's cigar store on Main Street as Hank headed home. Wood figured Hank had been celebrating although he seemed to be riding straight in the saddle. He watched as Hank spurred his horse to a fast gallop, heading south along Main.[2] With disbelief, he saw Hank's horse lose its footing and fall sideways, pinning its rider beneath him. Some said recent rains had soaked the ground and as Vaughan's horse made the turn at the Bowman corner, it slipped and fell throwing Hank to the ground.[3] Others said the horse caught the calk of its new shoe in the railroad track which caused it to fall and throw its rider. Others recalled the horse shied violently at a pile of rocks near the depot, catapulting its rider into the rocks. The *East Oregonian*, May 31, 1893, carried this version of the accident:

HURT AGAIN
Hank Vaughan Has a Fearful Fall
From a Horse in Pendleton

Hank Vaughan was out celebrating to some extent Tuesday afternoon. Mounted on his handsome sorrel horse, and wearing chaparejos and an air of bravado, he rode up and down the streets to give a gratuitous "wild west" show for the benefit of the Pendleton public.

About 5:30 o'clock in the evening Hank put spurs to his steed and rode furiously down Main Street toward the depot, rider and horse being nearly concealed in a cloud of dust. At a cross street just beyond the depot, in an attempt to make a sudden turn, the horse stumbled and fell, hurling Hank over its head into the gravel, some of the spectators stated that the animal sprawled on top of its luckless rider.

The faithful horse arose and stood motionless, Hank's foot remained in the stirrup. He was picked up, bleeding, dirt-covered and insensible, his right eye nearly forced from its socket by striking the rocks, and it looked for a time that the man who appears to have nine lives and more too, so often has been hurt and wounded, had at last been the victim of his own recklessness.

He was taken to the Transfer House and Drs. [C.J.] Smith and [E.F.] Guymon (sic) summoned. From the effects of the hard fall he was for some time unconscious, and it was hard to say how his injuries would terminate. This morning, however, he rallied in good shape, and remarked, almost cheerfully: "It's pretty hard to kill me off." He is hurt somewhat about the chest, and may have a cracked rib. His eye is badly damaged and fearfully swollen; but it is thought that he will not lose it.

Hank's family were notified, and arrived on the evening train from Athena to attend him.

The *East Oregonian* continued to carry almost daily reports keeping its readers informed of Hank's failing condition:

> (June 5) Hank Vaughan is regarded by his physicians to be in pretty serious condition, and the outcome of his case is problematical. He began to grow worse Saturday, and part of the time since has been flighty and irrational, although able to sit up and walk about. The severe concussion to his head is the cause.
>
> (June 6) A slight improvement was noted today in Hank's condition.
>
> (June 8) Hank Vaughan took a turn for the worse, last evening, and his life seemed in danger. He worried through all night, however, and is better today. Physically he is strong, his mental condition does not improve.

Some of the family returned to the ranch bringing back some personal items to make his confinement more cheerful. Among the things they brought was Hank's pet monkey. Passersby were amused to see the monkey playing by the hour on Hank's bedroom window sill in the Transfer House.[4]

But Hank was taking no note of the monkey's antics, for as the *East Oregonian* observed, his coma continued:

> (June 13) Hank Vaughan appears to grow no better. He lies in a condition of almost stupor, and is unable to recognize those at his bedside. He is weaker physically, and there is no sign of restoration of his mental facilities, injured by the fearful fall upon his head. His case is considered very doubtful, and he may be claimed at last by death, after escaping many perils. The patient receives constant care from his friends and family.

One of those friends who showed concern was none other than Charlie Long:

> All the old animosity had been forgotten and Long looked upon Hank as a hero. At that time Pendleton was short of greenhouses. Long wanted to present Hank with flowers, but being unable to find any florist he entered a milliner's shop and bought ten dollars' worth of artificial flowers, which he placed in a basin with water and sent up to Hank's room, saying that while Hank had shot him several times in their difficulty at Long Creek [sic] he retained no grudge against him and desired to do him honor.[5]

Charlie himself was to come to a bloody end up in the Okanogan country in Washington State. He was homesteading a piece of land with George F. "Okanogan" Smith, Jr. in a partnership which didn't run too smoothly. At one time, according to Long's friend, Long threatened to kill Smith but Smith eventually got the drop on Charlie and killed him with an ax.

For two more days the medical reports in the *East Oregonian* continued with grave pronouncements on Hank's condition:

> (June 14) Hank Vaughan's condition is considered quite critical. His throat seems paralysed, and he is unable to swallow. It is believed there is little chance for his recovery, and death may occur at any time.
>
> (June 15) A surgical operation was performed today for the relief of Hank Vaughan. Dr. Kenneth McKenzie, of Portland, who stands high in the medical

profession, was telegraphed Friday by the patient's relatives, and arrived this morning.

A consultation was afterward held, and an operation decided upon as the only means of saving the injured man's life. It began at 11 o'clock this afternoon at the Transfer House, and was performed with care and skill by Dr. McKenzie, assisted by Drs. Smith and Guymon (sic), of this city. Three hours were consumed in the task. The patient lay in the stupor that has marked his condition for some time past, and was doubtless mercifully relieved, to a large extent, from pain.

The surgeons laid open the scalp, and removed at the seat of the injury a portion of skull about as large as a fifty cent piece. It was supposed that a clot of blood might have formed, but none was found. A very slight fracture of the skull was discovered, and pressure upon the brain will be relieved by the operation.

The patient seemed to be somewhat better at the close of the operation than when it began, and was alive at a late hour in the afternoon. It is impossible to say at present whether he has chance for recovery; yet Hank Vaughan has passed through many bad experiences, none of which an ordinary man could survive.

A late report from The Dalles *Times-Mountaineer*, June 15, 1893, told of the unsuccessful outcome of the operation:

Hank C. Vaughan died this evening from the result of an accident. He was thrown from a horse last week and was rendered unconscious. He had been lying in a semi-comatose condition ever since. This afternoon Dr. McKenzie, of Portland, assisted by Drs. Vincent, Smith, and Guymon, performed a surgical operation upon him, but he never rallied, and died at 9 o'clock this evening. The result of the operation showed that his skull was fractured, and 12 or more pieces of shattered bone were removed. The operation was too long delayed to save his life. Vaughan although having been somewhat of the character of a desperado in his early life, has many friends in this part of the state who will be pained to hear of his tragic end.

Back in Pendleton, the *East Oregonian*, of June 16, 1893 told of Hank's death and funeral and lamented his passage in prose that reached literary heights:

HANK VAUGHAN DEAD
The Life of One of the Wild West'
Best Known Characters is Ended

At 8 o'clock last night, death closed an eventful career. The operation upon Hank Vaughan could not save the life that was almost extinct before it began. And in a few hours afterward the quick disturbed breathing that was the sole evidence of the fast-dimming vital spark ceased abruptly, and the soul of one of the most daring of the reckless beings who have given the "wild west" its title was called to its maker. Oh. Hank, that was a fatal ride, the last time you mounted your trusty sorrel in the streets of Pendleton and sped with him like a tempest until even his true feet could not keep pace with your impulse, and you were plunged headlong upon the rocks.

The funeral took place this afternoon from the Transfer House, and the remains which had been encased in a handsome casket, were followed by a long line of carriages. Services were conducted in an appropriate manner by Rev. W.W.

> Brannin. Mrs. Vaughan is quite ill as the result of her care and anxiety, and was unable to attend the funeral.

A disturbance occurred along the route on the day of the burial that would have delighted Hank. The *East Oregonian*, June 16, 1893, reported:

> A runaway occurred this afternoon on the way to the cemetery, during Hank Vaughan's funeral. A fractious team attached to a hack containing five men collided with a buggy occupied by J.C. Misell and Sam Hillie, badly wrecking it. The horses were tangled up together for a time but were finally gotten under control.

The cortege of mourners followed the casket out of town to the Olney Cemetery which lay along the Pilot Rock road south of Pendleton. They watched as the body was lowered into the ground. Hank was buried in Plot 3 of Block 9, Lot 26 which his family purchased for $10.[6] No marker has been placed on his grave (fig. 36).

Those who watched Hank knew that one day his luck had to run out and he would surely fall victim to his own recklessness. He had placed himself face to face with death too many times. Whiskey-braced courage and a flare for show finally caught up with Hank in that hell-bent ride down Pendleton's main street. Although he was one of the best horsemen in a time when the whole of the west was moving

FIGURE 36—Hank Vaughan's final resting place is in an unmarked lot in the Olney Cemetery, Pendleton, Oregon.

on horses and he had suffered from dozens of previous falls from horses, this day the odds were against him.

It was symbolic that a horse and a railroad played a part in Hank's death for they had both been significant to him during his lifetime. He loved horses and rode and owned the best available. The railroads provided much of his livelihood. During the great period of western expansion, he sold horses used in railroad construction activities.

These same railroads were a symbol of progress and the arrival of civilization which began to threaten Hank's illegal trade. He wasn't the only one who felt the threat of these bands of progress. Only four years earlier, according to the *East Oregonian*, October 4, 1888, some citizens of Pendleton recognized the town would be permanently crippled by taking something so dangerous as a railroad right into its heart. Since Pendleton lay between hills and didn't have much room to spare, there was much protest when G.W. Hunt's line proposed to serve the town:

> A few threatened an injunction to prevent entrance on Webb street, but tracklayers got busy at four o'clock Thursday morning, August 29, 1889, and by eight o'clock Thursday morning, the track was laid down as far as the Watson & Luhrs Planing Mill.
>
> The next Sunday morning, bright and early, another forced march was made by Hunt's graders and track layers and before citizens realized what was being done rails were down and the first engine passed down Webb and across Main street.[7]

Hank profited with the building of the railroads, but once they were built, their value to him was gone. From then on, the railroads brought people and restrictions on those like Hank who had little regard for law and order. No longer was Hank's territory wide open and unfenced where a man could make his own rules so long as he could enforce them. The country was becoming settled with people who expected and were beginning to receive law enforcement to protected them from the rowdies like Vaughan.

In the era before railroads, horses were the main mode of travel and horses were suited to the Vaughan character. It is easy to imagine him astride a fast steed leading the dust into a sleepy western town, heading for the nearest saloon. With his horse tied to the hitching rack, he would be inside quenching his thirst with hard liquor while he planned a joke to take the starch out of some luckless person.

It wasn't so much that Vaughan was mean as it was he liked excitement. He gave little thought to the pain his actions would bring on flesh and bones. His own body scars told of a history of abuse. Billy Mays said, "I saw Hank stripped once and he was a regular sieve. . . . He had scars all over him where he had been shot or cut. He used to do lots of things playfully that finally gave him a reputation as an ugly customer."[8]

In his obituary, the *East Oregonian*, June 16, 1893, said, "Vaughan, it is related, carried thirteen bullets in his body." The writer must have meant bullet holes, as Drake's story said, "The physicians reported his body carried thirteen bullet wounds."

Records and authenticated stories only account for six of the thirteen bullet holes. It would be interesting indeed if something were known about the encounter which produced each scar. Perhaps there was some truth to the stories of Sagebrush Brown, the Lewiston confrontation in the Green Front Saloon, and the gun fight at Ainsworth. It is regrettable John Bentley didn't give more details when he reminisced:

> . . . One time he [Hank] and I had a long friendly talk. He cleared up several murder mysteries for me. He told me he had, for business or social reasons, had to kill 13 men. Some of them may have deserved to be killed, but Hank's method of disposing of them was too irregular.[9]

Bentley had many difficult run-ins with Vaughan while serving as Umatilla County Sheriff in the late 1880s, but when he served as Deputy U.S. Marshal in 1892-93, he got to know Hank in a better mode. In one position, Bentley was protecting citizens of the State whereas in the latter post he was maintaining federal law and order. Since Vaughan was too wise to get involved in federal violations, Bentley did not find Hank much of a threat.

Most so-called bad men of the early west preferred to die with their boots on as a sign they went out fighting, but Hank Vaughan never wanted it to end that way. Walter Meacham said, "Hank's old dad always told him that he would die with his boots on."[10] Although the prophecy became near reality on many occasions, somehow Hank pulled through but only after having his boots removed. To the end, Hank was obsessed with the idea of fooling his dad and he did. He died in bed like a gentlemen.

Hank was known to have kept a private safe in the Transfer House. This was according to Attorney William Parsons who probably together with Sheriff W.J. Furnish had a court order to take charge of Vaughan's personal effect. Parsons said:

> Among these were six hundred dollars in ten cent pieces, about a score of seal finger rings, some of them very beautiful, diamond pins, gold studs, a nugget of gold of the value of six hundred dollars from the mines of Southern Oregon, and a dozen or more elegantly mounted revolvers.[11]

What was Hank doing with 6,000 dimes? It may have been loot from a bank robbery traded with his McCarty in-laws. Hank was fond of giving rings as gifts, so perhaps that explains his collection of seal rings. The diamond pins and gold studs were purchased by him at various jewelry stores. Some stores, like Charles St. Johns in Baker City, never received payment for what he charged. The gold nugget was undoubtedly the one he purchased in 1891 from D.F. Smyer at a reported cost of $356.61.

Some time in the summer of 1892, Hank bought a pair of six shooters with pearl grips from Browning Bros. of Ogden, Utah. It is likely that these new acquisitions were among those stored at the Transfer House. One of these pistols is now in the museum collection of the Oregon State Sheriffs Association (fig. 37).[12]

Since Vaughan left no will, Stephen L. Morse was appointed by the court to administer the estate. Named as appraisers were W.J. Furnish, Pat Kine, and W.P. Lathrop. These men were appointed August 5, 1895, more than two years past the date of Hank's death.[13] In the probate of Vaughan's estate, it was estimated that he

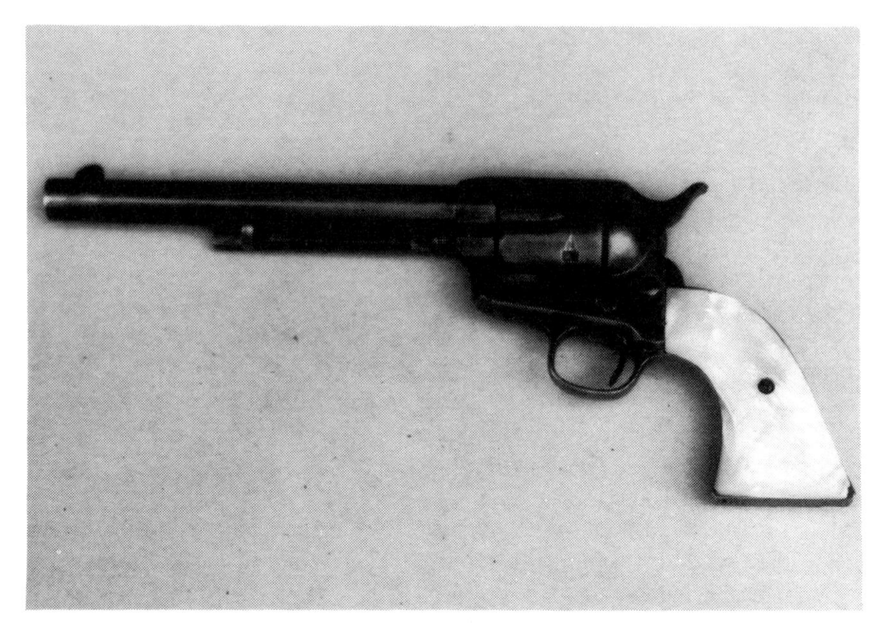

FIGURE 37—This Colt single action army revolver that once belonged to Hank Vaughan is in the museum collection of the Oregon State Sheriffs' Association. It was obtained by H. William Hawley, historian, from the son of W.J. Furnish who was sheriff of Umatilla County at the time of Hank's death.

had personal property valued at only $500. This does not tally with the value of the contents of his lock box. The gold nugget was said to be worth $600 and the dimes would have been worth $600. The revolvers would have increased the value of his personal property considerably more.

It would appear Hank Vaughan did not die a wealthy man. Any liquid assets he may have possessed at the end would have been absorbed covering his medical care and lodging at the Transfer House after his accident. As to any money due Hank through his stock trading ventures, the only record of such accounts would have been lost when he died.

Most of the property Vaughan had managed these past few years belonged to Martha through virtue of her inheritance from A.H. Robie and her claim to land on the reservation through her Indian heritage. Martha lived to be eighty-eight years old. She died in 1930. Her body was cremated and the ashes taken to Idaho to be placed beside her first husband, according to the Athena *Press*, March 28, 1937.

Some said the world was a better place without the likes of Hank Vaughan but those expressing that sentiment didn't appreciate the entertainment value he provided his contemporaries in this period of the developing west. He was the kind of person who never accepted humdrum as an inevitable condition of life. Although his method of creating excitement seems violent in this day, his antics with guns when liquored up were not unusual at that time. Some claimed he was just an overgrown boy. In a genteel society, Hank would have been an uncouth misfit, but in the frontier community of his day, he was distinguished only by the excessive commotion he created.

One of Hank's contemporaries remembered how he and his environment suited each other:

> I rode the range with Hank in the hills. Hank loved the hills. And a man can't fool the hills, either. They know a man. If there's orneriness in a man the hills will bring it out. For weeks at a time we'd be alone, and if there's any time or place when two men will get on each other's nerves, its when they ride in the hills together. I never saw Hank the least bit out of sorts. . . .[14]

Lawmen have expressed widely different opinions of Vaughan. Matt Taylor, who was at various times a marshal at Centerville, a deputy sheriff in Pendleton, and always a highly respected citizen of Umatilla County, said of Hank:

> He wasn't a bad man ordinarily, but when he "liquored up" he was somewhat of a desperado. . . . I never carried a gun when I went to arrest Hank, I was afraid he would take it from me. . . . I arrested Hank many times but never had any difficulty in doing it, as I never attempted it when he was drunk.[15]

From most accounts, Vaughan respected any man who displayed courage and could meet him on his own ground. But others saw him in a different light. James F. Johnson, another deputy from Pendleton, who had trouble with Hank on several occasions, didn't have such a good opinion of him: "A dirty yellow coward he was unless he had the drop on you."[16]

People's opinion of Hank seemed to improve with age. Oliver White, a lawman of sorts, spoke of Vaughan's younger days, saying, "As a boy, he was an outright thief." However, in later years while a newspaper man at Dayton, White developed a reasonable tolerance toward Hank.[17]

Hank's newspaper friend, Clark Wood, also had a mellowed remembrance of him:

> With ordinary citizens he was happily harmless, a good natured, soft-spoken person of more than average height with splendid shoulders and engaging manners. Yet he always had guns under his long coat and marvelous facility in producing them when the occasion seemed auspicious.[18]

From the many stories of his intoxicated revels, one might have expected Hank to be a slovenly drunk, but he wasn't. People remembered he was neat in appearance, choosing clothing that cultivated his appearance as a respectable professional man.

The profession Hank knew best was horse trading. He showed skill and thoroughness in the way he developed his business—illegal though it was in most instances. He became the agent for the ordinary lot of horse thieves, most of whom were of an antisocial, churlish nature who relied on Hank to fence their stolen products. He was knowledgeable as to markets and he cultivated those people who were in a position to buy his stock. He knew how to procure horseflesh and deliver it with a minimum of problems. And he learned early the worth of a competent lawyer and how to manipulate the intricacies of the law in case he did get caught.

According to Billy Mays:

> Hank engineered a lot of deals that were outside the law. He was the brains for a lot of fellows who could pull off a holdup or rob a stage if Hank would do the headwork.
>
> They didn't get the best of Hank very often. He could usually find a trail out of any fix he got in.[19]

When a former companion and fellow prison inmate of Hank's was sentenced to hang in 1896 he revealed in a death row confession his association and earlier escapades with Vaughan. The man, William Mason Roe, had been arrested for murder in Nampa, California, in the fall of 1891. He had several aliases, William Moore or "Desperate Dick." He was an inmate in the Oregon penitentiary with Hank and according to the Boise *Statesman*, of November 22, 1896, ". . . claimed, among other things that while in Idaho in the mid 1870s he was identified with Hank Vaughn in numerous daring stage robberies and other crimes." At one time Roe was sentenced to prison for attempting to kill a bartender in Middleton, Idaho Territory, a known hangout for Hank. That Hank took part in stage robberies is not known except through the death-row confession of "Desperate Dick." Roe was declared insane on several occasions, so could not be counted as a reliable informant.

The reputation Vaughan had in Kittitas County, Washington Territory, after the Roslyn bank robbery was of a man who knew how to execute robberies but who was not involved personally:

> . . . Old-timers, in on the know, asserted that he was the master mind for many years behind a gang that were guilty of all kinds of law violations from petit larceny to highway robbery. Hank himself did not take an active part, but was alleged to have made the plans and directed activities. His part being to furnish bail, defense and advice for all members of his gang who ran afoul of the law.[20]

As a family man, Hank left much to be desired. His first two wives may have expected more of his time than he was willing to give from what he considered his business—a common complaint of wives of many dedicated businessmen! His sons were ignored until they neared manhood and developed a degree of reasonableness. It seems improbable that Hank would ever have had the patience necessary to nurture and rear the boys. It is questionable that he could have given them much moral guidance.

In retrospect, the third woman in his life, Martha Robie, must be credited with playing a very significant role in Hank's later activities. Through her, Vaughan acquired the responsibilities attached to landownership and with it a certain amount of respectability. That he was capable of handling the management of her affairs was shown by the productive ranch they ran on the reservation. Theirs was a congenial relationship and they apparently enjoyed each others company as evidenced by their many trips together. Without this stabilizing influence, Hank might well have advanced no further than a rough, punk horse thief.

Responsibility may have been a stabilizer for Hank, but liquor was his agitator. Those who knew him said he was a reasonable sort until he had a few drinks and then there was no stopping his wild behavior.

Hank had to be accepted for what he was—shrewd in a business deal whether lawful or unlawful, a demon for excitement with no thought of fear, and much adversely affected by liquor. His exploits filled the newspapers of his day and when his contemporaries were interviewed years later their memories were still vivid with stories of the desperado, Hank Vaughan.

A few references to Hank claim he was called "Bunchgrass" by his friends. This nickname was seldom found in print but it seemed a descriptive title, one that linked him with bunchgrass, a prairie grass that once covered the whole of the interior west from the Rocky Mountains to the Cascade-Sierra Nevada Range.

However, the bunchgrass began to disappear after the mid 1870s when great concentrations of cattle were trailed from the Northwest to stock the former buffalo ranges in Montana, Wyoming and Colorado Territories. Overlapping the cattle drives were activities of farmers bent on plowing up the native range to replace it with grain and exotic feeds for livestock. Along with plows came fences to protect the fields. After each successful harvest, more people arrived and the population grew, clustering into towns and villages. With that, law and order arrived.

While it lasted, bunchgrass was a source of wealth to all kinds of stockmen. For them the bunchgrass was a bonanza. Hank's life spanned this period. In his heyday, he could move at will with his bands of horses and find abundant feed most anywhere. No barbed wire crossed his path. His territory covered the range from Arizona to Nevada across Idaho, Oregon and Washington.

The bunchgrass complemented Hank's way of life but it like him was forced to bow to the pressure of increased population and use. As Billy Mays observed about this frontier period and how it suited Hank:

> . . . a wild goose never laid a tame egg nor neither does a hawk or an eagle. Hank Vaughan was just wild by nature. He lived wild and he died wild. Settlement and civilization have killed off the buffalo and the carrier [passenger] pigeon, and it has killed off the Hank Vaughans, too.[21]

When Hank died, some of the spirit of the wild west died with him. The rough and tumble setting of the frontier times that allowed him to act out his boisterous ways was being replaced by the refinements which accompany civilization. These refinements could only stifle the earthy energies of the likes of Hank Vaughan. Perhaps that last wild gallop down the streets of Pendleton was his protest to that suffocation.

REFERENCES

Chapter 19

1. *East Oregonian*, March 2, 1968.
2. *Ibid.*, March 27, 1948.
3. *Ibid.*, April 10, 1948.
4. Drake, *op. cit.*, 10.
5. *Spokesman Review*, August 31, 1913.
6. Cemetery Records, City Hall, Pendleton, Oregon.
7. Pioneer Ladies Club, *op. cit.*, 238.
8. *Spokesman Review*, August 16, 1913.
9. *Oregon Journal*, August 13, 1923.
10. Meacham, *op. cit.*
11. Parsons and Shiach, *op. cit.*, 259. *Also* Royal Robie, Mountain Pass, California. Personal correspondence. November 6, 1972.
12. Hawley, H. William, Oregon State Sheriff's Historical Association, Lake Oswego, Oregon. Personal correspondence. August 24, 1972.
13. Umatilla County Court, Probate-Henry C. Vaughan, Probate Book F. 113-116. Filed August 27, 1895, Pendleton.
14. *Idaho Statesman*, May 23, 1937.
15. Taylor, *op cit.*
16. Kelly, John, *op. cit.*, 12.
17. The Dalles *Chronicle*, September 23, 1926.
18. *East Oregonian*, March 27, 1948.
19. *Spokesman Review*, August 16, 1913.
20. Ballou, *op. cit.*, 61.
21. *Spokesman Review*, August 16, 1913.

BIBLIOGRAPHY

BOOKS

Angel, Myron (ed.). *History of Nevada.* Oakland: Thompson & West, 1881.

Anon. *History of the Pacific Northwest: Oregon and Washington.* Vol. 2. North Pacific History Company. Portland, 1889.

Anon. *Portrait and Biographical Record of the Willamette Valley Oregon.* Chicago: Chapman Publishing Co., 1903.

Bailey, Robert G. *River of No Return.* Lewiston: R.G. Bailey Printing Co., 1947.

Ballou, Robert. *Early Klickitat Valley Days.* Goldendale: The Goldendale Sentinel, Printers, 1938.

Bancroft, Hubert Howe. *History of Washington, Idaho, and Montana, 1845-1889*, Vol. 31. San Francisco: The History Company, 1890.

Bancroft, Hubert Howe. *Popular Tribunals*, Vol. 1. San Francisco: The History Company, 1887.

Becher, Edmund T. *Spokane Corona, Eras and Empires.* Spokane: C.W. Hill Printers, 1974.

Blankenship, Russell. *And There Were Men.* New York: Alfred A. Knopf, 1942.

Brimlow, George Francis. *Harney County, Oregon, and Its Range Land.* Portland: Binfords and Mort, 1951.

Clark, Keith, and Lowell Tiller. *Terible Trail: The Meek Cutoff, 1845.* Caldwell: Caxton Printers, Ltd., 1966.

Eastern Washington Directory, compiled by D. Allen Miller, Walla Walla: Harris, The Printer, 1883.

Edwards, Jonathan. *An Illustrated History of Spokane County.* Spokane: W.H. Lever Co., 1900.

Fargo, Lucile F. *Spokane Story.* New York: Columbia University Press, 1950.

Gard, Wayne. *Frontier Justice.* Norman: University of Oklahoma Press, 1975.

Geer, T.T. *Fifty Years in Oregon.* New York: Neal Publishing Co., 1912.

Gilbert, Frank T. *Historic Sketches of Walla Walla, Whitman, Columbia, and Garfield Counties in Washington Territory, and Umatilla County, Oregon.* Portland, 1882.

Hiatt, Isaac. *Thirty-one Years in Baker County.* Baker City: Abbott and Foster, Printers, 1893.

Holmes, Kenneth L. *Ewing Young: Master Trapper.* Portland: Binfords and Mort, 1967.

Hunter, George. *Reminiscences of an Old Timer.* San Francisco: H.S. Crocker and Co., 1887.

Josephy, Alvin M., Jr. *The Nez Perce Indians and the Opening of the Northwest.* New Haven: Yale University Press, 1965.

Kelly, Charles. *The Outlaw Trail.* New York: Bonanza Books, 1959.

Lewis, William S.. *The Story of Early Days in the Big Bend Country.* Spokane: W.D. Allen, Publisher, 1926.

Lockley, Fred. *Reminiscences of Colonel Henry Ernst Dosch.* Eugene: Koke-Tiffany, 1924.

McArthur, Lewis A. *Oregon Geographic Names.* Portland: Binfords and Mort, 1952.

McCarty, Thomas. *A History of Tom McCarty.* Reprint. Hamilton, Montana: Rocky Mountain House Press, 1986.

Macnab, Gordon. *A Century of News and People in the East Oregonian 1875-1975.* Pendleton: East Oregonian Publishing Co., 1975.

Moore, Lucia. *The Wheel and The Hearth.* New York: Ballentine, 1953.

Oliphant, J. Orin. *On the Cattle Ranges of the Oregon Country.* Seattle: University of Washington Press, 1968.

Osgood, Ernest Staples. *The Day of the Cattleman.* Chicago and London: University of Chicago Press, 1929.

Parsons, William, and W.S. Shiach. *History of Umatilla and Morrow County.* Spokane: W.H. Lever Company, 1902.

Pioneer Ladies Club. *Reminiscences of Oregon Pioneers.* Pendleton: East Oregonian Publishing Co., 1937.

Rollinson, John K. *Wyoming Cattle Trails.* Caldwell: Caxton Printers, Ltd., 1948.

Ruby, Robert H., and John A. Brown. *The Cayuse Indians: Imperial Tribesmen of Old Oregon.* Norman: University of Oklahoma Press, 1972.

Searcy, Mildred. *Way Back When.* Pendleton: East Oregonian Publishing Co., 1972.

Sheller, Roscoe. *Bandit to Lawman.* Yakima: Franklin Press, 1966.

Splawn, Andrew J. *Kamiakin-Last Hero of the Yakimas.* Portland: Metropolitan Press, 1944.

Waggoner, George A. *Stories of Old Oregon.* Salem: Statesman Publishing Co., 1904.

Walla Walla Valley Genealogical Society, compilers. *Early Marriages of Walla Walla County 1862 thru 1899, Washington Territory and State.* Walla Walla: Walla Walla Valley Genealogical Society, 1976.

Warner, Matt. *The Last of the Bandit Riders.* Caldwell: Caxton Printers, Ltd., 1940.

Villard, Henry. *The Early History of Transportation in Oregon.* Eugene: University of Oregon Press, 1944.

Western Historical Publishing Company. *An Illustrated History of Union and Wallowa Counties.* Spokane: W.H. Lever Company. 1902.

Western Historical Publishing Company. *History of Baker, Grant, Malheur and Harney Counties.* Spokane: W.H. Lever Company. 1902.

MANUSCRIPTS

Curtis, John T. Idaho *Daily Statesman*, November 26, 1933, sec. 2, p. 4, from Thomas Teakle Collection, *Pacific Northwestern Transcripts*,: Vol. 72, Idaho Vigilantism, Penrose Library, Whitman College, Walla Walla.

Drake, Lee D. Original Manuscript. No Date, 10 p., typescript in possession of James H. Sturgis, Curator. Blue Mountain College Museum, Pendleton.

McCarty, Thomas. "A History of Tom McCarty," No Date, 98 p., Manuscript, Utah State Historical Society, Salt Lake City.

Meacham, Walter. Original Manuscript. No Date, 1 p., typescript in possession of James H. Sturgis, Curator. Blue Mountain College Museum, Pendleton.

Meyer, Bette E. "Ainsworth: A Railroad Town." No Date, Copy in the Northwest Collection, Spokane Public Library, Spokane.

Sharon, Julian L. "Pendleton-Umatilla County and the Oregon Country," 1940, 136 p., Manuscript, Umatilla County Library, Pendleton.

Tucker, Gerald J. "The Pilot Rock Emigrant Road." No Date, 10 p., Umatilla County Library, Pendleton.

ARTICLES

Beal, Merril D. "Rustlers and Robbers." *Idaho Yesterdays*, Spring, 7:24-28 1963.

Kelly, John W. "Hank Vaughan: A Story of the Old West." *Oregon Motorist*, September 1930.

Mires, Austin. "The Great Roslyn Bank Robbery," ed. by Terry Abraham, *The Record*, 32:27-72, Pullman: Washington State University, 1972.

Pfeifer, William. "The Men Who Wore The Oregon Boot." *Old West*, Winter 1966.

Tucker, Gerald J. "Hank Vaughn's Fatal Ride." *Frontier Times*, April-May 1966.

Tucker, Gerald J. "Massacre for Gold." *Old West*, Fall 1967.

West Shore, 9: September 1883; 10(4):117-118, April 1884; 11(1):13-15, 23, January 1885; 11(10):298-299, 303, October 1885.

NEWSPAPERS

Adams Times, Adams, Oregon

Ainsworth *Budget*, Ainsworth, Washington Territory

Baker County *Reveille*, Baker City, Oregon

Bedrock Democrat, Baker City, Oregon

Boise *Tri-Weekly Statesman*, Boise City, Idaho Territory

Centerville *Home Press*, Centerville, Oregon

Centerville *Examiner*, Centerville, Oregon

Chief Joseph Herald, Joseph, Oregon

Daily Record, Pioche, Nevada

Daily Oregonian, Portland, Oregon

East Oregonian. Pendleton, Oregon

Elko Independent, Elko, Nevada

Elko *Post*, Elko, Nevada

Elko *Weekly Post*, Elko, Nevada

Harrington *Times*, Harrington, Washington

Idaho Daily Statesman, Boise City, Idaho Territory

Idaho Free Press, Mount Idaho, Idaho

Idaho Statesman, Boise City, Idaho Territory

La Grande *Gazette*, La Grande, Oregon

Morning Oregonian, Portland, Oregon

Oregon Journal, Portland, Oregon

Pendleton *Independent*, Pendleton, Oregon

Pendleton *Tribune*, Pendleton, Oregon

Portland *Telegram*, Portland, Oregon

Prescott *Weekly Arizona Miner*, Prescott, Arizona

Salem *Statesman*, Salem, Oregon

Silver City *Idaho Avalanche*, Silver City, Idaho Territory

Silver State, Winnemucca, Nevada

Spokesman Review, Spokane, Washington

Spokane Falls Chronicle, Spokane Falls, Washington Territory

Standard, Portland, Oregon

Sunday Oregonian, Portland, Oregon

The Dalles *Chronicle*, The Dalles, Oregon

The Dalles *Weekly Chronicle*, The Dalles, Oregon

The Dalles *Mountaineer*, The Dalles, Oregon

The Dalles *Sun*, The Dalles, Oregon

The Dalles *Time-Mountaineer*, The Dalles, Oregon

Times Review, Tuscarora, Nevada

Union Scout, Union, Oregon

Walla Walla *Journal*, Walla Walla, Washington

Walla Walla *Union*, Walla Walla, Washington Territory

Wallowa County *Chieftain*, Enterprise, Oregon

Weekly Mountaineer, The Dalles, Oregon

Weston *Leader*, Weston, Oregon

Wenatchee *Daily World*, Wenatchee, Washington

INTERVIEWS

Ayers, Charles R., Star, Idaho, February 28, 1974.

Barrett, Areta, Athena, Oregon, May 10, 1973.

Knight, William J. "Bill," Sr. La Grande, Oregon, February 2, 1967.

O'Kelly, John, Prineville, Oregon, July 28, 1974.

Riede, Sophia, Boise, Idaho, February 7, 1973.

Robie, Royal, Mohave Valley, Arizona, January 26, 1987.

Rogers, Laura Bell, Foster, Oregon, December 29, 1972.

Stickler, Ted, Starkey Cow Camp, Union County, Oregon, August 12, 1967.

Strack, Ray, Starkey, Oregon, June 16, 1974.

Whitney, F. G. "Whit," Ukiah, Oregon, June 23, 1967.

LETTERS

Contreras, Ina, Chula Vista, California, July 26, 1973.

DelCurto, Courtney, Sunnyside, Washington, January 15, 1973.

Hawley, H. William, Lake Oswego, Oregon, August 24, 1972, February 4, 1973.

Martin, Thelma, Bremerton, Washington, February 9, 1973.

Robie, Royal, Mountain Pass, California, November 6, 1972.

Tucker, Gerald J., Imnaha, Oregon, March 14, 1974.

COURT RECORDS

Ada County, Book of Marriage Intentions, Book 1., Vol. 2, 183, 209.

Ada County Circuit Court, Criminal Case File 3, 284-290. The People vs. H.C. Vaughan, Boise, Idaho Territory.

Baker County Circuit Court, Civil Case No 1. 96-149, Chas. St. Louis vs. Hank Vaughn, Baker, Oregon.

Baker County Circuit Court, May Term 1865, Criminal Case File No. 19, State vs. Henry Vaughn, Auburn, Oregon.

Elko County Circuit Court, Civil Case File No. 104, C. Zimmerman vs. William A. Moody, Elko, Nevada.

Elko County, Deeds, Grantee, Vaughan, Henry Clay, and Alexander H.; Book 6, 365, 400 and 633, respectively. Elko County Courthouse, Elko, Nevada.

Elko County, Marriages, Book No. 1, 84, dated May 8, 1875, Elko, Nevada.

Umatilla County Circuit Court, Civil Case No. 44-53, Book 11, Hollis and Cleve vs. A.H. Robie, Pendleton, Oregon.

Umatilla County Circuit Court, Case No. 270-31. Frank Rayburn vs. H.C. Vaughan.

Umatilla County Circuit Court, Criminal Case File No. 26-416, State vs. Hank Vaughn and S.P. Whitley, Pendleton, Oregon.

Umatilla County Circuit Court Divorce Case No. 191-30, Louisa J. Vaughan vs. H.E. Vaughan, Pendleton, Oregon.

Umatilla County Circuit Court Divorce Case No. 191-31, H.C. Vaughan vs. Lois Vaughan.

Umatilla County Court, Book of Marriages, Page dated August 31, 1878, Pendleton.

Umatilla County Court, Probate-Henry C. Vaughan, Probate Book F, 113-116, Filed August 27, 1895, Pendleton, Oregon.

Union County Circuit Court, Civil Case F.S. Ladd vs. Henry C. Vaughan and A.R. Matoon.

Wallowa County Circuit Court, Docket A.

Wasco County Circuit Court, Criminal Case, File No. 55-51, State of Oregon vs. Henry Vaughn, Oregon State Archives, Salem, Oregon.

GOVERNMENT DOCUMENTS

Census, Umatilla Indian Reservation, 1887, 1890, 1891, Office of Indian Affairs, National Archives, General Services Administration.

Census, United States, Report of the Census Bureau, Oregon, Washington, D.C., 1850, 1860, 1870.

Commitment Record, Convicts Received, Nevada State Prison, 1877, Biennial Report of the Warden of Nevada State Prison for the Years 1877 and 1878, Appendix, 36. Ninth Session of the Nevada Legislature, 1879.

Governor's Executive Documents, Records of the Secretary of State, Oregon State Archives, Salem, Oregon.

Idaho, Statistics of, Silver City, Owyhee County, Idaho, L.D.S. Genealogical Library, La Grande, Oregon.

Military Department Records, Oregon State Archives, File 59-36 and 60-28, Salem, Oregon.

Office of Indian Affairs, Census of Mixed Bloods of the Umatilla (Confederated) Tribe of Indians, Umatilla Agency, Oregon, June 30, 1891, National Archives, Washington, D.C.

Office of Indian Affairs, Letters Received, 1887-1907, No. 13337-E, May 13, 1889, National Archives, Washington, D.C.

Pendleton City Cemetery Records, City Office, Pendleton.

Report of Superintendent and Commissioners of the State Penitentiary, Fifth Regular Session of the Oregon State Legislative Assembly, September 1868.

Report of Superintendent and Commissioners of the State Penitentiary, Senate Proceedings, Messages and Documents, 1866.

The Great Register, Vol. 1. Commitment Papers, Oregon State Penitentiary, Vol. 1857-1878. Oregon State Archives, Salem, Oregon.

Umatilla County Tax Rolls, Secretary of State Bienniel Reports 1870-1877, Archives Division, Oregon State Library, Salem.

Works Project Administration, General Histroy 11, Inventory of Penitentiary, Petition No. 22, Oregon State Archives, Salem, Oregon.

Works Project Administration, General History 11, Umatilla County, Bibliographies-Hank Vaughn, Oregon State Archives, Salem, Oregon.

INDEX